Evaluating Educational Interventions

The Guilford Practical Intervention in the Schools Series

Kenneth W. Merrell, Series Editor

Books in this series address the complex academic, behavioral, and social–emotional needs of children and youth at risk. School-based practitioners are provided with practical, research-based, and readily applicable tools to support students and team successfully with teachers, families, and administrators. Each volume is designed to be used directly and frequently in planning and delivering educational and mental health services. Features include lay-flat binding to facilitate photocopying, step-by-step instructions for assessment and intervention, and helpful, timesaving reproducibles.

Recent Volumes

Clinical Interviews for Children and Adolescents: Assessment to Intervention
Stephanie H. McConaughy

Response to Intervention: Principles and Strategies for Effective Practice
Rachel Brown-Chidsey and Mark W. Steege

The ABCs of CBM: A Practical Guide to Curriculum-Based Measurement
Michelle K. Hosp, John L. Hosp, and Kenneth W. Howell

Fostering Independent Learning: Practical Strategies to Promote Student Success
Virginia Smith Harvey and Louise A. Chickie-Wolfe

Helping Students Overcome Substance Abuse: Effective Practices for Prevention and Intervention
Jason J. Burrow-Sanchez and Leanne S. Hawken

School-Based Behavioral Assessment: Informing Intervention and Instruction
Sandra Chafouleas, T. Chris Riley-Tillman, and George Sugai

Collaborating with Parents for Early School Success: The Achieving–Behaving–Caring Program
Stephanie H. McConaughy, Pam Kay, Julie A. Welkowitz, Kim Hewitt, and Martha D. Fitzgerald

Helping Students Overcome Depression and Anxiety, Second Edition: A Practical Guide
Kenneth W. Merrell

Inclusive Assessment and Accountability: A Guide to Accommodations for Students with Diverse Needs
Sara E. Bolt and Andrew T. Roach

Bullying Prevention and Intervention: Realistic Strategies for Schools
Susan M. Swearer, Dorothy L. Espelage, and Scott A. Napolitano

Conducting School-Based Functional Behavioral Assessments, Second Edition: A Practitioner's Guide
Mark W. Steege and T. Steuart Watson

Evaluating Educational Interventions: Single-Case Design for Measuring Response to Intervention
T. Chris Riley-Tillman and Matthew K. Burns

Evaluating Educational Interventions

Single-Case Design
for Measuring Response to Intervention

T. CHRIS RILEY-TILLMAN
MATTHEW K. BURNS

THE GUILFORD PRESS
New York   London

© 2009 The Guilford Press
A Division of Guilford Publications, Inc.
72 Spring Street, New York, NY 10012
www.guilford.com

Printed in Canada

This book is printed on acid-free paper.

Last digit is print number: 9   8   7   6   5   4   3   2   1

Library of Congress Cataloging-in-Publication Data

Riley-Tillman, T. Chris.
    Evaluating educational interventions : single-case design for measuring response to intervention /
T. Chris Riley-Tillman, Matthew K. Burns.
        p. cm. — (The Guilford practical intervention in the schools series)
    Includes bibliographical references and index.
    ISBN 978-1-60623-106-7 (pbk. : alk. paper)
    1. Learning disabled children—Education—United States.   2. Special education—United
States—Evaluation.   3. Single subject research—United States.   I. Burns, Matthew K.
II. Title.
    LC4705.R55 2009
    371.9′043—dc22

                                                                    2008049412

About the Authors

T. Chris Riley-Tillman, PhD, is Associate Professor and Director of Graduate Studies in School Psychology and Pediatric School Psychology at East Carolina University. His research focuses on improving education through the effective application of a problem-solving model. Specifically, he is interested in social behavioral assessment, intervention, single-case design, and consultation. Dr. Riley-Tillman has written numerous articles, books, and book chapters related to these research interests.

Matthew K. Burns, PhD, is Associate Professor in the Department of Educational Psychology at the University of Minnesota. His research focuses on improving instruction for children with varying abilities and disabilities. Dr. Burns explores the application of learning and ecological theories to assessment and subsequent instruction, and is interested in systemic change to reform the education of children with unique learning needs through measuring children's response to intervention. He has written numerous articles, books, and book chapters related to these research interests.

Preface

Although trends in education come and go, the general development of the field is undeniable. Education is becoming increasingly data driven, accountability based, and generally more scientific. While we applaud this maturation, there seems to be a significant component of a fully scientific model of education that is missing from the conversation. For a discipline to be scientific, it must embrace and incorporate an experimental methodology. While the use of evidence-based interventions and outcome data are positive developments, optimal outcomes cannot be realized without an experimental approach. This book presents single-case design (SCD) as the experimental methodology for measuring response to educational intervention. The primary goal of this book is to provide guidance in the use of experimental methods in daily educational practice. Throughout, we emphasize that the benefits of educational intervention are maximized when a truly scientific approach is adopted. As such, this book is intended to be a road map to the ongoing transformation of educational practice into a scientific endeavor.

The specific purpose of this book is to bring together two educational technologies: SCD and response to intervention (RTI). SCD may be generally unknown to most educational professionals, but it is a class of experimental methodology that has been utilized for decades in a number of disciplines (Kazdin, 1982). The limited use of SCD in day-to-day educational practice is unfortunate, because in an applied setting SCD allows educational professionals to defensibly document the effect of interventions, assess the role of an intervention in the observed change, and decide if that information has some general programming utility. Educational systems that embrace a problem-solving orientation require statements about intervention effectiveness, particularly if they result in educational planning, to be backed up with data.

One of the most visible examples of data-based educational planning is the nationwide movement to an RTI service delivery model. RTI is an educational problem-solving model with the principal goal of providing the most effective instruction and intervention to each student through the efficient allocation of educational resources. RTI utilizes a three-tiered model of service delivery, with increasing levels of intervention and related educational services provided to each student based on need. Using an RTI model, special education becomes the funding source for children who need the most significant levels of support (Burns & Gibbons, 2008), as eligibility for special education services is based on a child's response to intervention.

The role of academic and social behavior intervention is magnified in an RTI environment. The success or failure of an intervention (i.e., the student's response to evidence-based intervention [EBI]) is a critical diagnostic tool as long as the intervention is functionally relevant, evidence based, and implemented with integrity (Riley-Tillman & Walcott, 2007). Regrettably, these elements are necessary but not sufficient for an RTI process to work effectively. Even if a functionally relevant EBI is conducted with integrity, we still may not simply conclude that the child was responding (or not responding) to that particular intervention as opposed to other extraneous factors. This statement requires the use of fully experimental methods like SCD. The use of SCD allows for educational professionals to "know what they know, and know what they don't know" in terms of RTI. In an environment where the stakes of a successful intervention are dramatically higher than in years past (in particular, in schools using an RTI model of service delivery), using a defensible methodology to determine the effectiveness of an intervention is critical.

There are other advantages to SCD beyond clearly demonstrating the effectiveness (or lack thereof) of an intervention. First, it is a highly feasible method of conducting applied research, as it does not require the use of a control group or randomization of subjects. In addition, SCD is highly flexible and can be adapted to most situations in educational environments. In essence, SCD is the ideal technology for educational professionals to make more defensible decisions in an RTI model as well as the ideal experimental basis for making the field of education truly scientific.

This book is intended to be a guide for educational professionals who aspire to make educational intervention an applied research endeavor. To accomplish this goal, eight chapters and two appendices are presented. Three chapters are dedicated to an understanding of SCD and a review of specific methods. Two chapters are devoted to a variety of relevant analytic methods, and one chapter is focused on brief experimental analysis. Also included are introductory and concluding chapters that embed SCD in modern education in general and an RTI service delivery model in particular. These chapters include guiding questions to facilitate effective and efficient use of SCD and analysis in an educational problem-solving model. Throughout the book, examples of SCD used for educational intervention are presented. These examples are author simulated, drawing upon previous experiences using these design and analysis strategies in educational settings. As such, no identifying information or actual outcome data have been included in the book.

In light of the nationwide push to increase the scientific nature of education, this book is appropriate for anyone working with students in schools. Any educators interested in effective and efficient data-based decision making about educational intervention should find this material immediately usable and worthwhile. It is our belief that the field of education is past the point where ignoring the benefits of a fully scientific approach to education is acceptable. The importance of a scientific approach is especially true with children who are failing. For education to fully emerge as a mature scientific discipline, problem-solving approaches that incorporate EBI, formative evaluation, and experimental methods must become standard educational practice for all educational professionals. It is our hope that this book will be one small step in the direction of schools finally embracing a complete scientific approach to education, and thus committing to the highest standards of educational practice.

Acknowledgments

We begin by thanking our many mentors who have helped shape our beliefs and practices over the years. We would also like to thank Craig Thomas, Editor at The Guilford Press, and Kenneth Merrell, Editor of The Guilford Practical Intervention in the Schools Series, for their editorial support and guidance. We also are grateful to Ajlana Music for her editorial eye. Finally, we would like to thank our spouses, Erin and Mary Beth, and our families for their continuous support.

Contents

List of Figures and Tables

FIGURES

TABLES

1

Introduction to Design and Analysis for Educational Intervention

A recent documentary television program showed two men trying to attract sharks, from the safety of a shark cage and a boat, using different kinds of sounds. They tried several sounds for short periods of time, each with no luck. The disappointing experiment was about to end when all of a sudden a large great white shark appeared. The two would-be scientists concluded that the sound being projected at that time was the exact auditory stimulus that would attract sharks. Many people would probably, and correctly, interpret this "experimentation" as completely lacking validity, yet this approach to empirically answering questions happens in K–12 schools every day. Sometimes this unscientific decision-making model is acceptable, but often examining data collected in a manner from which causality cannot be inferred can have disastrous results.

While it would be ideal if general education instruction and curricula would meet the needs of all children, this is all too often not the case. A significant percentage of students have some academic or social behavior difficulties at school due to reasons that range from various environmental issues to student disabilities. Regardless of the cause, it is the school's obligation to attempt to intervene in order to solve the problem when students do not progress at the same rate as their peers or are behaving in an inappropriate manner. Doing so fulfills the school's legal obligation to provide a free and appropriate public education (FAPE) while keeping in mind the availability of limited resources.

The FAPE obligation stemmed from the Education of All Handicapped Children Act of 1975 (Public Law 94-142), which initially mandated special education, and was reauthorized with the Individuals with Disabilities Education Improvement Act of 2004 (IDEIA 2004). Moreover, the 2001 No Child Left Behind Act (NCLB) mandated that children with special needs be included in state accountability testing. Historically, children with special needs were removed from standardized assessment (state/district) tests, which resulted in public snapshots of schools and districts not adequately representing the educational outcomes for children with special needs. Current NCLB mandates require that students with special needs also experience positive academic outcomes, which often motivates the school to maximize the academic development of all children. Thus, we engage in individual and small-group interventions to try to solve academic and social behavior problems for personal, professional, and ultimately legal reasons.

WHAT IS INTERVENTION?

Before we move on, it is critical that we define the model of "intervention" that we use throughout the book. Without doing so, we risk readers applying their own version of educational intervention as they read and reflect. An intervention is "a planned modification of the environment made for the purpose of altering behavior in a prespecified way" (Tilly & Flugum, 1995). An intervention can be at the whole-school (e.g., curriculum) or individual level.

Because interventions are preplanned modifications to the environment, the method with which they are planned is equally important as the target. Previously used intervention heuristics emphasized intuitive appeal over empirical data. Interventions for children with learning difficulties in the 1960s, 1970s, and early 1980s were frequently developed by matching instructional modality with the student's preferred learning style or by identifying areas of psycholinguistic difficulty (Kavale, 2001). However, meta-analytic research found such small effects for these interventions that relying on them was presented as an example of philosophical and clinical beliefs overshadowing research data (Kavale & Forness, 2000).

Recent research developments led to interventions with greater likelihood for success if based on formative data and implemented with integrity (Daly, Martens, Dool, & Hintze, 1998; Daly, Martens, Hamler, Dool, & Eckert, 1999; Graham, Harris, & MacArthur, 2004; Poncy, Skinner, & O'Mara, 2006; Shapiro, 2004). Moreover, current educators and interventionists rely on student outcomes as an empirical indicator of the value of innovations. This movement toward empiricism represents a more scientific approach that relies on experimental, rather than correlational data (Reschly & Ysseldyke, 2002). The emphasis on student outcomes is also apparent in efforts to implement and study response to intervention (RTI) and in policy recommendations (Donovan & Cross, 2001; Gresham, 2002b; No Child Left Behind Act, 2001). Instructional decisions based on student learning data inexorably lead to techniques with a strong research base and away from popular but less effective approaches.

This book clearly adheres to the empirical foundation of interventions with the effectiveness being best documented by observing the outcome data. In our opinion, outcome data gathered in a scientific manner drive the intervention process, which suggests that educators are not only effective in selecting appropriate and scientifically based interventions, but also in collecting academic and social behavior outcome data.

There are a number of excellent resources for intervention selection (Daly, Chafouleas, & Skinner, 2005; Rathvon, 2008; Shapiro, 2004) but the data analysis aspect of an effective intervention has yet to be the focus of intervention resources. This creates a critical problem because although selecting research-based interventions increases the likelihood of a positive effect, it does not insure it. Further, while collecting defensible outcome data for interventions allow educational professionals to judge the effectiveness of the intervention, that data must be collected in a systematic manner (experimental) and analyzed appropriately. In other words, without effective intervention methods and analysis, the final step of problem solving cannot be taken. This book attempts to fill that critical void by focusing on the design and analysis of data to evaluate the effectiveness of interventions.

RAISING THE STAKES: RESPONSE TO INTERVENTION

Response to intervention (RTI) is an educational problem-solving model with the primary goal of providing the most effective instruction and intervention to each student through the efficient allocation of educational resources. Through a three-tiered model (Tier 1: Universal, Tier 2: Targeted, and Tier 3: Intensive), increasing levels of intervention and related educational services are provided to each student based on need. Through this process, special education becomes the funding source for children who need the most significant levels of support (Burns & Gibbons, 2008). In other words, eligibility for special education services is based on a child's response to intervention.

RTI and Special Education

Because the goal of RTI is to identify an intervention that allows a child to be successful, special education is primarily seen as the funding avenue for children whose needs are so intense that they exceed the resources typically allocated to general education (Burns & Gibbons, 2008). Thus, the primary jurisdiction over RTI functionally falls within general education, but the origins lie in special education.

We have long understood that children who are referred for special education eligibility assessments are likely to be placed into special education, often due to variables other than educational need or consistency with eligibility criteria (Gerber & Semmel, 1984; Potter, Ysseldyke, Regan, & Algozzine, B., 1983; Ysseldyke & Thurlow, 1984). As a result, special education policy recommendations have focused on using RTI to enhance eligibility decisions (Donovan & Cross, 2001; Gresham, 2002b; Public Law 89–10). Thus, RTI is the latest installment of the data-based decision-making movement that began with Deno and Mirkin's (1977) seminal work and culminated with IDEIA 2004's provision that a local education agency "may use a process that determines if the child responds to scientific, research-based intervention as a part of the evaluation procedures" (Public Law 108–446 § 614 [b][6][A]; § 614 [b][2 & 3]). However, several important events and movements occurred along the way that facilitated interest in data-based decision-making education including dissatisfaction with special education, educational accountability, and research about human learning.

Dissatisfaction with Special Education

There has been a considerable amount of controversy surrounding special education since it was first mandated in 1975 (Ysseldyke, Algozzine, & Thurlow, 2000). Much of the dissatisfaction was focused on the diagnostic procedures for determining eligibility. Initially, learning disabilities (LD) were defined in federal regulations for Public Law 94–142 as severe underachievement as compared to the child's intelligence, which was little more than a compromise due to a lack of an accepted LD diagnostic model at the time (Gresham et al., 2004). However, shortly after being institutionalized in federal regulations, the discrepancy model of LD was questioned by research conducted by the Institute for Research on Learning Disabilities (IRLD) at the University of Minnesota. After almost 30 years of research the LD diagnostic approach outlined in special education mandates is considered a failed model (Aaron, 1997; Fletcher et al., 1998).

Unfortunately, the shortcomings of the discrepancy model are compounded by disappointing results of special education effectiveness research. Specifically, research by Kavale and Forness (1999) using meta-analytic techniques found small average effects for commonly used instructional methods in special education such as perceptual and psycholinguistic training. In addition, their research found that the average effect size for special education in general was actually –0.12. This stunning finding suggested that children receiving special education services actually did worse than those with similar disabilities but who did not receive special education. Fortunately, subsequent research with children identified as LD found large effect sizes for direct instruction, explicit comprehension instruction, and mnemonic strategies (Kavale & Forness, 2000). This finding suggests, though, that students in special education are not consistently receiving the interventions that result in a large effect. These data caused many to ask, "If intervention methods that work are not being used in special education, what is special education?" Special education was originally, and remains defined as, "specially designed instruction, at no cost to the parents or guardians, to meet the unique needs of a child with a disability" (§ 300.39). Sadly, it seems that that all aspects of that definition are not met in traditional special education settings where interventions are designed based on categories of deficits rather than based on individual student needs.

Research into Human Learning

Meta-analytic research has questioned the effectiveness of special education and has identified effective practices for children with learning difficulties (Kavale & Forness, 1999; Swanson, Hoskyn, & Lee, 1999). This research provides an excellent starting point for a pathway to success when working with struggling students.

Another relevant line of research has examined the physiological effects of effective interventions. Simos et al. (2002) studied a group of children who were diagnosed as LD with a discrepancy model. Moreover, the study participants all demonstrated a brain imagery pattern when reading in which the right hemisphere of the brain was activated or no clear pattern was evident. This is consistent with patterns associated with children diagnosed as LD, whereas skilled readers tend to focus their neurological activity in the portion of the brain's left hemisphere where language functions are centered. Simos and colleagues implemented an intervention with a strong research base and then repeated the imaging of the children while reading and found that the activity pattern had changed and now focused on the left hemisphere such as associated with skilled reading. Think about the potential implications of this finding. Effective intervention with children whose neurological activity previously was consistent with an LD population resulted in typical neurological activity. The term *brain chemistry* is often discussed in schools, but current research suggests that changing behavior modifies brain chemistry, which is a far more plausible option among educational interventionists. Ironically, it appears that in many instances, the best way to change the child is to alter the environment to maximize educational success. It seems that in schools it is not only more feasible to focus on effective intervention than a medical approach to diagnosis, but also more prudent if one is truly interested in positive outcomes.

Accountability

The data-based decision-making movement took a somewhat surprising twist in 1983 with the *Nation at Risk* report (U.S. Department of Education, 1983). The report's claim that American schools were failing led to a general increased interest in educational accountability (Ravitch, 1999). The interest in accountability spilled over into special education through the report of the President's Commission on Excellence in Special Education (2002). Subsequently, IDEIA (2004) specified that children could be diagnosed as LD if "the child fails to achieve a rate of learning to make sufficient progress to meet state-approved results in one or more of the areas identified in paragraph (a)(1) of this section when assessed with a response to scientific, research-based intervention process" (Public Law 108–446, §§ 300.309). Thus, NCLB's mandate for including all children in outcome assessments and RTI became married as extensions of the same construct.

The implications of including children with disabilities in accountability assessments are significant. Systems with a significant rate of failure will be questioned. In addition, all children, including those in special education, will be incorporated in this analysis. As a result, school districts are held accountable not only for the success of the whole, but also the success of the children who are most at risk. Considering the general failures of special education as noted above, this is clearly a difficult situation for most educational environments. Luckily, as also noted above, there are intervention strategies that are effective with children who have traditionally been placed in special education. The challenge is simply to match the appropriate strategy with the child, and then monitor the effectiveness and react accordingly. This is otherwise known as a *data-based decision-making model*.

RTI and Intervention

Educators in settings that implement an RTI model clearly place a significant value on intervention and data-based decision making. As such, it is critical to consider the varying nature of interventions in education. When one considers intervention from a whole-school perspective, the importance of intervention methodology is clearly not consistent throughout each level of service delivery. Intervention begins with curriculum, and then becomes more and more individualized as it proves to be ineffective. At each stage, the amount of resources allocated to the intervention increases and the implications of intervention failure rise. Figure 1.1 presents the three-tiered model of RTI with intervention, assessment, and services typically associated with each level (Burns, Deno, & Jimerson, 2007).

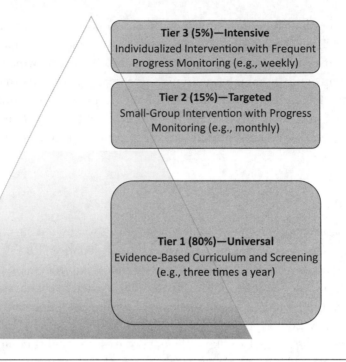

FIGURE 1.1. A continuum of assessment and intervention activities.

In Tier 1 the standard intervention practices, or curriculum, are utilized in a somewhat uniform manner across all children in the school. While schools tend to spend a good deal of time and energy on the selection of curriculum, this selection process is not tailored to one individual student, rather it is designed to encompass the general education population. The assessment of the effectiveness of this curriculum is also not individualized for each student, rather standard grading methods and periodic standardized assessment procedures are utilized to judge how individual students are progressing. At this level, essentially all we know is that either a student is progressing acceptably, or is not. We can never be sure if the observed progress or lack thereof is directly related to the general education program. Realistically, a student could be doing quite well due to other supports (e.g., tutoring, home support, superior abilities) that are unknown to the school. Further, a student could be failing due to reasons that are not directly related to the primary intervention.

In the case of a failing student he/she is moved to Tier 2 so that schools can accomplish two goals. The first goal is obviously to attempt more rigorous interventions to help the child in relation to his/her academic or social behavior difficulties. The second goal is to administer the intervention in a more systematic manner in terms of selection, assessment, integrity, and intervention methodology so that we can better understand a child's academic or social behavior problem more thoroughly. In Tier 2 the first goal takes precedence. At this stage daily small-group interventions with weekly or biweekly progress monitoring are often the norm (Burns, Hall-Lande, Lyman, Rogers, & Tan, 2006). Tier 2 should service approximately 15% of the total school population.

Students who do not respond adequately to intervention in the first two tiers are moved into Tier 3. In Tier 3, thoroughly understanding a child's academic or social behavior problem becomes increasingly more important as assessment and intervention efforts attempt to identify the causal variables or functional relationship between the instructional setting and student learning. At this stage, a fully problem-solving approach is essential for the development of intervention. Children for whom interventions within Tier 3 are not effective, or for whom the successful intervention is so intense that it exceeds the resources associated with general education, are considered for special education eligibility in order to provide a FAPE.

RTI and Problem Analysis

As student needs become more intense, measurement becomes more precise and frequent, and problem analysis becomes more in-depth. Problem analysis involves identifying the important elements of a problem by examining possible causes, seeking additional information, and framing possible solutions (Thomson, 1993). In Tier 1, problem analysis simply involves identifying whether a problem exists. Often the data gathered in Tier 1 can be similar to the shark seekers discussed earlier. If the sound attracts the shark (i.e., students are learning), then there is no need to consider the situation any further because it does not matter *why* students are being successful at this point. Thus, the measurement can be simplistic and the assumption of causality can be minimal.

Students for whom the general curriculum and instruction are not effective require a slightly more in-depth analysis. Remembering that Tier 2 essentially involves small-group interventions, the primary analysis task is to identify a category of deficit and then monitor the effectiveness of interventions to address that deficit. Monitoring the progress requires sound data collection techniques, but a lack of sufficient progress heightens the need for psychometric adequacy and experimental rigor. As students' needs become more intense, the need for experimental control and assumptions of causality become more prominent. Students for whom the Tier 2 intervention was not successful then are provided individualized intervention, which requires that the primary problem-analysis focus in Tier 3 is to identify the causal variables of the deficit based on idiosyncratic behavior and idiographic principles.

THE IMPLICATIONS OF AN RTI MODEL ON INTERVENTION METHODOLOGY

The role of academic and social behavior intervention, which has always been significant, is magnified in an RTI environment. In this setting, the success or failure of an intervention (i.e., the student's response to an evidence-based intervention [EBI]) is a critical diagnostic tool as long as the intervention is functionally relevant, evidence based, and implemented with integrity (Riley-Tillman & Walcott, 2007). These three criteria highlight the many critical issues educational professionals must deal with when implementing an RTI model. First, the intervention must be appropriate for the problem. If an intervention is not functionally relevant, then a lack of response is predictable rather than a signal of a more serious problem. Once a function has been proposed, it is critical that the intervention is considered "evidence based," or supported by research as an effective remedy to a particular referral concern. As with the use of functionally irrelevant interventions, using interventions that have no empirical support is not considered evidence of a larger problem but rather preliminary evidence that the intervention is not effective. Finally, the intervention must be implemented with integrity. If the intervention is altered or degraded, then that is the most likely reason for the lack of success.

Fortunately, each of the aforementioned criteria has received a good deal of attention (e.g., Berninger, 2006; Burns & Coolong-Chaffin, 2006; Noell & Gansle, 2006; Wagner, McComas, Bollman, & Holton, 2006). Regrettably, these elements are necessary but not sufficient for an RTI process to work effectively. Even if a functionally relevant EBI is conducted with integrity, we still may not simply conclude that the child was responding (or not responding) to that particular intervention as opposed to other extraneous factors. This statement requires the use of fully experimental methods.

Burns and Gibbons (2008) suggest that RTI is a series of problem-solving decisions in which measurement becomes more frequent and precise, and problem analysis becomes more exact as the student's needs become more severe. Thus, as the decisions being made with the intervention outcome data become more serious, it is essential to start considering the issue of causality. Specifically, educational professionals must document both whether academic or social behavior changes have occurred, and if the intervention in question was responsible for those substantiated changes. The issue of causality becomes most relevant when academic or social behavior problems are dramatic or when the results of the intervention will be used for special education eligibility decision making. At this step it is critical that one can attest that it was the intervention that resulted in a change or that the intervention truly did not show an effect.

Some have suggested that a documented "lack" of an intervention effect triggers special education services in an RTI model (Fuchs, Mock, Morgan, & Young, 2003; Speece, Case, & Molloy, 2003). While this is logical from an educational perspective, it is rather unique experimentally (as researchers tend to look for an effect rather than a lack of an effect). To be able to take this next step, we need to employ a defensible intervention methodology within the framework of a single-case research design.

SINGLE-CASE DESIGN AND ANALYSIS

Single-case designs (SCD) are a class of experimental methodology that has been utilized for decades in a number of disciplines including psychology and education (Kazdin, 1982). While known by a number of different names, such as *single subject*, *intrasubject*, and *N = 1*, we use the term *single case* throughout the text. Before we move on, it is important to note that a number of the names used for this class of experimental design imply defining features that are not always accurate. For example, the terms *single subject* and *N = 1*, which suggest that this class of methodology is to be used with only one subject, are incorrect, as SCDs are often used with small groups. Another term used for this class of design, *intersubject replication*, also can be a bit misleading for two reasons. First, as Kazdin noted in his classic SCD book, some designs actually depend on comparing intervention effects across subjects. Second, while replication is a key figure in the classic research application of these designs, in an applied educational setting we do not always have a replication phase. It is our belief that the most common feature of SCD is the very philosophy on which it is based, baseline logic, which we further explore in Chapter 2.

Perhaps the best manner to introduce the concept of SCD is to consider what this class of design was developed to accomplish (Riley-Tillman & Wallcott, 2007). SCD is a collection of experimental methods that are developed to essentially document three things:

1. If there is an observable and important change in some dependent variable.
2. If the observed change in the outcome data postapplication of the independent variable is a result of the application of the independent variable.
3. If this change is something that is generalizable across time, setting, and target.

When applied to an educational environment in general and educational intervention specifically, the three general purposes of SCD read as follows:

1. Did the outcome variable (e.g., percent of time on task) change when the intervention was implemented?
2. Was the observed change due to the implementation of the intervention and *only* the implementation of the intervention?
3. Can the information learned from this educational intervention be generalized to other similar educational problems and settings?

Although each of these three purposes are discussed further in Chapter 2, at this point it is important to know that SCDs allow for educational professionals to defensibly document the effect of interventions, assess the role of the intervention in the observed change, and decide if that information has some general programming utility. Obviously, documenting intervention effectiveness is of critical importance in today's educational environment. Gone are the days where it was acceptable for an educational professional to simply state that some intervention was or was not effective. In the accountability era, such statements, particularly if they result in educational planning, must be backed up with data.

The second and third goals of SCD are a bit more advanced, but have become critical in modern education. As noted above, when the success or failure of an intervention is used as evidence for special education eligibility for a struggling student, clearly we should be sure that it was indeed the intervention that created the effect rather than some random external factor. To be sure of the relationship between the intervention and the outcome data experimental control is critical. Experimental control is what SCD is built to accomplish as discussed in Chapter 2. While this idea of documenting causality may seem novel, to avoid this issue with high-stakes cases is hardly defensible.

The final goal of SCD is to collect evidence regarding the generalization of some intervention finding. In other words, can this same intervention be used in the future with the same child, or can this intervention be used with another child who has a similar issue? As shown in Chapter 2, the only way to gather evidence to support that a current intervention effect will work in the future or with another child is systematic replication. SCD gives educational professionals a path to conduct systematic replication, and thus a path to defensible claims as to the generalizability of intervention results.

WHY IS SCD IDEAL FOR EDUCATIONAL PRACTICE?

Perhaps the most attractive element of SCD is that it is a family of experimental methods that are designed for use with one student (or a small group of students). If you pick up a journal that publishes educational research, you will undoubtedly find that most studies compare groups of subjects in some manner. This type of experimental design is focused on collecting data from a large number of subjects who are considered to be a good representation of some larger population. This form of experimentation is effective for the development of generalizable knowledge. Research using one child is typically not as suited for this purpose. For example, it would be risky to say that outcome data on one child with some specific reading problem would be predictive for other children with the same reading problem (Kazdin 1982; Kratchowill & Williams, 1988; Walcott & Riley-Tillman, 2007). The one child being observed could be unique in a number of ways that might make him/her an atypical representative for the larger population of children with that specific reading problem. On the other hand, if you were to collect data from say, 150 children with that specific reading problem, their outcome data would start to describe the larger population (all children with that specific reading problem), but might miss important idiosyncrasies for the individual student. Moreover, while a group orientation is logical if you are attempting to produce knowledge about a population, most educational professionals work at the level of one child or a small group of children.

Through systematic replication of observed intervention effects (across setting, situations, and interventionists) we gain confidence that the intervention will be effective in future applications if used with targets similar to those represented in the large-group efficacy studies. While this is clearly valuable information, it does not mean that we can confidently assume that an EBI will always have a positive effect on an individual child who is a member of that group. To illustrate why this is the case consider an intervention that is consistently effective (e.g., showed a positive intervention effect with 90% of children studied). Even with such a consistently effective intervention, it was ineffective in 10% of the cases. A practitioner can never truly know before implementation if he/she is working with a child who falls in that 10% and thus the intervention would likely prove ineffective. In the end, the label of EBI does not imply that an intervention will work with a similar child, but rather that it is probable that it will be effective (assuming it was selected appropriately). The implications of this reality are critical. Even a well-selected EBI that is delivered with perfect treatment integrity may prove ineffective for an individual child. As a result, in practice it is critical that educational professionals determine whether an EBI proves effective for each child after implementation. This obligation is even more critical when a child's response to an EBI will be a part of special education eligibility determination. Indeed, understating what an EBI is and what the label of EBI really means, it is clearly not defensible to simply select, implement, and assume that the child will respond. When the level of interest is the specific child, then SCD is the ideal choice of research methodology.

The use of SCD allows for educational professionals to "know what they know, and know what they don't know" in terms of response to intervention. By adhering to an appropriate SCD, educational professionals can make defensible judgments about the impact of interventions (independent variables) on outcome data (dependent variables) with only one student. As discussed above, in an environment where the stakes of a successful intervention are dramatically higher (particularly, schools using an RTI model of service delivery), being able to use a defensible methodology to determine whether an intervention was effective is critical.

There are other advantages to SCD beyond clearly demonstrating the effectiveness (or lack thereof) of an intervention. First, it is a highly feasible method of conducting applied research as it does not require the use of a control group or randomization of subjects. Obviously, in schools it is not typically appropriate to have a "control group" of students who are intentionally denied an intervention. One can only imagine a parent's response when they find out that their struggling child is receiving a placebo intervention. While a SCD requires baseline data to be collected (and thus, some delay in implementing an intervention), there is no need for a group of children in need to be denied the appropriate services. Ethically, this is a significant advantage of single-case methodology. In addition, SCD is highly flexible. As discussed in Chapter 2, single-case logic (or baseline logic) can be used to build a number of different designs. This range of options makes it much more likely that there will be an appropriate design for each situation. In essence, SCD and analysis is the ideal technology for educational professionals to make more defensible educational decisions in an RTI model.

HOW READY ARE EDUCATIONAL PROFESSIONALS?

It is clear that intervention practices in schools are changing and there are technologies such as EBIs, problem-solving models, direct academic/social behavior assessment strategies, and single-case methodology and analysis that exist for educational professionals to utilize in this transition. Unfortunately, it is somewhat questionable how prepared teachers and other educational professionals are to use these technologies. Preservice teachers report receiving very little instruction in behavior practices or direct academic assessment (Begeny & Martens, 2006) and practicing special education teachers frequently report using instructional practices with little research support (Burns & Ysseldyke, in press). Moreover, graphing procedures remain remarkably underutilized in elementary and secondary classrooms (Moxley, 2007). These studies only confirm the widely held belief that national implementation of an RTI model will be a difficult task (Burns, 2007; Burns, Vanderwood, & Ruby, 2005; Vaughn & Fuchs, 2003). Clearly one of the major challenges in transition to an RTI model is a significant amount of training for teachers and other educational professionals in some of the most basic skills associated with RTI implementation.

While these issues are of concern, there are clearly individuals in the schools who should be the conduits for distributing information and training educational professionals to adopt RTI. Given that group-based data management is a critical component of RTI (Kovaleski & Pedersen, 2008) one or two individuals with expertise in SCD and analysis should be able to use this technology to assist in individual cases as well as model it for other members of the team. While this task can seem daunting, in our experiences such demonstrations are effective training opportunities that can help team members develop the skill set to effectively launch an RTI model.

CONCLUDING COMMENTS

The purpose of this chapter was to consider the role of SCD in a modern model of special education service delivery. Clearly, as the stakes of using academic and social behavior intervention increases, the integrity of such intervention must also increase. As such, it is critical that educational professionals steep themselves in the literature focusing on intervention selection and the measurement of intervention effects. This book is not a comprehensive guide of intervention selection or the measurement of the effects of an intervention; therefore, professionals who desire development in reference to those to topics should consult texts on intervention selection (e.g., Rathvon, 2008), academic assessment (e.g., Hosp, Hosp, & Howell, 2007), and social behavior assessment (e.g., Chafouleas, Riley-Tillman, & Sugai, 2007).

While the selection, implementation, and monitoring of educational interventions are necessary elements of a defensible and effective RTI model, they are not sufficient. RTI can best be conceptualized as the systematic use of assessment data to most efficiently allocate resources in order to improve learning for all students (Burns & VanDerHeyden, 2006). Moreover, in order to inform a valid RTI framework, data need to model academic growth, distinguish between ineffective instruction and unacceptable individual learning, inform instructional decisions, and be sensitive enough to detect treatment effects (Gresham, 2002a). Thus, the terms *RTI* and *data* are essentially synonymous, but it is not the collection of data that makes an effective system, rather the systematic use of the data. In our opinion, RTI cannot happen without defensible data collection *and* valid analytical techniques for which to consider data from individuals and groups of students.

This book is not intended to be a complete overview of the philosophy and basis of SCD nor is it intended as a guide for traditional researchers. There are a number of excellent texts that already accomplish those goals (e.g., Cooper, Heron, & Heward, 2007; Kazdin, 1982; Kennedy, 2005; Tawney & Gast, 1984). Rather this book is intended to be a guide for educational professionals who desire and are now more often required to make educational intervention an applied research endeavor. As such, the remainder of this book is a detailed description of SCD, the analysis of intervention data, and guidance as to how to use this technology in schools. In the next chapter, we consider baseline logic in order to have a full understanding of SCD. Chapters 3 and 4 build on the foundation of baseline logic to present a number of SCDs. Chapters 5 and 6 outline the numerous strategies that educational professionals can use to effectively analyze intervention outcome data. Chapter 7 presents a unique application of SCD for assessment of interventions called *brief experimental analysis*. Finally, in Chapter 8, additional guidelines are discussed to enhance the use of SCD and analysis in RTI environments.

2

The Nuts and Bolts
of Single-Case Design

WHAT IS THE PURPOSE OF EXPERIMENTATION?

Consider for a moment a simple question. What is the purpose of experimentation? While there are many possible answers to that question, they all should revolve around some idea of generating defensible knowledge. The nature of knowledge has been discussed from Plato's *Theaetetus* to modern study in educational psychology and philosophy departments. Within the context of applied decision making, we are most interested in "defensible" knowledge that rises above personal beliefs and experiences through scientific inquiry.

There are a number of definitions of the scientific method, but the classic explanation of experimental inquiry by Cohen and Nagel (1934) is quite to the point: "Scientific method we declared as the most assured technique man has yet devised for controlling the flux of things and establishing stable beliefs" (p. 391). The act of experimentation is the gathering of evidence to support or refute hypotheses, or the formal statement of an educated guess. Using a three-stage hypothesis–initial experiment–replication model of the scientific method, experimentation is the second and third steps of scientific inquiry. Thus, experimentation is at its core the implementation of controlled procedures to test a hypothesis. We engage in that process so that we can gain confidence in the "facts" that we consider sound, so the evidence is both defensible and useful.

In the schools, the same general ideas regarding experimentation can be applied. In fact, the scientific method is the preferred basis of practice for school psychology (Ysseldyke et al., 2006), special education (Odom et al., 2005), and education in general (Shavelson & Towne, 2002). There is an endless supply of educated guesses that are the basis of decisions in schools. These can range from the guess that a particular curriculum or behavior management system will be effective to the guess that a particular child needs to be educated in a particular manner. In reality, the aforementioned curriculum, behavior management system, and intervention method have some degree of effectiveness. Each one of these educated guesses can be tested, and decisions can be made accordingly. Considering the importance of many educational decisions, an experimental path is most defensible.

Perhaps the better question in relation to experimentation and school environments is, "Why don't we use experimentation in the schools?" There seem to be a number of answers to that question, including:

1. It is just not feasible to treat every question in an experimental manner.
2. Traditional experimental methods are not considered realistic in the schools.
3. The goal of education is not to produce generalizable knowledge but rather to educate children, and education is not something that can be quantified.

Each of these arguments probably sounds rather familiar to anyone who has worked in the schools, or more specifically tried to promote science in the schools. Frankly, each of these statements has some merit. It is not feasible to make every decision that takes place in the schools into a formal experiment, and most educational professionals are not trained to apply social science experimental methodology. Experimental methods requiring a control group are often not realistic in the schools, and methods that examine groups are often not useful for individual children. However, there is a potential solution to each of the reasons for a lack of experimentation in schools. Many of those solutions are found in the particular research methods of SCD.

It is generally suggested that experienced teachers understand what methods work, and which methods are ineffective. This idea, while attractive, assumes that the teacher can detach personal beliefs from any specific intervention case. In other words, this assumes that the teacher is not influenced in some manner based on his/her belief about the educational practice in question. This assumption has long been understood to be incorrect. The educational professional is more likely to observe supporting evidence than evidence that contradicts preconceived notions. This is commonly known as a *confirmation bias*. Thus, the educator who is sure the intervention will succeed is likely to focus on evidence supporting this belief while ignoring or minimizing evidence to the contrary. As a result, we are often prone to believe the intervention is effective. Likewise, the educational professional who believes that the intervention will fail will focus on evidence supporting this belief. Sadly, there is little reason to trust that educational professionals will accurately judge the effectiveness of the intervention in the absence of a scientific, or experimental, approach. This is not a judgment on the ethics of teachers, but rather a reality of how individuals process information that either confirms or refutes their beliefs. The results of this pattern are predictable, ineffective methods that are thought to work will be considered effective even in the face of evidence to the contrary. Likewise, effective methods that were not originally believed effective are likely to be dismissed. In addition, the vigor of the beliefs held by teachers in regard to the success or failure of intervention is not sufficient for critical educational decisions. Another quote from Cohen and Nagel eloquently expresses this point: "Science is not satisfied with psychological certitude, for the mere intensity with which a belief is held is no guarantee of its truth. Science demands and looks for logically adequate grounds for the propositions it advances" (p. 394). In the end, it is critical that educational professionals apply the scientific method to their work to ensure that best practices are actually being utilized. As such, before considering SCD, it is important to take a step back and consider the general process of the scientific method.

STEP 1. DEVELOPMENT OF A HYPOTHESIS: EXPERIMENTAL THINKING

While we all have beliefs about the way things work, scientists attempt to make testable statements about those beliefs. Such statements, called *scientific* or *research hypotheses*, are stated as predictions about some observable phenomena based on existing knowledge or theory. For example, a teacher with 20 years of experience might draw upon his/her experience to say that a particular reading program is more effective than another. A school principal might rely on the research literature to conclude that positive behavior supports would lead to a number of desired outcomes in regard to behavior in his/her school. In either case, a body of information was used to make an informed prediction. While this informed prediction or belief is clearly a useful tool, it is critical to take one more step and create a formal hypothesis. This formal hypothesis will turn this belief into a statement that can be used to create a research plan. There are three critical elements to a formal hypothesis: an independent variable, a dependent variable, and a statement of the direction of the expected change.

The *independent variable* is the set of experimental conditions (or treatments) that is expected to bring about some observable change in the participants. Educational examples of independent variables range from primary whole-school procedures to tertiary specific intervention procedures for a target student. For example, full-day preschool (as compared to half-day preschool) could be an independent variable. Regardless of the nature of the independent variable, it is critical that it is well-defined so that the experience in question is consistent across participants and fully understood by the applied experimenter. For example, if we are interested in the effect of a particular reading intervention, we want the specifics of that intervention (activity, materials, frequency, and so on) to be clearly spelled out. It would be imperative to know that the "reading intervention" is a repeated reading activity using instructional-level text conducted for 30 minutes five times a week.

The second critical element of a hypothesis is a clear statement of the behavior that will change as a result of the application of the independent variable. This target behavior is called the *dependent variable*. While it is not unusual for the dependent variable to start as a rather general construct (e.g., reading achievement or appropriate social behavior), it is important that it is refined into a specific form of outcome data (e.g., curriculum-based measurement of reading fluency results, or systematic direct observation). This specification is critical in that while we often think of the more general construct, we actually study what is specifically measured.

Finally, hypotheses should include a clear statement about the nature and direction of the expected change (e.g., increase, positive relationship, or lesser gain). Once the independent variable, dependent variable, and direction of the change are stated in objective terms, the hypothesis is ready to be examined. In addition, creating a complete hypothesis statement automatically generates an alternative hypothesis predicting that no change will be observed. This "no change" version is called a *null hypothesis*. As we discuss later in this chapter, in an RTI model the null hypothesis is quite important.

STEP 2. OBSERVATION OF A FUNCTIONAL RELATIONSHIP FOR THE FIRST TIME

After developing a hypothesis that indicates the anticipated relationship between the independent and the dependent variable, the next step is to test this hypothesis in a controlled manner to determine if the statement is correct. Researchers consider this stage the actual experiment, which is conducted by observing the outcome data with and without the presence of the independent variable (e.g., application of the intervention). In typical research, the experiment is accomplished by randomly assigning groups of people into two conditions. The randomization process, if done correctly, allows for the assumption that each group is essentially equivalent at the study onset. Post randomization, in one condition the intervention is applied, while in the other condition some "placebo" is applied. If as predicted in the hypothesis the group that receives the intervention looks different than the placebo group on the dependent variable, then the hypothesis is supported. Another model would be to measure the group (again looking at the dependent variable) before the intervention, and then again after the intervention. If there is a significant change as outlined by the hypothesis, this again would be considered supporting evidence. If one were to outline the logic at this stage, it would look something like this:

> If X, then Y.
> Y, therefore, X.

The experimental adaptation of this is (Cooper et al., 2007):

> If the independent variable is a controlling factor for the dependent variable (X), then the outcome data will show a change when the independent variable is present (Y) (if X, then Y).
> The outcome data show a change when the independent variable is present (Y is true).
> Therefore, the independent variable is a controlling factor (effective in changing) for the dependent variable (therefore, X is true).

The intervention adaptation of this is (Cooper et al., 2007):

> If the intervention is a controlling factor for the behavior (X), then the data will show a change when the intervention is present (Y) (if X, then Y).
> The outcome data show a change when this intervention is present (Y is true).
> Therefore, the intervention is a controlling factor (effective in changing) for the behavior (therefore, X is true).

Regardless of the presentation, any student of logic will quickly note that this is a classic formal fallacy called *affirmation of the consequent* (Audi, 1999). In any of the conditions there could have been other reasons that Y occurred, rather than X. Simply because X means Y will occur does not mean that X is the *only* reason that Y can occur. For example, consider the following:

> If you have food poisoning, you will feel nausea.
> You feel nauseous.
> Therefore, you have food poisoning.

Clearly there are a number of reasons you could feel nauseous, food poisoning being only one of them. In the case of experimentation, the researcher will do his/her best to control as many other factors as possible. Unfortunately, even in the most rigorous of experimental situations, there are always known and unknown variables for which the effects are not accounted. Some potential confounding variables could include inherent measurement issues and the possibility that the right dependent variable or the right combination of dependent variables are not being measured (Sidman, 1960).

Given that in an educational environment the luxury of a rigorous experimental situation rarely occurs, it is clear that any "fact" that is discovered must be considered tenuous at best. In the end, affirming the consequent really only tells us that we have observed something that would support the hypothesis. Without further work, one cannot be sure that the application of the independent variable (or intervention) was indeed the manipulation that caused change.

STEP 3. REPLICATION

The end goal of experimentation is to produce some form of usable knowledge. While the use or application of the knowledge will vary, one of the core necessities for information to be usable is that it be reliable. While it is tempting to declare that an initial observation of the relationship between an independent and a dependent variable is real, such a statement may be premature. In an attempt to make stronger assertions as to the reliability of a relationship between an independent and dependent variable, we must replicate this initial observation. By observing the relationship several times, one can gain confidence in the dependability or reliability of the relationship (with some specific stipulations based on the form of replication undertaken). It has been long understood that the reliability of information is a matter of degree rather than an absolute. While it is clear that theories can be shown to be consistently incorrect, they cannot be declared absolutely correct (Sidman, 1960). Replication helps us to make much stronger statements about the relationship between an independent and dependent variable, but never absolute ones.

Based on this lack of absolute understanding, it becomes obvious that the scientific endeavor is one that is centered on gathering evidence to support and gain confidence in a theory, or finding out that theories do not have support. Replication is the process in experimental design that allows us to make stronger statements as to the reliability of a particular situation or relationship. While there are different types of replication that result in different types of confidence, the general principle is consistent. There are two general forms of replication: direct and systematic (Sidman, 1960).

Direct Replication

Direct replication refers to the simple repetition of the experimental procedures. There are two general classes of direct replication: intrasubject and intersubject (Cooper et al., 2007; Sidman, 1960). The distinction between these two classes is particularly important for educational researchers. Intrasubject replication refers to repeating the same procedure with the same research participant. The goal of such a replication is to increase the reliability of the findings, or the believability of the suggested functional relationship (Cooper et al., 2007), by holding the ecology (the environment during the observation) static. Reliability or believability is on a continuum from highly reliable (extremely trustable) to minimally reliable (cannot really be trusted). As discussed above, the goal of replication (intrasubject, in this case) is not to obtain absolute reliability but to simply determine where on the continuum this functional relationship lies. In educational terms, if one is suggesting that a particular intervention changed a child's on-task behavior, finding a way to replicate that procedure makes it more believable that it was the intervention that indeed changed the child's behavior. It is critical to note that in much of the scientific community, this is seen often as a first step to a second issue that we discuss next. In an educational community though, the believability of such a functional relationship is in fact a critical goal in and of itself. This form of replication allows us to increase the confidence with which we can make the statement that the child did, or did not respond to a particular intervention. Obviously this is a critical statement in an RTI service delivery model.

The second general class of direct replication, intersubject replication, has a very different goal in mind. When replicating the exact procedure with other participants, we are examining the generalizability of the information (Cooper et al., 2007). In other words, we are determining how confident we are that the observed functional relationship would be observed in other similar subjects as well. The amount of generality, much like the amount of reliability, is on a continuum from generalizable only to similar subjects/environments to generalizable to different subjects/environments. Some relationships are not relevant to anyone other than the first subject, while others could be close to universal.

In the life of a researcher, the generality of a finding is often critical. Generality suggests that the discovered knowledge is considerably important because it will affect a broader audience. In contrast, this type of generality is not nearly as important to an educational professional. For the most part, educational intervention is conducted on a subject-by-subject, or case-by-case basis. When a child is having difficulty learning to read, or staying on task, the primary objective is to help that specific child learn to read or increase task engagement. The reinforcement for success is significant, and is likely the very reason why many go into teaching. Finding that a successful intervention would help a number of children is clearly exciting, but the initial case is the most important in the applied setting because good teachers find success one student at a time.

Systematic Replication

Systematic replication is the process of altering one or more of the experimental conditions or aspects of the intervention to observe whether the relationship between the independent and dependent variable is reliable within the original setting and under the new set of experimental conditions. For example, while direct replication can increase confidence in the effectiveness of an intervention that has been experimentally observed to increase a target child's on-task behavior in a reading class, this does not necessarily mean that the intervention will be effective in the same manner in the child's math class. Through the process of systematic replication, we can alter the setting of the experimental conditions (e.g., reading versus math class) to see if that relationship is present in the math class. Systematic replication can be important because it allows a researcher to systematically extend findings. For example, one could change the intervention slightly to see if a briefer version is as successful, or to see if a different teacher can implement the intervention.

Interestingly, intersubject systematic replication happens to be a notable assumption in most modern consultation models. It is typical for school consultation models to suggest that one of the key benefits of working with a teacher in a problem-solving consultation process is that the teacher can then apply the intervention to other students in his/her class that are similar to the target student (Erchul & Martens, 2002). In other words, the hope is that if the intervention with Johnny was successful, then in the future the teacher will implement the same intervention or a slightly varied version of the intervention with children who are perceived similar to Johnny and are experiencing the same issue. As each applied intersubject replication is successful, the teacher uses the method more consistently and thus, increases his/her general skill as a teacher.

TARGET BEHAVIOR AND ASSESSMENT METHOD

As previously discussed, before we examine formal SCD, we must have a target behavior and some measurement of that behavior. Both of these issues are critical because the result of this process will be the dependent variable. As such, it is critical that a clear definition of the problem is developed, and a defensible assessment strategy is selected. While it is beyond the scope of this book to comprehensively present the process of selecting, defining, and measuring a target behavior, a brief outline is presented below. Readers are encouraged to consult other resources (e.g., Chafouleas et al., 2007; Merrell, 2003; Hosp et al., 2007) for an in-depth analysis.

First it is necessary to refine the definition of the problem into a clear target behavior. Students are often referred for a general pattern of problematic behavior. Unfortunately, while this general pattern of behavior may be something the teacher can define, it is not the type of focused variable needed for intervention, much less experimental design. In any problem-solving model it is important to develop a clear definition of the target behavior.

Hawkins and Dobes (1977) provide the classic criteria to define a target behavior suggesting that the behavioral definition should be objective, clear, and complete. The definition of the target behavior should be composed of clearly observable behaviors. It is preferable to have examples and nonexamples so that there is no ambiguity as to what is the target behavior. Thus, it is essential that any educational professional read the defined target behavior and understand if the behavior was or was not present (and other relevant features) after an opportunity to observe the target student in an appropriate setting. This behavioral definition can be enriched by including other relevant details (e.g., a list of who is present, a description of the typical setting when the behavior occurs).

Several strategies have been suggested to assist in the procedure of developing operational definitions (Alberto & Troutman, 2003), including stating both examples and nonexamples of the target behavior (Lewis & Sugai, 1996) and presenting an extensive list of representative behaviors (Todd, Horner, & Sugai, 1999). Regardless of the method, a behavioral definition that meets the three conditions suggested by Hawkins and Dobes (1977) of objectivity, clarity, and completeness is essential to eventually gauge the effectiveness of an intervention in general.

Once the target behavior has been defined a decision as to how that behavior will be measured must be made. Chafouleas et al. (2007) suggest that this decision should be based on four questions (see Table 2.1). First, why do you need the data? It is important that the source of outcome data is relevant to the type of decision being made. Second, which tools are best matched to assess the behavior of interest? It is clear that assessment tools do not all adequately measure the same behaviors (McDougal, Chafouleas, & Waterman, 2006). As such it is important to consider the strengths and weaknesses of available assessment methods and select one that is appropriate for the current target behavior (Riley-Tillman, Kalberer, & Chafouleas, 2005). Third, what decisions will be made using these data? As the stakes of the decisions that will be made using the data increase, so must also the quality of the outcome data. While in low-stakes cases it may be acceptable to use less rigorous data sources, only defensible outcome data should be used as the stakes increase. Finally, what resources are available to collect these data? This final issue focuses on feasibility. Outcome data must actually be collected, and thus, the strategies selected need to be realistic considering the availability of resources.

The results of this process should be the selection of a feasible and defensible assessment for the target behavior that is appropriate for the intended use. Once the target behavior has been defined and the assessment methodology has been selected, it is possible to consider baseline logic, which is the very basis of SCD and experimentation.

TABLE 2.1. Questions to Ask When Selecting an Assessment Tool

- Why do you need the data?
- Which tools are best matched to assess the behavior of interest?
- What decisions will be made using the data?
- What resources are available to collect the data?

Note. From Chafouleas, Riley-Tillman, and Sugai (2007). Copyright 2007 by The Guilford Press. Reprinted by permission.

BASELINE LOGIC

In order to formalize the three general steps of hypothesize, observe, and replicate, it is important to establish a formal set of guidelines. For SCD, those guidelines are baseline logic (Cooper et al., 2007; Riley-Tillman & Walcott, 2007). Baseline logic is to SCD as grammar is to writing. As such, an understanding of baseline logic allows one to "diagram" the experimental design (Riley-Tillman & Walcott, 2007), which is critical in an applied educational setting as things often do not go as planned. Although typically described as a three-step model (Cooper et al., 2007), we use a four-step model in this book (Riley-Tillman & Walcott, 2007). Specifically, we include the first *affirmation of the consequent* as a separate phase. While in a traditional experimental presentation one typically thinks of affirmation of the consequent as a form of replication (Sidman, 1960), in applied work the first demonstration is also important (and sometimes the final stage). Specifically, our model of baseline logic is comprised of four steps, including (1) prediction, (2) affirmation of the consequent, (3) verification, and (4) replication by affirmation of the consequent.

Prediction

Given that the goal of SCD is to defensibly document whether an intervention does or does not have a direct impact on the student behavior, the starting point of baseline logic is to determine what the preintervention behavior looks like. This stage, often called *baseline*, is a bit more complicated than what one might think. Of course, we know that the behavior in question is a problem, or we would not spend time considering an intervention. It may be difficult to explain to educational professionals why we need to start collecting outcome data to estimate the target behavior *before* the intervention begins. Teachers usually refer a student for consultation based on their perception of a problem, not some clear absolute level. Some teachers delay referring until the problem is significant, others call for intervention services as soon as minor problems present themselves. Unfortunately, while we know that there is a problem, we must formally assess the target behavior to provide a foundation from which we can build.

The collection of preintervention, or baseline, data allows for the documentation of how the behavior is naturally changing over a period of time without a change in the ecology (e.g., implementing an intervention). The collection of a stream of outcome data at this stage can help us ask a series of questions:

"What is the level of the behavior?"
"Is the behavior stable or is it changing (getting better or worse)?"
"How variable is the behavior?"

When it comes time to ask the question, "Did the intervention work?" we will consider each one of these issues. Thus, it is essential to have an understanding of the behavior, as represented in the outcome data, before we implement the intervention and observe to see if a change occurs. Without this information, we will always be left guessing about how the behavior looked prior to the intervention.

At this point, it is important to consider the actual statement made in the prediction phase of baseline logic:

If we do nothing, this is what we can expect the child's behavior to look like in the future.

By collecting a sufficient and steady stream of outcome data we are able to predict future levels of the behavior if nothing were to change (Cooper et al., 2007). Figure 2.1 displays a baseline data path and the predicted level of outcome data in the future with no intervention (or other change). Obviously, there is a critical assumption that nothing will change built into this statement. We know that no matter how much data are collected, we cannot with absolute accuracy predict future levels of behavior. Naturally at some point in time, there will be a change in some aspect of the child or the ecology that will result in alterations in the outcome data. For example, as the curriculum alters over time, the curricular match will likely shift and on-task behavior of a target student changes as the task becomes too easy or too difficult (Treptow, Burns, & McComas, 2007). Thus, the prediction statement must be rather tentative and include an unknown expiration date. We come back and readdress this issue in the third stage of baseline logic, verification. In addition, the actual

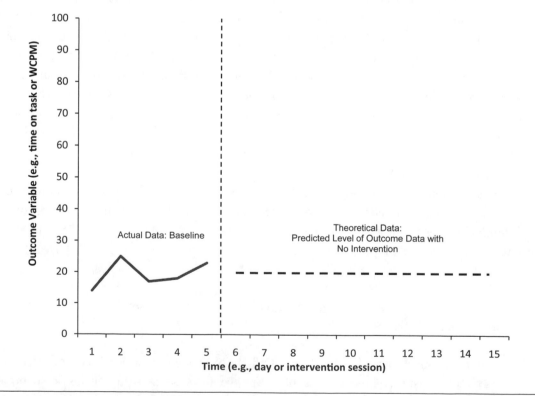

FIGURE 2.1. Baseline logic: Prediction. Adapted from Cooper, Heron, and Heward (2007). Copyright 2007 by Pearson Education, Inc. Adapted by permission.

amount of outcome data needed for a stable baseline is a critical issue, and one that is not easily answered. This issue is addressed in depth in Chapter 3.

It is fair to assume that in an applied setting, the importance of measuring preintervention behavior will not be readily apparent to all educational professionals. In order to describe the implication of not taking the time to establish a defensible baseline, consider the question, "What happens if we don't establish a defensible prediction statement?" Simply put, without such data one can never say with confidence that an observed pattern in the target behavior represents any "change" or was due to a particular intervention. Without baseline data, we can talk about the progress that a child is making toward some goal, but not that anything we are doing is necessarily responsible for that progress. We discuss in Chapter 3 some cases where this level of analysis may be fine, but if it is important to defensibly document response to intervention, then baseline data are clearly essential.

Affirmation of the Consequent

Once a prediction statement has been made, it then becomes possible to move into the second stage of baseline logic, affirmation of the consequent. This stage is where we have the opportunity to first test our hypothesis that some evidence-based, functionally relevant intervention will have an impact on the child's behavior. To do this, we must make the following series of assumptions. First, we start with the prediction statement of "If nothing is done, the outcome data will remain stable." Second, if the intervention is functionally relevant to the target behavior, then there will be some predictable change in the outcome data after implementation of the intervention (Cooper et al., 2007; Johnston & Pennypacker, 1993).

Figure 2.2 presents an example of affirmation of the consequent in the case of an intervention thought to increase on-task behavior. The baseline data suggest that without intervention the child's time on task will remain in approximately the 10–30% range centering at about 20%. After the intervention was applied, we observed the consequent (which was predicted in the hypothesis) of the prediction statement. In this case of an effective intervention, and thus a change in the outcome data, we start to build evidence to support that the intervention does indeed impact the outcome data in the predicted manner. Although the first observation of an intervention impacting the outcome data provides some evidence that there is a functional relationship, the strength of such evidence is questionable because it is based on a logical fallacy as discussed previously. There could have been some other factor, or a number of other unaccounted factors that were responsible for the observed change in the child's behavior. The subsequent steps of baseline logic will address potentially confounding variables, but before proceeding, let us consider what we know and do not know after the first two stages of baseline logic.

Your perception regarding what we know after the first affirmation of the consequent phase is likely heavily affected by whether you consider yourself a researcher or an educational professional. It is essential for the researcher to document some change in the outcome variable and to be able to tie that change back to some specific intervention. However, a causal statement cannot be made with confidence when it is based on only the prediction and a single change in the observed outcome data.

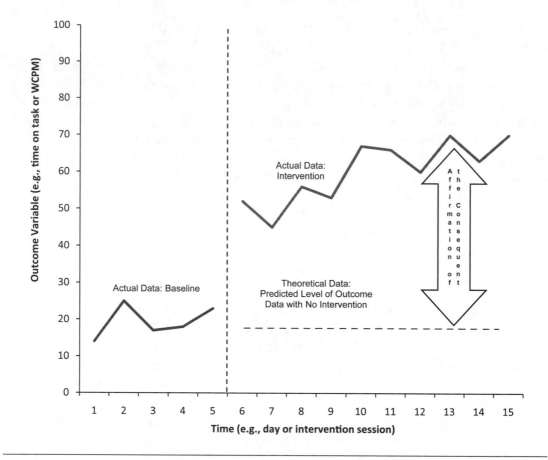

FIGURE 2.2. Baseline logic: Affirmation of the consequent. Adapted from Cooper, Heron, and Heward (2007). Copyright 2007 by Pearson Education, Inc. Adapted by permission.

Causal statements are critical for the researcher, but may or may not be essential for the practitioner. However, in an RTI model it is important to apply the causal criteria associated with research when documenting a sufficient response. It is the response to the intervention that is being documented and not the response to just anything. It is also true that a causal level of understanding is arguably a luxury in the lower-stakes cases. Indeed, in most instances, it would be more than acceptable to document whether a change was or was not observed, and make no specific claim as to the locus of that change. This is particularly true if the intervention process brought the child's behavior to an acceptable level so that intervention is no longer required.

Verification

If you remember back to the prediction phase of baseline logic, it was pointed out that the statement made was understood to be suspect. We know that over time there are a number of reasons that the level of some behavior could change. Thus, the verification phase is conducted in order to strengthen the original prediction statement. The goal of the verification phase of baseline logic is to ensure that the initial prediction of a stable baseline was accurate (Cooper et al., 2007). In other words, we are verifying the prediction statement in this stage of baseline logic.

The cleanest example of verification is to simply remove the intervention so that the dependent variable returns back to baseline levels. For example, in the case where on-task behavior was in the 10–30% range in baseline, and increased to 45–70% after a reinforcement-based intervention was applied, the next step would be to remove that intervention. If the removal of the intervention results in a decrease of on-task behavior back to the 10–30% range, then the prediction is verified. As shown in Figure 2.3, the baseline–intervention design is extended into a baseline–intervention–baseline design, and verification is observed in the second baseline phase. We observe the child's on-task behavior in the second baseline phase return to similar levels as was observed in the first baseline (before the intervention). In this case, the prediction statement has been verified, which increases our confidence that (1) the target behavior would have remained consistent had nothing been done, and (2) changes observed during the intervention phase were related to the introduction of the intervention rather than some other factor. If verification did not occur when the intervention was withdrawn, then some other factor was probably responsible for the observed change. Such a situation (a lack of return to baseline) may or may not be of concern in an applied educational environment.

There are many situations where removal of the intervention will not result in a return to preintervention levels of the outcome data such as with skill-acquisition interventions.

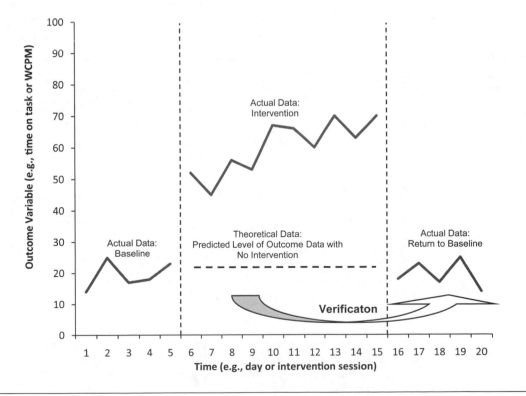

FIGURE 2.3. Baseline logic: Verification. Adapted from Cooper, Heron, and Heward (2007). Copyright 2007 by Pearson Education, Inc. Adapted by permission.

While this presents a challenge, verification is still possible as the discontinuation of the intervention should result in a number of other changes. First, the intervention withdrawal should result in a decreasing rate of learning. This decreasing rate of learning can be used as a path to verification of the prediction statement. Second, more complicated designs can be used to verify the prediction statement. Both of these possibilities are addressed more fully in the next two chapters.

Replication by Affirmation of the Consequent

The replication stage is an attempt to strengthen the initial intervention effect observed in the affirmation of the consequent phase. This is done by repeating the intervention (in some manner) and thus, creating the opportunity to again observe the change or lack of change in the outcome data. Figure 2.4 extends our previous example to show all four stages of baseline logic. If done correctly, replication will reduce the chance that any observed intervention effect when the intervention was first applied was due to some other factor. As a result, successful replication increases the probability that there is a functional relationship between the intervention and the target behavior (Cooper et al., 2007; Riley-Tillman & Walcott, 2007). Of course, any subsequent replication of this effect will further our confidence of the functional relationship.

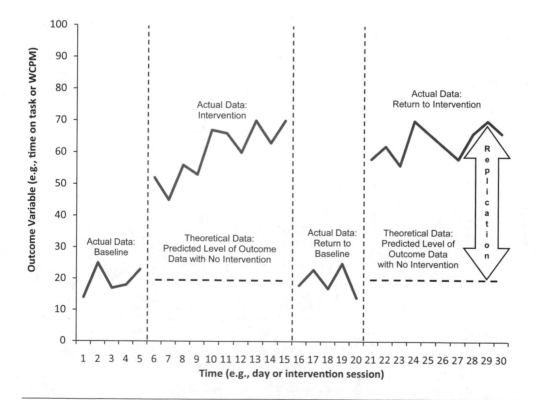

FIGURE 2.4. Baseline logic: Replication by affirmation of the consequent. Adapted from Cooper, Heron, and Heward (2007). Copyright 2007 by Pearson Education, Inc. Adapted by permission.

Think of different intervention cases in your career. In many, if not most, you do not really need to say, "I am confident that there is indeed a functional relationship between the intervention and the target behavior." In such cases, one would not take this final step because it could make the intervention methodology much more cumbersome. There are other cases, though, where the stakes are much higher. In these situations, this confidence in the presence or absence of a relationship between the intervention and the behavior becomes critical.

If the application of an intervention (independent variable) results in a change in the outcome data (dependent variable), then the effectiveness of the intervention can be cautiously positively evaluated. However, we also cannot immediately proclaim the intervention as unsuccessful when the relation is not observed. The importance of this caution is increased by the reality that the null hypothesis (that the invention did not work as predicted) is a high-stakes hypothesis in an RTI environment. Second, as with an affirmation statement where one must be tentative as other factors could be controlling the dependent variable, there could be a number of factors limiting the effectiveness of an otherwise effective intervention. As a result, schools using an RTI orientation should cautiously present both answers, and replicate each until one is truly confident as to the statement of the child's response to intervention. Another quote by Cohen and Nagel (1934) address this general caution: "Science is thus always ready to abandon a theory when the facts so demand. But the facts must really demand it. It is not unusual for a theory to be modified so that it may be retained in substance even though "facts" contradicted an earlier formulation of it" (p. 394).

BASELINE LOGIC, SCD, AND RTI

In Chapter 1, the utility of SCD for educational practice was explored. At this point, we look at a more in-depth question: Why look at "baseline logic" rather than a tradition presentation of SCD? For example, most SCD books present designs that if adhered to would be considered defensible. Using such designs the practical benefit of design adherence is that one can then use this design to defend the statements made about the results.

While this process is reasonable for researchers, such an approach is not realistic for practitioners. In a K–12 classroom, clinic, or other educational setting, if a design is violated, the data cannot simply be thrown away for a number of reasons. First, a great deal of work goes into any intervention, and it is not realistic to expect that educational professionals will be able to function on such a lean schedule of reinforcement. Second, it is much more typical for designs to be violated, and thus, much more typical in a traditional view of SCD that the information is meaningless. Consider the following differences between an experimental and an applied setting:

Experimental setting
- A small number of projects at any time (10–15 active research studies would be considered a massive research agenda).
- Weeks to even months to come up with hypotheses.

- Weeks to months to consider the design.
- A large number of individuals who are a part of the process (e.g., graduate assistants, faculty, and others).
- Individuals are typically trained in experimentation design and analysis.
- Individuals are reinforced for adhering to research rigor.
- Ample time to analyze and write up the data.

Applied setting
- A large number of cases at any time (if 10% of a school is in some phase of intervention at any time, the number of student cases would be in the hundreds for most school psychologists).
- Limited time to come up with hypotheses.
- Limited time to consider the design.
- Few individuals to collect data/run the experiment.
- Individuals have minimal or no training in experiential design and analysis.
- Individuals are not traditionally reinforced for adhering to research rigor.
- Limited time to analyze and present the data.

Essentially, the researcher is in an environment that has been developed to support research behavior, while educational professionals are in an environment not suited for traditional research practice. The result of this is that traditional publication quality research is simply not typical in an applied environment. Also consider that in general, a researcher can simply redo an experiment, while such an option is often not possible in practice. Fortunately, the rigor associated with experimental control and causality is not always needed in practice.

We have chosen to embrace several realities. First, in an RTI environment the experimental and the null hypotheses are at least equally important, and the null is arguably the higher-stakes finding. Second, much work will be done with no expectation of a traditional research design, yet we need to interpret the results. Finally, everything that can go wrong will typically go wrong, and thus we will be left figuring out what we know from what we have, rather than dictating what will happen. While this seems like a quagmire from which one cannot recover, in reality the situation is rather bright as an understanding of baseline logic allows for a defensible decision even in the worst of conditions. In the end, when things do not go well, the questions that educational professionals who use SCD must ask are "What do I know?" and "What can't I defensibly say?" The answers to these questions are found in baseline logic by asking, "What steps of baseline logic have we accomplished?" If we know, for example, that prediction, affirmation of the consequent, and verification occurred, but replication was not observed, we know that we can say whether a change occurred at the time the intervention was applied and that the prediction statement was verified. However, we cannot say that we observed a direct or systematic replication and thus, the dependability and/or generality of the first observation of the affirmation of the consequent is tentative at best. As shown in Table 2.2, there are a series of questions that can guide the evaluation of baseline logic. This same process can be taken for any combination of predicted relationships or circumstances that an applied setting throws at an educa-

TABLE 2.2. Questions to Ask When Considering an SCD

Question	If yes	If no
Were sufficient baseline data collected so that a defensible *prediction* can be made regarding the likely outcome if nothing is done?	It is possible to judge the effectiveness of a subsequent intervention.	It is not possible to judge the effectiveness of a subsequent intervention in a defensible manner.
Has the *affirmation of the consequent* been documented?	Assuming that the prediction step of baseline logic has been followed, this is evidence of RTI, although another variable may have caused the observed change.	Assuming that the prediction step of baseline logic has been followed, this is initial evidence of a lack of an RTI.
Was the baseline prediction *verified*?	This supports the prediction statement and makes conclusions about the effectiveness of the intervention more defensible. However, it does not preclude that some other variable caused the change as opposed to the intervention.	This weakens the degree of certainty about the effectiveness of the intervention.
Was the affirmation of the consequent *replicated*?	This strengthens the affirmation of the consequent and makes the final conclusion about the effectiveness of the intervention highly defensible.	This weakens the final conclusion about the effectiveness of the intervention.

Note. Based on Riley-Tillman and Walcott (2007).

tional professional. It is critical to remind the reader that this stage of analysis is contingent on the defensible selection of a target behavior and assessment method. If the outcome data is irrelevant, or the data is suspect, then any subsequent use of the data will be dubious.

CONCLUDING COMMENTS

The purpose of this chapter was to outline the philosophy behind SCD. In the next two chapters we review a series of formal designs that to varying levels utilize baseline logic. Some designs only incorporate the first few stages (e.g., prediction or prediction/affirmation of the consequent). Other designs incorporate all of the stages of baseline logic and thus, reach the level of an experimental design that can document the functional relationship between the intervention and the outcome data. While these formal designs can be quite helpful, one of the primary purposes of this overview of baseline logic was to present a more complete understanding of single-case experimentation so that when a design is violated, the implications are understood. This level of understanding is critical for educational professionals who often deal with interventions not implemented according to plan.

In addition, as is outlined in Chapter 8, when using SCD as a component in an RTI model, it seems prudent to consider both formal designs and atypical applications of baseline logic. It is clear that as RTI cases proceed from Tier 1 into Tiers 2 and 3, the implications of a child's response to intervention become more serious. Thus, the importance of using a defensible intervention methodology should accordingly increase. It may be acceptable to simply track a student's progress in Tier 1, but designs that incorporate prediction and affirmation of the consequent phases are more important in Tier 2. In Tier 3, as the stakes again increase, it is necessary to consider using all four stages of baseline logic. While such designs are clearly resource intensive, the intensive levels of intervention design should only be necessary with a small percentage of students.

3

The Classic A-B-A-B Design

TRANSFORMING BASELINE LOGIC INTO FORMAL DESIGNS

An understanding of baseline logic makes the components of an ideal intervention design clear. First, a stable series of baseline data allow for a prediction to be made. Second, the intervention is implemented to see if, using the logic of "affirmation of the consequent," it appears to be related to the target behavior in the predicted manner. Third, an ideal design would remove the intervention and observe whether the prediction was correct. This removal would verify the prediction statement and confirm that the baseline data were an accurate forecast of the target behavior if a change in the ecology had not occurred. Finally, the ideal design would then reinstate the intervention to replicate it using affirmation of the consequent. As we discuss in the next chapter, there are a number of inventive manners in which to accomplish each facet of baseline logic in an SCD, but we start with the most direct approaches, typically called *withdrawal* and *reversal designs*. Each of these designs starts with the most basic A-B (or baseline–intervention) component, then adds on a withdrawal (or verification), and finally a replication phase.

Prediction–Intervention–Verification–Replication

(A)   (B)   (A)   (B)

The purpose of this chapter is to build up to the A-B-A-B design by looking at a series of initial designs. Specifically, the B design, A-B design, and finally, A-B-A design will be reviewed before a formal presentation of the full A-B-A-B design.

Before proceeding, it is important to review the typical coding system used in SCD, called an *ABC notation system* (Tawney & Gast, 1984). By using a common language, knowledgeable individuals can quickly understand what design is being used. Armed with this language and an understanding of SCD, the analysis phase will be much more efficient. This general system is presented below:

- A refers to the baseline condition.
- B refers to the intervention condition.
- B^1, B^2, and so on, refer to minor alterations to the intervention. This can also be noted by the use of a prime symbol ('), so B', B'', and so on, represent minor alterations to the intervention.
- C, D, and so on, refer to subsequent different interventions.
- When a hyphen (-) is placed between two condition (e.g., A-B), it signifies that there is a change in phase.
- When two conditions are presented together (e.g., BC), it signifies that two interventions are being introduced concurrently.

Using SCD language, A-B signifies a baseline phase followed by an intervention phase. A-BC signifies a baseline phase followed by two interventions incorporated concurrently. A-B-B^1 or A-B-B' signifies a baseline phase, followed by an intervention phase, and then a phase with an altered version of the intervention. While we could continue with examples, the utility of the ABC notation system should be clear. Using this system to communicate a design is an efficient and clear process between individuals knowledgeable in SCD.

B DESIGN

While rarely discussed, the arguably most utilized SCD in educational environments is a B design. In the case of a B design, it is understood that some intervention is currently in place. This is the case in any school environment where some formal instructional practices are instituted in every regular classroom. From a problem-solving perspective, this is the Tier 1 level where all children participate in a set of empirically supported instructional approaches (academic and social behavior). If the Tier 1 practice is evidence based, appropriate for the school population, and implemented correctly, then it should be effective for a majority of students. Teachers have always assessed the effectiveness of Tier 1 practices, usually with measures that are often administered to the whole class in the form of unit tests and standardized assessments. Outcome data collected in Tier 1 can be compared to historical rates of production to answer the question, "Is the target child progressing as children have in the past?" In addition, the observed level of response can be compared to current students in the same educational environment to answer the question, "Is the target child progressing in a similar manner as his/her peers?"

The simulated data presented in Figure 3.1 are an example of a B design in an applied setting. In this example, weekly (for the fall) frequency counts of office discipline referral (ODR) data are presented for a whole class. This presentation allows for the teacher or other educational professional to consider both the pattern of the class behavior using this data source, as well as observe whether there are any students who seem to be problematic. As can be observed in the data, there is a general decreasing trend in the overall class rates of ODR, but two of the students seem to be increasing their weekly rates. In this case, while the social behavior pattern of the whole class appears to be positive, the behavioral pattern of the two students should be considered using a problem-solving approach.

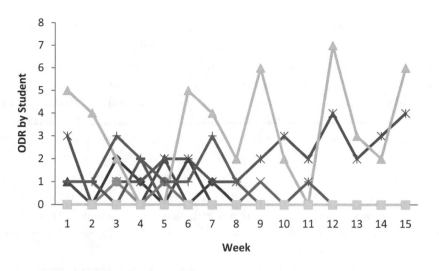

FIGURE 3.1. Example of a B design.

Three critical decisions must be made when constructing a B design; selecting the target student/group, the outcome data, and the comparison methods. The first decision is the selection of the target of the B design. Ideally, a whole class or group will be monitored. The advantages of monitoring a whole group are twofold. First, all students' progress should be monitored, and thus all should be included in this most basic design. Second, the whole-group outcome data will prove highly useful when it comes time to consider individual students. In some instances, however, smaller groups or a specific student will be the target of the design. Once the target is determined, some behavior and assessment method that will measure that behavior must be selected. As previously discussed in Chapter 2, the target behavior should be clearly defined and relevant. The assessment method for a B design must be repeatable, appropriate for the target behavior, and highly feasible in terms of data collection.

The final critical element of a B design is the method of comparison. The outcome data of the target student (or group) must be compared to some standard; there are a number of options for this standard. The first option, which is most useful at the whole-group level, is to use some growth standard to gauge the progress of the whole group or specific students in the group. This growth standard can be some researched norm (e.g., the typical growth in words correct per minute [WCPM] in the third grade) or something specific to the incorporated protocol (e.g., the number of correct math questions on end of chapter tests needed to progress to the next level). Any such standard can be graphed with the outcome data to look for children who are not on pace. A second option, which is particularly useful when a specific student is being considered, is to compare the target student to current students in the same educational setting. Usually, these comparison students are selected due to their representativeness of a "typical" student. A logical extension of this option is to compare a target student to a whole class or group when outcome data are available for a whole group. Finally, the target student or group outcome data path can be compared to itself for changes in level, trend, or variability in the outcome data. This option is most appropriate when looking for a general increase or decrease in the outcome data.

As discussed in Chapter 2, to consider if an SCD allows for internal validity (or experimental control), each element of baseline logic (prediction, affirmation of the consequent, verification, and replication) needs to be present. If each element is present in a design and the outcome data show the predicted change in each phase, then it becomes possible to suggest that the change in the target behavior is functionally related to the intervention. In the case of a B design none of the steps in baseline logic are present. Baseline data are not collected (although the collected data could be used as baseline data for subsequent interventions). The initial affirmation of the consequent is not observed due to the lack of baseline data. Obviously, verification and replication are impossible as there was no baseline to verify, and no affirmation of the consequent to replicate. Thus, a B design is not to be confused with an experimental design.

Despite being nonexperimental, there are some considerable advantages to a B design in an educational system that incorporates a schoolwide problem-solving model. It is common for consistent outcome data to be collected to gauge the effectiveness of instruction, but when educational professionals understand how these data can be appropriately graphed and analyzed, it opens up a great deal of information for use in the problem-solving process.

Steps to a successful B design (adapted from Tawney & Gast, 1984)
1. Clear description of the target, target behavior, and ecology (time, place, instructional activities, and all other relevant features).
2. A defensible data collection method.
3. As frequent data collection as possible.
4. Data on similar target students for comparison purposes. Another comparison option would be some growth standard.

What a B design can tell you
1. That the target student is increasing or decreasing in the target behavior.
2. That the target child is progressing at a pace that is typical for his/her peers (assuming that outcome data on target peers is available).
3. What the target behavior looks like in a standard (Tier 1) environment. This can be used as baseline data for subsequent designs.

What a B design cannot tell you
1. That some particular intervention is responsible for any observed change.
2. That an observed change would not be present in the absence of *any* instruction.

A-B DESIGN

While a B design may be the most utilized version of SCD in educational environments, an A-B design is the most basic design to monitor intervention effectiveness. Any intervention has at its base, the goal of "changing" something. A social behavior intervention focused on increasing time on task is only initiated when there is some reason to increase time-on-task behavior for some specific target student or group of students. Likewise, a reading fluency intervention with the goal of increasing the number of words a child can read correctly per minute (as a proxy for reading fluency) is based on the decision that the current performance of the target student is not at the desired level, and thus a change needs to occur. As discussed in Chapters 1 and 2, the very concept of intervention is steeped in the idea of change. An intervention is indeed a planned alteration in the environment (e.g., a new reading program) with the goal of changing some target outcome variable. With that in mind the role of the intervention design and subsequent analysis is rather obvious. It is critical that the design documents the presence or absence of a change in the target outcome variable. In the case of the B design, a change is not actually documented as there is no measure of the behavior before the intervention is initiated. In an A-B design, preintervention, or baseline data, are collected so that a comparison of the state before the intervention and during the intervention can be made.

The A-B design has been called the *most basic quasi-experimental version of SCD* (Tawney & Gast, 1984). In terms of baseline logic, the first two stages, prediction and affirmation of the consequent, are observed in an A-B design. The collection of baseline data allows for the prediction statement (What would happen if nothing was done?). Once the baseline data are collected, any intervention (experimental hypothesis) can be tested by simply implementing it in a controlled manner, and then observing if the outcome data change from baseline in the predicted manner. As stated in Chapter 2, this is called *affirmation of the consequent* in baseline logic. Specifically, the consequence of the intervention was affirmed by demonstrating the change in the target outcome data.

The simulated data presented in Figure 3.2 is an example of an A-B design in an applied setting. In this example a classroom teacher is monitoring the effect of a peer tutoring intervention on a target student's reading fluency as measured by WCPM on curriculum-based measurement (CBM) probes collected three times each week. In the intervention condition

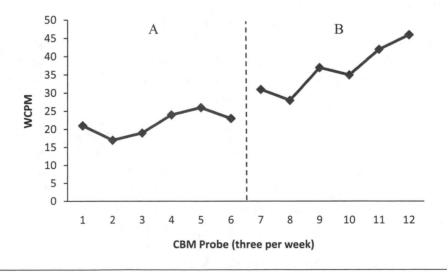

FIGURE 3.2. Example of an A-B design.

the target student was making little progress in the 2 weeks prior to beginning the intervention. It can be observed that after starting the intervention the target student's WCPM increased at a steady pace. While it would be inappropriate to say that the peer tutoring intervention caused the documented change in reading fluency, it can be stated that there was a positive change in reading fluency. In this case the teacher decided to continue the intervention and monitor progress.

The successful application of an A-B design can provide two pieces of information. First, there is a clear documentation of a change in the preferred direction. While this may seem like a minor step, any educational professional knows the alarming frequency of intervention cases that do not have data-based demonstrations of change. The second piece of information that a successful A-B demonstration provides is a bit more nuanced. The first affirmation of the consequent begins to provide evidence that the intervention (independent variable) is functionally related to the outcome data (dependent variable). This is called *experimental control*. It is critical to note that this affirmation of the consequent must be replicated for one to assert that experimental control is documented. As discussed in Chapter 2, replication is critical so that the possibility that the change in behavior was due to some other uncontrolled variable (such as an unknown intervention, maturation, and so on) can be ruled out. Thus, this first presentation is not sufficient for claiming that the intervention changed the target outcome behavior, but it is a necessary step. Technically, it has long been understood that A-B designs suffer from significant threats to internal and external validity (Campbell & Stanley, 1966; Kratochwill, 1978; Tawney & Gast, 1984). One simply cannot be sure that it was the intervention that caused the change (internal validity or experimental control), which in turn suggests that it is not safe to generalize the results (external validity).

What statements may an educational professional make when interpreting an A-B design? It is defensible to say that a change occurred or did not occur. It is not defensible to say that a change was due to the intervention or interestingly, that a lack of change means that the intervention was not effective. Furthermore, the results of an A-B SCD cannot be generalized due to the threats to external validity. This is significant in educational practice as it is typical to take a limited sample of behavior and inappropriately make a broad and general statement about the child, such as the child is generally "inattentive." One must resist this urge at this point and stick to what can be said. Specifically, when the intervention was implemented in X environment at Y time, the behavior changed or did not change. It will take a more complex design to defensibly make a more general statement.

One practical question at this point is, "What are enough data for each phase?" The traditional answer is you need to collect enough data so that a stable pattern is demonstrated. This concept goes back to the role of the prediction statement in baseline logic. As a reminder, the prediction phase of baseline logic attempts to estimate what the outcome data would be if there were no intervention (Cooper et al., 2007). By collecting a sufficient and steady stream of outcome data we are able to predict future levels of the behavior if nothing were to change. Of course the problematic issue is defining "sufficient." There is no simple definition of sufficient because it is impacted significantly by what outcome behavior is being measured. If a very stable behavior is being measured, then it could be argued that three data points are defensible. For example, a child who has not learned a specific skill, such as single-digit to single-digit addition problems, and never demonstrates the skill will produce a very stable series of outcome data points (all zeros). After three data points it is clear that the data are flat, there is no upward trend, and most importantly they are consistent with reports that the skill is not evident. The number three is still selected as a minimum defensible criterion as the first two stable outcome data points could simply be by chance. The chances that all three are in agreement, and are not an accurate estimate of the child's level of function, is rather remote.

Unfortunately, most cases do not include such consistent outcome data. In cases where there is some variability in the outcome data, it is suggested that a minimum of five data points are collected in both the baseline and the intervention phases. With five data points there starts to be able opportunity to observe the level, variability, and trend of the behavior. It is critical to note that it is only acceptable to stop at five data points *if* a prediction statement can be made. Consider Figures 3.3 through 3.5. In Figures 3.3 and 3.4 the data are stable, and a prediction (the grey box) can be made. Figure 3.3 is a rather simple case with a stable pattern of level data. The benefit of having five data points is that the variability of the outcome data can be observed consistently. Figure 3.4 is a bit more complex in that a trend is being observed. With five data points it is clear that the trend is stable and thus can be predicted to continue. It is important to note, however, that any prediction with a trend is understood to end at some time in that behavior cannot accelerate forever. For example, in the case of a reading fluency intervention a child will not continue to acceler-

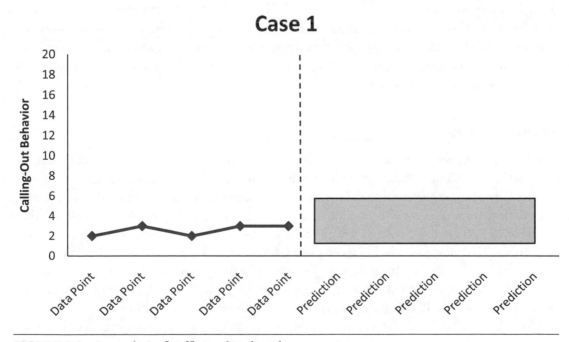

FIGURE 3.3. Example 1 of sufficient baseline data.

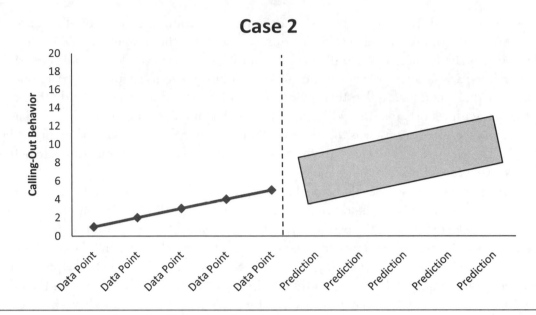

FIGURE 3.4. Example 2 of sufficient baseline data.

ate his/her reading in terms of WCPM forever. While a trend of gaining 3 words correct per week may be appropriate when he/she is reading 30 WCPM, it will likely not continue when the child is reading 150 WCPM. At some point, it is understood that there will be a ceiling. In Figure 3.5, however, the collection of additional outcome data is critical as either of the prediction statements made are a possibility. As with all decisions in SCD, one must go back to the purpose of the data and ask if the baseline logic statement can be made with confidence. In Case 1 and 2, the prediction statement can be made. In Case 3, additional data are needed. In the end, it is critical that baseline data are observed before the decision to begin an intervention. Only when one observes stable baseline data can the prediction statement be made with confidence.

Baseline Issues

This brings us to what we call the *baseline dilemma*. While it is clear that baseline data is essential in the documentation of a change, any educational professional recognizes that it can be difficult to argue for this data collection in practice. Most educational professionals and parents want a change to happen quickly. As parents ourselves, we understand that when a child is being difficult, or struggling, the urge is to remedy that situation as quickly as possible. This is of course even more of an issue when the target behavior is highly problematic. When a child is hitting, or acting out in an extreme manner, the immediacy of the intervention effect is critical. Indeed, one can argue that is it unethical to wait to implement an intervention in dangerous situations. Unfortunately, by definition the collection of baseline data will delay the start of the intervention. In our own applied practice this issue has been raised on a number of occasions. Teachers and parents rightly ask, "Why wait?"

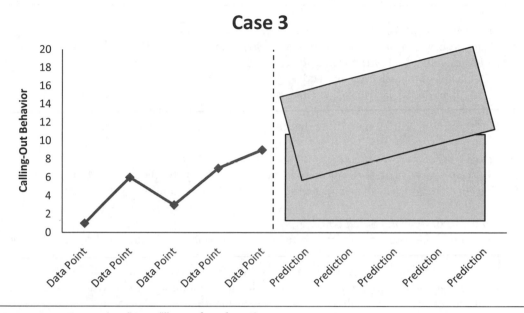

FIGURE 3.5. Example of insufficient baseline data.

Rather than dismiss this question, we think it is a logical step when considering a design. Do you need to document a change in the target child's behavior? Is that need more important than the significance of changing the behavior immediately? In other words, is the problem so significant (e.g., dangerous) that is it essential to start the intervention as soon as possible, and therefore not collect baseline data? A child with significant and frequent violent outbursts or a child who is injuring him/herself comes to mind. Obviously in these cases the benefits of baseline data collection (documentation of change in target behavior) do not outweigh the costs (injury to child). Thankfully these cases are rare. In most cases the argument, "Why wait?" will be focused on less critical issues. While delaying a reading intervention a week may seem unfair, the potential information acquired from baseline data collection can be well worth it. If anything, it is only ethical in such a case to make sure that an intervention is working (that a change has occurred) and thus should be continued. The rush to intervene in mild and moderate cases without baseline data only increases the likelihood that ineffective interventions that don't actually change the outcome behavior will be retained.

Before ending discussion about the baseline dilemma we need to point out that it is this baseline dilemma that makes the consistent collection of formative assessment data critical (Chafouleas et al., 2007). In educational environments where potential outcome data are consistently collected (e.g., schools who have adopted positive behavior support or Dynamic Indicators of Basic Educational Literacy [DIBELS]) there is likely some outcome data that can be used to estimate baseline functioning. In highly problematic situations, or even mild/moderate cases, this consistent collection of outcome data minimizes or altogether removes the need to delay the intervention. While it is often difficult to begin schoolwide formative assessment practices, this is a significant argument to make this a priority.

Steps to a successful A-B design (adapted from Tawney & Gast, 1984)
1. Clear description of the target, target behavior, and ecology (time, place, instructional activities, and all other relevant features).
2. A defensible data collection method.
3. As frequent data collection as possible.
4. Sufficient baseline data (A) so that the pattern of outcome data is stable.
5. Sufficient intervention data (B) so that the pattern of outcome data is stable.

What an A-B design can tell you
1. That there was a change in outcome data from the baseline to the intervention phases.
2. The specific nature of that change (e.g., level, trend, or variability).

What an A-B design cannot tell you
1. That the change observed was due to the intervention. Or, in practical terms, that the intervention was effective.
2. That a lack of observed change suggests the intervention is not functionally related to the target behavior. Or, in practical terms, that the intervention was ineffective.
3. That the results are generalizable to another setting, time, or target.

A-B-A DESIGN

A rather unique, but important SCD in an RTI service delivery model is an A-B-A design. This design builds on the A-B design by adding a return to baseline (the second A). In terms of baseline logic, the second baseline is called the *verification phase*. It is easy to remember the purpose of this phase by thinking of it as the "verification of the prediction statement." A successful return to baseline increases our confidence that the original prediction made from the baseline data was accurate. While this is not a fully experimental design as replication has not been included, it is a significant step beyond an A-B design. As Tawney and Gast (1984) outline, the A-B design allows correlational conclusions, while A-B-A design allows for tentatively functional conclusions.

The simulated data presented in Figures 3.6 and 3.7 are examples of an A-B-A design in an applied setting. In these examples, a classroom teacher is monitoring the effect of an intervention on academic engagement as measured by direct behavior ratings (DBR) (Chafouleas et al., 2007) using a 10-point scale (ranging from 1, "not engaged," to 10 "fully engaged"). In the first case, the initial intervention was observed to be effective, and the withdrawal of the intervention was to strengthen the evidence a functional relationship. In the second example, the initial intervention did not seem effective. The teacher thought that there might be some external factors inhibiting the effectiveness of the intervention, and thus the withdrawal phase was incorporated. The outcomes of the full A-B-A design suggest that there is no functional relationship between the intervention and the outcome data. In this case, there was no documented response to intervention.

The most basic benefit of an A-B-A design is that the statement of change is strengthened with the return to baseline. With an A-B design, the conclusion can only be that when *X* intervention was put into place, we observed (or did not observe) a concurrent change in

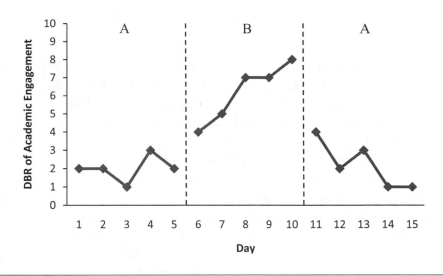

FIGURE 3.6. Example 1 of an A-B-A design.

the target behavior. This correlational conclusion can in no manner insinuate that it was the intervention that caused the documented change. Adding the return to baseline adds a second documentation of change in a predicted direction. This in turn allows us to increase our confidence that any change in the intervention phase was not something that would have occurred without some change in the environment. This does not yet mean that the change can be attributed directly to the intervention, but it is becoming more and more likely. Without replication of the treatment, there are still significant internal validity threats. The return to baseline simply strengthens our confidence that something occurred that was different from the initial situation, and that the intervention is the most likely candidate. This same logic can be used when there appears to be no change in the B phase.

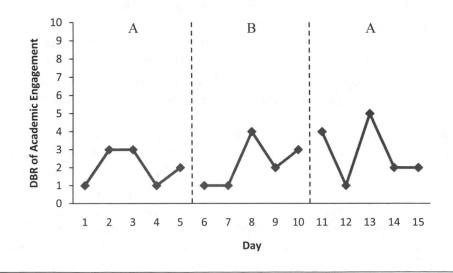

FIGURE 3.7. Example 2 of an A-B-A design.

The return to baseline is arguably more critical in an RTI environment when the intervention does not appear to be effective. As discussed in Chapters 1 and 2, in an RTI model the lack of a sufficient response results in increasing levels of service delivery. Given that this path can lead to the educational diagnosis of specific LD, it is critical that we are sure that a change did *not* occur. It is tempting after implementing an A-B design with no demonstration of an intervention effect to simply stop the process or immediately start a new intervention. Unfortunately, we cannot be sure that there was not some other variable that was actually negatively impacting the target behavior and thus counteracting the impact of the intervention. Considering the importance of a line of "failed" interventions in an RTI model, it is critical that a more robust design be implemented than a simple A-B. This statement is even more critical as one approaches Tier 3 decisions. An A-B-A design in the case of an intervention that appears not to be effective meets this criteria.

Baseline Issues Revisited

While the baseline dilemma discussed previously can be difficult in an educational environment, advocating for return to baseline is a significantly more difficult challenge. There are two distinct situations where the return to baseline can be complicated and perhaps even unethical. In the case of an effective intervention, advocating returning to baseline technically means that the intervention must be discontinued. To stop doing something that is effective, particularly in cases where there has been a great deal of failure, is simply not a typical procedure in a school environment. At this point, it is critical to ask several questions. First, do you need to move from a correlational conclusion to the beginnings of a functional conclusion? It is honestly necessary to assign causality for the observed change to the intervention. In many cases, the documentation of change will be sufficient. However, if preceding through the RTI tiers of service delivery, then it becomes important to document that it was the intervention that was cause of the change in the target behavior.

The second question, assuming that the answer to the first was "yes," concerns whether a return to baseline is ethical. As discussed above, there are cases where it is not ethical to delay or withdraw an intervention due to the severity of the problem behavior. For such cases, we explore SCDs in Chapter 4 that deal with this issue in a rather inventive manner. In most cases where a return to baseline is necessary, the situation will not be so significant that it is unethical to return to baseline. As such, it is critical for school psychologists and other educational professionals to explain why this procedure is necessary to those less experienced with SCD.

Two very common A-B-A issues that impact any design that incorporates a withdrawal of the intervention to return to baseline are slow or partial returns to baseline. A slow return to baseline is observed when it takes a concerning number of sessions for the outcome data to return to preintervention levels after the intervention has been removed. A partial return to baseline is observed when preintervention levels of the outcome data are never observed. Slow and partial returns to baseline should be addressed separately as they have different impacts on the analysis of withdrawal-based designs. In the first case, a slow return to baseline, baseline logic can be obtained but it is required that the withdrawal phase be extended so that a full return to baseline be observed. As such, it is critical to avoid rushing the reinstatement of the intervention. It is not atypical in both applied settings and research environments for phases to be rushed. In the applied setting, as discussed above, there is a tense balance between establishing experimental control and providing a perceived effective intervention. The urge to restart the intervention can be quite powerful, and in some cases is the ethically correct action.

Applied researchers are of course affected by rushed phases as well. A considerable amount of applied educational research takes place in schools based on the idea that there is a win–win opportunity. The school receives services from the research staff that would not be available while the researcher receives access to participants. This win–win is contingent on ethical practice, which makes the withdrawal of an intervention problematic. In addition, it is not atypical for the realities of the academic calendar to impact the research timeline. If the school year ends in 2 weeks, and the design will only be completed with an immediate return to the intervention condition, there will be pressure to make a premature phase change. Unfortunately, rushing a phase in the case of a slow return to baseline can make it impossible for verification of the prediction statement to be fully established. It is critical in practice that one has the patience to allow for the full return to baseline if it is important to document experimental control. It is also critical to consider this issue when scheduling so that time does not simply run out before the design can be completed.

The second issue, a partial return to baseline, is a bit more complex. In some cases, it is difficult or impossible to ever fully return to the original baseline level. Logically, the experience of the intervention could result in some semi- or fully permanent changes that make it unlikely that the target will ever fully return to baseline levels of behavior. This may be due to something that has been learned as a result of the intervention, or simply a carryover effect. A partial return to baseline is a clear threat to experimental control as it is impossible to know if the partial change from baseline was due to the intervention (e.g., something learned) or whether there is some other variable that is also controlling the outcome data. Essentially, the partial return gives you confidence that the intervention is partially responsible for the observed change in outcome data. There are two manners with which to deal with a partial return. First, if you know in advance that it is unlikely that the withdrawal of an intervention will result in a return to baseline levels of functioning you should consider designs that do not require a withdrawal phase. Another option to address the potential for a partial return is to consider alternative approaches to document a treatment withdrawal. While historically it has been argued that learning tasks are not likely candidates for designs that rely on a withdrawal phase, there are means to return to baseline in other ways than going back to the original level. For example, if you are interested in the rate (e.g., WCPM) that a child is learning to read, the baseline data can be expressed in terms of how many WCPM the child gained each week. If in baseline this trend is rather flat (e.g., gaining 1 WCPM per week from a starting level of 10 WCPM), and increases in the intervention phase to gaining 3 WCPM per week, an interesting opportunity arises. Even though after 2 weeks of baseline data and 2 weeks of the intervention the current level is up to 18 WCPM, if the intervention is withdrawn, the trend could go back to the baseline level of gaining 1 WCPM per week. This return to baseline is based on a return to the baseline "trend" rather than the level as it is unlikely that the child will regress from the newly established level. This same strategy could be used with the variability of the data (e.g., high amounts of variability in baseline and withdrawal as opposed to low amounts of variability intervention conditions) if that is a logical way to gauge the effectiveness of an intervention. In Chapter 5 we discuss analysis strategies in more depth. One must be careful, however, with these manners of returning to baseline levels as they are not as powerful in terms of experimental control as a return to baseline that incorporates all aspects of analysis.

Steps to a successful A-B-A design (adapted from Tawney & Gast, 1984)
1. Clear description of the target, target behavior, and ecology (time, place, instructional activities, and all other relevant features).
2. A defensible data collection method.
3. As frequent data collection as possible.
4. Sufficient baseline data (A) so that the pattern of outcome data is stable.
5. Sufficient intervention data (B) so that the pattern of outcome data is stable.
6. Sufficient return to baseline data (A) so that the pattern of outcome data is stable.

What an A-B-A design can tell you
1. That there was a change in outcome data from the baseline to the intervention phases.
2. The specific nature of that change (e.g., level, trend, or variability).
3. Whether the prediction statement from the baseline data was correct (observed in the return to baseline data).
4. That a lack of observed change suggests the intervention is not functionally related to the target behavior. Or, in practical terms, that the intervention was ineffective. This assumes that the return to baseline phase verified the prediction statement.

What an A-B-A design cannot tell you
1. That an observed change was due to the intervention. Or, in practical terms, that the intervention was effective. While this design comes close, without replication there is still not enough evidence to claim experimental control.
2. That the results are generalizable to another setting, time, or target.

A-B-A-B DESIGN

One of the most well-known and incorporated single-case methods is the A-B-A-B design. In circles where SCDs are used commonly, the A-B-A-B design is often simply referred to as a *reversal* (Baer, Wolf, & Risley, 1968; Risley, 2005) or *withdrawal* (Leitenberg, 1973) *design*. Procedurally, a reversal design is suggested to refer to situations when the intervention is actually reversed, whereas a withdrawal design refers to situations when the intervention is simply removed (Poling & Gossett, 1986). Cooper et al. (2007) argue that the most appropriate term for A-B-A-B design is a reversal design as it refers to both the withdrawal and reversal of the intervention in an attempt to demonstrate behavioral reversibility (Baer et al., 1968; Thompson & Iwata, 2005). After stepping through B, A-B, and A-B-A designs, the purpose and logic of the A-B-A-B design should be obvious. This is the first design presented that allows for experimental control, and thus the true documentation of a response to specific intervention.

As with any design, stepping through the A-B-A-B design in terms of the stages of baseline logic is an excellent path to understand how experimental control is established with this method. The first A phase presents the prediction statement or what would happen if nothing was done. The first B phase allows for the affirmation of the consequent, or observing the intervention effect. The second A phase, the withdrawal of the intervention, allows for the verification of the prediction statement. Finally, the full model of baseline logic, and thus the opportunity for experimental control, is completed with the second B phase. In this phase, replication of the intervention by affirmation of the consequent is attempted. For experimental control to be obtained, it is critical that a standard pattern is observed in the outcome data. After a stable baseline (A) and the intervention is applied (B), it is important to observe an immediate change in the outcome data in the predicated manner. After the first B phase has continued long enough for the outcome data to stabilize, the intervention can be removed, thus starting the withdrawal phase (A). At this stage, it is critical that the data return so that it is consistent with the data observed in the prediction phase. When the outcome data have stabilized back at the original baseline level, the intervention can be reapplied (B). The reapplication of the intervention should result in the return of the hypothesized change in the outcome data that was observed after the first intervention application. It is only at this stage, and with this pattern of outcome data, that experimental control can be claimed. In other words, it is only after this process that one can start to make the argument that the intervention was functionally responsible for the observed change in outcome data.

The simulated data presented in Figure 3.8 is an example of an A-B-A-B design in an applied setting where a classroom teacher is monitoring the effect of an intervention on academic engagement as measured by DBR using a 10-point scale (ranging from 1, "not engaged," to 10, "fully engaged"). In the baseline condition the teacher rated the target student's academic engagement as very low. The initial application of the intervention showed a positive effect. When the intervention was withdrawn, behavior was reported to return to levels observed in baseline. Finally, when the intervention was restarted, the initial affirma-

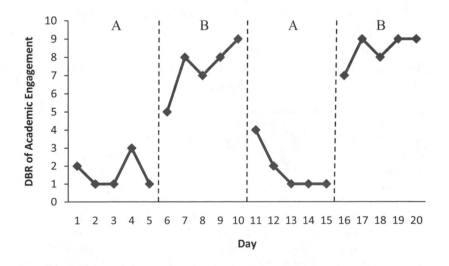

FIGURE 3.8. Example of an A-B-A-B design.

tion by the consequent was replicated. This pattern strongly suggests that the target student responded to the intervention. In other words, the intervention was functionally related to the outcome data. In an RTI model, this is an ideal presentation of a response to intervention.

The advantages of an A-B-A-B design in an educational environment utilizing an RTI service model are somewhat obvious. The A-B-A-B design incorporates a direct replication component that results in the highest opportunity for experimental control in single-case research. In addition, the decisions that can be made based on intervention cases using an A-B-A-B design are clear. If intervention is effective in both B phases and a return to baseline is documented, it is defensible to say that the intervention was responsible for the change in the outcome data, or the change in the target behavior. If on the other hand the intervention was not effective, one can state that there was a clear lack of response (as with an A-B-A design). While these statements seem rather simple, they are the basis for a defensible RTI service delivery model.

The limitations of this design are also fairly obvious. There are clear, practical, and ethical implications of withdrawing an intervention. These ethical issues are magnified when the target behavior is more problematic, which is often the case with Tier 3 RTI cases. As noted, the withdrawal phase can be extended in order to fully observe a return to baseline. A second limitation, which has been discussed previously, is that some target behaviors can never exhibit a complete "return to baseline." In the case of learned behaviors only a partial return, or a return based on rate of learning or variability, can be demonstrated. As a result, only a weaker version of a reversal design is possible in many academic situations. As a result of these serious limitations, we present a series of designs in Chapter 4 that do not require a traditional withdrawal.

Despite these limitations, the A-B-A-B design should not be simply dismissed. The benefits of intrasubject direct replication are significant. Most notably, this is the only method that uses intrasubject direct replication of the intervention. As discussed in Chapter 2, the use of intrasubject direct replication allows for clearer conclusions in cases when the intervention is effective or ineffective. We find that models that use systematic replication or intersubject direct replication can become quite complex and can be difficult to analyze. As such, the A-B-A-B design should be strongly considered when possible. Even when this design is not appropriate for a particular case, it is critical to understand this design as it is the building block that more complex designs are considered against.

Steps to a successful A-B-A-B design (adapted from Tawney & Gast, 1984)
1. Clear description of the target, target behavior, and ecology (time, place, instructional activities, and all other relevant features).
2. A defensible data collection method.
3. As frequent data collection as possible.
4. Sufficient baseline data (A) so that the pattern of outcome data is stable.
5. Sufficient intervention data (B) so that the pattern of outcome data is stable.
6. Sufficient return to baseline data (A) so that the pattern of outcome data is stable.
7. Sufficient replication of the intervention data (B) so that the pattern of outcome data is stable.

What an A-B-A-B design can tell you
1. That there was a change in outcome data from the baseline to the intervention phases.
2. The specific nature of that change (e.g., level, trend, or variability).
3. Whether the prediction statement from the baseline data was correct (observed in the return to baseline).
4. That the change observed was due to the intervention. Or, in practical terms, that the intervention was effective. This assumes that all four phases of baseline logic are supported by the pattern of the outcome data.
5. That a lack of observed change suggests the intervention is not functionally related to the target behavior. Or, in practical terms, that the intervention was ineffective. This assumes that the return to baseline phase verified the prediction statement.

What an A-B-A-B design cannot tell you
1. That the results are generalizable. This can only be accomplished through further replication across the targets of generalization (e.g., subject, setting, outcome variable, and so on).

OTHER DESIGNS

While this chapter has focused on the classic A-B-A-B design and some subversions (B, A-B, and A-B-A) this should by no means be seen as an exhaustive list of all designs that fall into this general class of SCD. For example, a quick review of the literature yields the use of B-A-B, A-B-C, A-B-A-C, A-B-A-B-A-B, and many other similar designs. In addition, as discussed previously it is likely for the applied educational practitioner to work with cases where a predetermined design is altered in practice. While alterations of this class will each have unique features and associated strengths and weaknesses, each will also be based, to varying degrees, on using a baseline–intervention–withdrawal–intervention pattern to establish experimental control. Using the information in this chapter and Chapter 2, these other designs should be readily understandable.

B-A-B Design

The B-A-B design is understood as an intervention followed by a withdrawal phase and finished with a replication of the intervention. Such a design could prove useful in an applied setting after an intervention has been applied without the collection of baseline data, but when it is important to document that there is some change in behavior when the intervention is not present. While the withdrawal and replication phases have the potential to increase confidence in the relationship between the intervention and the behavior, it is understood that without baseline data the true effect of the intervention on prebaseline behavior cannot be known. In addition, without baseline data a causal relationship between the intervention and outcome data cannot be suggested. While this is not ideal, such a design often occurs in an educational setting where new interventions are frequently attempted.

CASE EXAMPLE 3.1: CHRIS

Chris was experiencing some academic difficulties when he began the first grade last year. In particular, it appeared that he was having some difficulty learning to read fluently, which resulted in his classroom teacher placing him in the lowest reading group. However, Mr. Jones, his classroom teacher, also started to systematically collect outcome data on Chris using curriculum-based measurement of reading (CBM-R) with weekly first-grade second-quarter (1–2) probes. This progress-monitoring data were then compared to the median data collected on three typical children in Chris's class. Figures 3.A and 3.B present the weekly data for WCPM and number of errors, respectively, throughout the first half of the first grade for Chris and the median of the typical students. In terms of SCD, a B design was used to gauge Chris's progress.

At the conclusion of the second quarter of the first grade it was clear that while Chris had made some progress, he was not catching up to his peers in regard to WCPM or number of errors. What was most concerning about Chris's academic progress was that he was falling further behind his peers as the year progressed. As a result of these data, it was decided that Chris would move to Tier 2 and receive more intensive intervention for his reading problems.

The low reading group in Chris's classroom focused considerably on repetition and exposure to reading but without a great deal of direct instruction of phonics. While this was effective for a number of children in Mr. Jones's class, Chris continued to struggle as the second half of the year approached. It was decided that a more intensive approach to direct instruction of phonics was the logical intervention pathway, and there was a 4-day-a-week small-group intervention program available in the school. Thus, Chris joined this group for the remainder of the first grade, while still participating in his core first-grade reading instruction.

The outcome data from the first half of the year were used as baseline for an A-B SCD. The results of this intervention are presented in Figures 3.C and 3.D (WCPM and errors, respectively), and were mixed. Chris decreased the number of errors across the third and

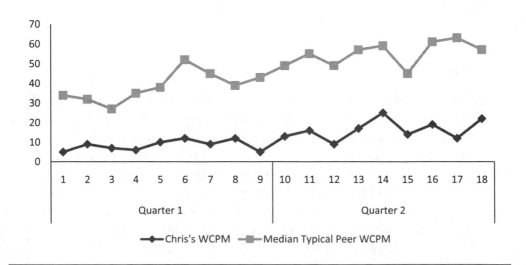

FIGURE 3.A. Tier 1 intervention outcome data (WCPM) for Chris using a B design.

(continued)

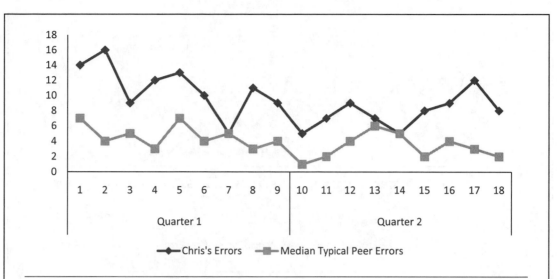

FIGURE 3.B. Tier 1 intervention outcome data (errors) for Chris using a B design.

fourth quarters. While the use of an A-B design precluded the ability to state that the intervention was the cause of this change, the progress was evident. Despite this positive finding, Chris's WCPM did not progress in a manner that was acceptable. Although Chris had clearly made some progress by the end of first grade, there were still significant concerns about his reading fluency.

In order to remedy this situation, it was decided that Chris required intensive individual intervention over the summer so that he did not fall any further behind. Thus, Chris was scheduled for 1 hour of daily individual reading instruction using primarily a practice-with-feedback method for 3 weeks in the summer. In addition, it was decided that it was important that his response to intervention was documented with more rigor. To accomplish

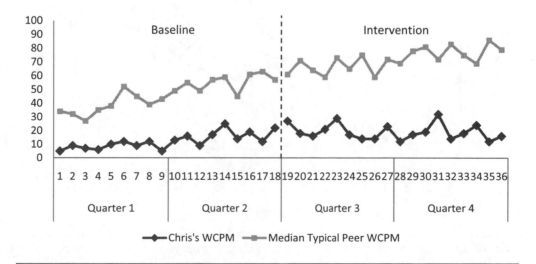

FIGURE 3.C. Tier 2 intervention outcome data (WCPM) for Chris using an A-B design.

(continued)

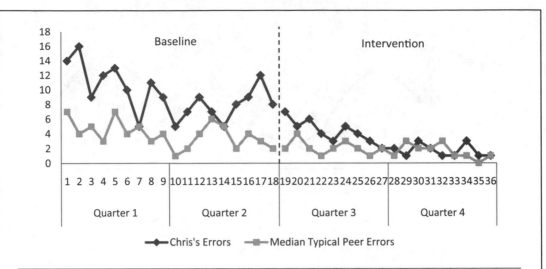

FIGURE 3.D. Tier 2 intervention outcome data (errors) for Chris using an A-B design.

this, an A-B-A-B design was selected, with the final 5 data points collected in first grade serving as initial baseline data. The results of this information are presented in Figure 3.E.

The intensive summer intervention seemed to be effective in the first B phase and Chris stopped increasing his WCPM when the intervention was withdrawn. Moreover, Chris immediately responded when the intervention was again applied. This outcome data pattern was consistent with an A-B-A-B design documenting a functional relationship between the intervention and the outcome data. In other words, it was clear that Chris responded to the intensive intervention. At the end of the summer intervention Chris's reading was at an acceptable level as compared to his peers and it was determined that he would participate in the typical second-grade reading instruction.

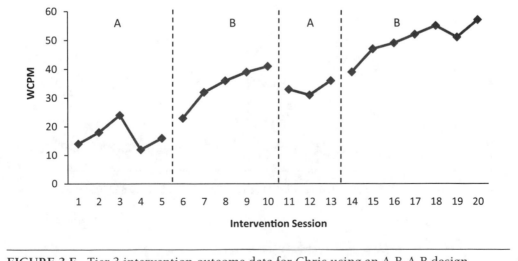

FIGURE 3.E. Tier 3 intervention outcome data for Chris using an A-B-A-B design.

A-B-C, A-B-A-C, A-B-C-A-C-B, and Related Designs

Another typical alteration of an A-B or A-B-A-B design is to incorporate a second intervention phase (C). As such, an A-B design would become an A-B-C design while an A-B-A-B design becomes an A-B-C-A-B-C design. In an applied educational setting this adaptation of an A-B-A-B design is attractive as the comparison of interventions is a typical goal. Obviously though, this additional comparison creates analysis issues. The primary effect of the introduction of a second intervention after the first is that those interventions may start to interact. Specifically, the intervention in the C phase is potentially impacted (in either a positive or negative manner) by the intervention in the B phase. As such, it would be inappropriate to attribute any observed intervention effect in the C phase only to the intervention applied. Rather, any effect should be attributed to that intervention after the presentation of the first intervention. Likewise, subsequent applications of the B intervention after the C intervention was presented must consider the potential of an interaction on the B intervention. One method to minimize intervention interactions is to return to baseline after each intervention phase. This addition would result in an A-B-A-C or A-B-A-C-A-B-A-C design. The return to baseline can provide both verification for the original prediction and a new prediction for the second intervention. In addition, the baseline can act as a buffer to minimize the impact of one intervention on the other. Another logical method to minimize the potential of an interaction effect between interventions is to include a counterbalance in the design. For example, A-B-A-C-A-B-A-C can be altered to A-B-A-C-A-C-A-B. This counterbalanced design will allow for the intervention presented in the C phase to be observed after the intervention in the B phase in the first half of the design, and then before in the second half. As such, if an order effect is present, it should be apparent in the pattern of the outcome data. For example, if the intervention in the C phase is made more effective by priming from the intervention in the B phase, then the outcome data in the first C phase should be more positive than in the second C phase. It is important to note that these methods are intended to minimize this issue rather than fully dismiss it. A return to baseline or counterbalancing will not remove any semipermanent impact of the previous intervention (e.g., an acquired skill). In the previous example, the original application of the intervention in the B phase could still provide a positive impact on the second application of the intervention in the C phase. In addition, such procedures can result in extremely extended designs that are unrealistic in most applied settings. In the next chapter we discuss designs that attempt to consider multiple interventions in a more feasible manner.

Regardless of the alteration (e.g., A-B, A-B-A-B, B-A-B, or A-B-C), each of these designs is based on the idea of withdrawing and replicating an intervention in an attempt to understand the relationship between that intervention and the outcome data. Considering the difficulties that a withdrawal of an intervention can cause, in the next chapter we address a series of designs that use other means of establishing experimental control.

4

Complex Single-Case Designs

As stated in the previous chapter, simple B and A-B designs can provide useful information to educators and psychologists in situations where experimental control and internal validity are not crucial. For example, if a child passes a test administered after a unit or increases reading skills after a simple intervention, then there is no reason to know why the positive behavior occurred. However, data collected within Tier 3 of an RTI model need to suggest a functional relationship in order to determine exactly what intervention is needed (Burns & Gibbons, 2008). Moreover, the identification of a functional relationship is the primary goal of SCD research. The A-B-A-B design was presented in Chapter 3 as the bedrock of single-case methodology, primarily because it provides the opportunity to go beyond simply documenting correlational relationships and delve into experimentation. The ability to document that an intervention caused a change in the target behavior is of critical importance in educational environments engaging in an RTI service delivery model.

While the potential of a fully experimental SCD is exciting, it is also clear that an A-B-A-B design may have significant disadvantages. Reversal designs can only be used when the behavior is reversible, which suggests that the behavior is likely to return to baseline levels when the intervention is removed. For example, student time on task may be substantially increased through simple modifications in the environment or reinforcing the on-task behavior, and when the modification or reinforcement is removed, time on task will likely return to its baseline level. However, reading continues to be the difficulty for which children are most frequently referred to school psychologists (Bramlett, Murphy, Johnson, Wallingford, & Hall, 2002) and reading is clearly not a reversible skill. It is not possible to implement an intervention so that a child increases reading skills from 30 WCPM to 75 WCPM, and then have the child forget the skills he/she learned in order to revert back to 30 WCPM during the next baseline phase, that is, unless the intervention is motivation oriented (e.g., reward for obtaining a criterion).

In addition to working with nonreversible behaviors, reversal designs may be unethical or impractical to implement in schools. A quality baseline should include at least three data points to ensure there is no naturally occurring trend, and should represent a condition severe enough to warrant an intervention. Thus, in order to establish experimental control it is necessary to have the child again exhibit severe behavior for a relatively extended period of time.

In this chapter a number of what we will call *complex SCDs* are presented as alternatives to A-B-A-B designs. We chose to call them complex designs because it is critical that users understand all of the elements of this class of single-case methodology. The following designs are based on systematic or intersubject direct replication rather than intrasubject direct replication for the development of experimental control. This issue was discussed in some depth in Chapter 2, so a brief review should suffice before we proceed. We replicate an intervention effect (first observed in a basic A-B-A-B design) so that we can be more confident that the first affirmation of the consequent was due to the independent variable and not some other unknown or external factor. There is a possibility that a change in target behavior is due to some other variable (known or unknown), even when the effect is large and immediately follows the application of the intervention (the start of the B phase).

There are two general means of replicating: direct and systematic. Intrasubject direct replication, as seen in A-B-A-B designs, tries to exactly replicate the original demonstration of the experimental effect. In practice, the same child, the same setting, and the same intervention is attempted again, which of course requires that the intervention be withdrawn in between the intervention phases. While this is not purely direct replication because there is a change in time and the impact of a behavioral history, it is as close as one can usually get in educational research. The benefits of direct replication lay in the clarity of what can be said about the results. If the original effect is replicated, then our confidence grows that there is indeed a functional relationship between the intervention and the target behavior. If on the other hand, the original effect is not repeated, we must be suspicious about the initial effect being caused by the intervention.

Systematic replication and intersubject direct replication are the alternatives to intrasubject direct replication. Intersubject direct replication is the process of repeating the intervention with a similar target student while holding all other variables consistent. Systematic replication is the process of closely replicating the original intervention while varying some element (e.g., an aspect of the intervention, the setting, the target, the dependent variable, and so on) in a logical manner. This is the very essence of complex SCD. Intersubject direct and systematic replication affords the opportunity to replicate, which is essential if the desire is to document causality, without the negative issues related to withdrawing an intervention. For example, one could replicate an A-B design over three settings or across three participants in a tight sequence. This approach allows for a full experimental model, but avoids the issues of an A-B-A-B design. Of course, these benefits come with some cost. Direct replication across participants and systematic replication are a tricky business, and designs that utilize these forms of replication are quite "complex." Moreover, when analyzing the outcome data it is important to remember that when systematically replicating, the decisions that are made can and probably will influence the relationship between the independent and the dependent variables. In addition, results from a direct replication across participants are influenced by the participants selected. As such, it is critical that when using a multiple-baseline, multielement, or other complex design that one fully understands the requirements described below.

MULTIPLE-BASELINE DESIGN

Baseline logic involves replicating the affirmation of the consequent, which is accomplished in an A-B-A-B design by removing and then reinstating the intervention. In a multiple-baseline (MB) design, replication is accomplished across participants, settings, or stimuli with a lag between phase changes across the multiple consequents. Thus, MB designs are essentially a series of A-B designs, using the same outcome variable and treatment, with staggered implementation of the treatment across conditions. The options for a condition in an MB design are typically participants, settings, or stimuli. The results are the commonly used names of this design, MB across participants, MB across settings, and MB across stimuli. It is possible to do an MB across other conditions as long as the same logic applies.

It is the lag between each A-B design that allows for the potential of experimental control. Logically, when the intervention is implemented in the first A-B condition (see Figure 4.1), one would expect a change in the outcome data for only that condition. Given that the intervention was not applied in conditions two and three, there should be no change in the outcome data for those conditions. The extended A phases for conditions two and three are acting as verification for the A phase in the first A-B design. After the intervention effect has stabilized, and assuming the baseline conditions remain stable for the remaining two cases, a second B phase is initiated. The same logic as in the first intervention application is applied. We expect a change in only the outcome data of the second A-B condition. Both the first A-B condition (currently in a B phase) and the third (currently in an A phase) should remain stable. This pattern then continues for each of the remaining A-B conditions (in Figure 4.1 there are three, but there is no maximum number). Internal validity is threatened when this pattern is not followed. For example, when the intervention is initiated in the first A-B case, if a change in baseline is observed in another case, there is a threat that some external variable is controlling the outcome data.

This method for establishing experimental control outlines several critical issues when developing an MB design. First, when developing the condition (typically participants, settings, or stimuli) it is important that they are as similar as possible in relation to the intervention so that the intervention logically impacts each in a similar manner. In addition, any external variable would impact each condition in the same way in regards to the target behavior. Remember that the goal is to catch any external variable impacting the first A-B condition at the same time an intervention is applied by observing a change in the outcome data in the second case.

As a rule, the goal when selecting the A-B cases (e.g., three subjects) is to make sure they are as similar as possible on all relevant features (e.g., age, developmental level, class, and so on). While it is tempting to provide a list of such features, they should be determined on a case by case basis considering the particulars of each situation. Unfortunately, similarity is not the only consideration when selecting conditions. While the targets of each A-B case should be similar, there should be no contamination of the intervention effect from case to case. For example, if triplets were in the same class, it would be tempting to use them as participants 1, 2, and 3 for an MB across participants design. While this may work, there is a fear that when an intervention is applied to the first target student, he/she would

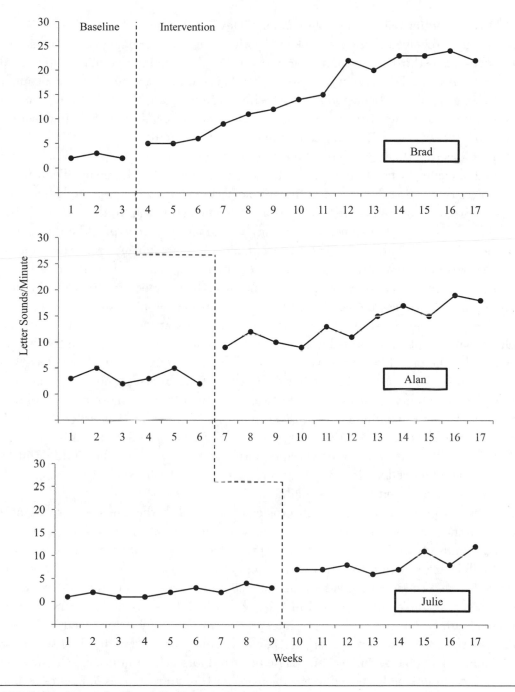

FIGURE 4.1. Example of an MB design across participants.

talk to his/her siblings about the intervention. "Hey, John, when I behaved today in Ms. Wilson's class I received three extra tokens!" This in turn could impact the outcome data in the second and third cases before the intervention is applied. Or, contamination could be as simple as a child observing the intervention being applied in the same setting and as a result changing his/her behavior. Any such effect would negatively impact the process of establishing experimental control. As such, when selecting conditions, it is important to consider independence while at the same time maximizing similarity.

When selecting the type of conditions to utilize, MB across participants design is ideally suited to evaluate the effectiveness of a particular intervention for a specific difficulty. This involves replicating the finding with multiple participants, with a repeated effect for at least three participants. As is often the case in experimental research, there is no definite rule as to how many participants are sufficient, but the more participants, the stronger the experimental control. Three would be an acceptable minimum because consistent findings across the participants would suggest a pattern of behavior. Data such as those presented in Figure 4.1 suggest an effective intervention because they immediately increased in level and trend after the phase change for all three students despite a lag of three data points between each successive student. A practitioner could look at the data in Figure 4.1 and conclude that the intervention led to increased fluency with which the students identified letter sounds. The practitioner could probably add that intervention to his/her repertoire to be used with students presenting similar deficits as these three students. However, there is little internal validity regarding the effectiveness of the intervention for any one of these three students. Thus, if an interventionist was interested in the effectiveness of a particular intervention, he/she could use MB across participants. However, if he/she was interested in the functional relationship between variables for a particular student, then a different MB approach would be needed. The two most common approaches to replicating the effect for one student are across settings and stimuli.

If the goal of an applied research project is to establish the functional relationship between an intervention and one target student's difficulty, an MB across settings or across stimuli design is ideal. For example, the data presented in Figure 4.2 are from a first-grade student exhibiting severe difficulties with penmanship. Thus, a formative evaluation was conducted to determine which letters the student made correctly and incorrectly, and an intervention was implemented with 15 letters with which he struggled to form correctly. The order with which the letters were intervened was randomly determined and placed into three sets of five each, except *b*, *d*, and *p*, which were presented in different sets. Given that an immediate change in level and slope occurred for each stimulus set, the intervention appeared functionally related to the behavior for this student. This MB across stimuli design allows for a clearer demonstration of a functional relationship for an individual student than is possible with an across participants design.

Number of Baseline Data Points

There is no hard or fast rule for the number of baseline data points needed or for the amount of lag between phase changes. Generally speaking, the greater the lag between phase

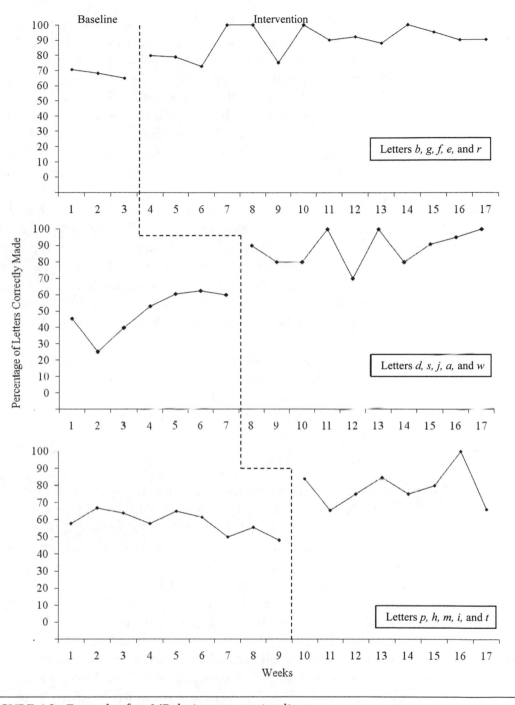

FIGURE 4.2. Example of an MB design across stimuli.

change with no unexpected change in outcome data, the less likely changes in behavior are due to variables external to the study and the stronger the experimental control. However, practitioners should collect baseline data until they appear stable and then consider if enough lag has occurred. For example, the data presented in Figure 4.2 includes three baseline data points for the first stimulus set, which suggests that five baseline data points would suffice for the second stimuli set. However, there was a clear upward trend in the baseline data after five points and an additional two data points ensured a more stable base to which intervention data could be compared. The baseline data for the third stimulus set were sufficiently stable after adding only two more points to the number obtained for the second stimulus set.

The baseline data in Figure 4.1 present another consideration. Three baseline data points were collected for Brad, and appeared sufficiently stable. Following the basic guideline, five data points should have been sufficient for the second student, but the third, fourth, and fifth baseline data points for Alan were upwardly trended. Thus, a sixth data point was collected, which approximated the third data point and ended the trend. Adding two data points would have resulted in eight baseline data points for the third student, but three additional points were included to be consistent among the participants of the across participants design.

It is important to note that all outcome data will not necessarily be at the same level across conditions. While ideally each target has the same level of the target behavior, this is often not the case. As long as baseline is established, and the preintervention level of the target behavior is documented, the logic driving an MB design can be utilized.

Concurrent or Nonconcurrent Designs

Data collection within an MB design classically occurs concurrently in the same or similar settings. This concurrent data collection reduces the influence of history effect on the data and enhances experimental control (Baer et al., 1968; Kazdin & Kopel, 1975). However, it may not be possible to collect these data simultaneously in an applied setting for various reasons including a lack of multiple students presenting similar problems and resources to concurrently intervene with those students (Winn, Skinner, Allin, & Hawkins, 2004). Thus, a nonconcurrent MB design may be used in which data are not collected for each A-B series until the previous series is completed (Watson & Workman, 1981). The nonconcurrent MB design can adequately address most threats to internal validity, including those associated with history, as long as instrumentation, conditions, observer accuracy, and stimuli remain as close to constant as possible (Christ, 2007). Moreover, if using at least three students, it is "unreasonable to assume that an uncontrolled extraneous variable would cause changes in each student's behavior at different times and those times coincide with the application of treatments to each student" (Winn et al., 2004, p. 112). However, the delay in the onset of data collection should be graphically displayed much like the approach used in Figure 4.3, so that practitioners can clearly evaluate the effect of the delay on the results.

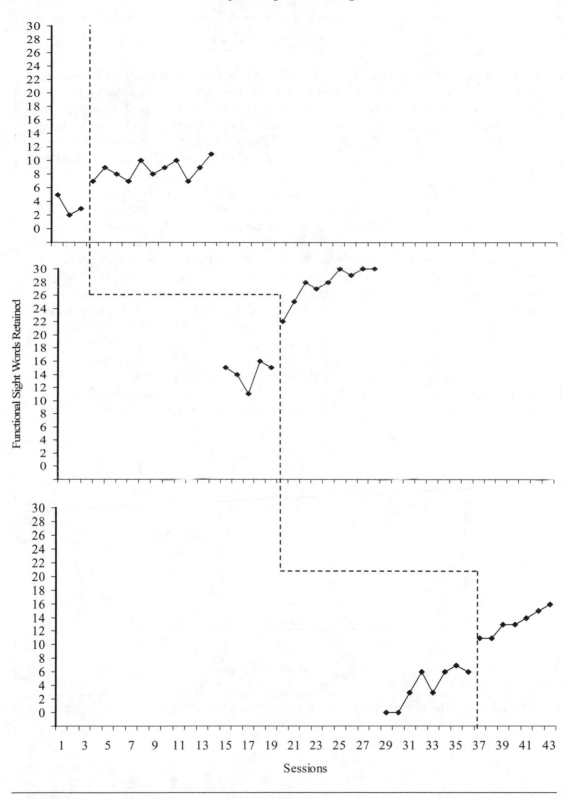

FIGURE 4.3. Example of a nonconcurrent MB design.

CASE EXAMPLE 4.1: CHELSEA

Chelsea has been through a series of interventions at Longwood Elementary School over the past 2 years. These interventions have attempted to increase her on-task behavior because high rates of off-task behavior have severely impacted her academic performance. Early screening and intervention found that Chelsea learned at a rate that was consistent with her peers when she was on task. In addition, consistent praise for on-task behavior with correction statement was effective in increasing Chelsea's on-task behavior in her science class (see Figure 4.A).

While this intervention success was good news, Chelsea's on-task behavior was a problem throughout the day. Due to the success of this intervention, and the significant concerns surrounding Chelsea's general performance in school, the intervention team at Longwood Elementary decided to conduct an intensive multisetting intervention plan to explore if this intervention was indeed responsible for the change in Chelsea's on-task behavior, and if it could be replicated in several settings. An MB across settings design was selected using the praise for on-task behavior with correction statement intervention in three classroom settings (reading, math, and social studies). Figure 4.B shows the results of this intervention plan. Unfortunately, the effectiveness of the intervention was not consistently replicated in two of the three settings. There appeared to be some success in reading class, but Chelsea's on-task behavior did not increase in math or social studies when the intervention was applied. Thus, some variable other than the intervention was likely responsible for the positive behavior in the science class. Clearly the intervention team needed to identify a different intervention program to increase Chelsea's on-task behavior across settings.

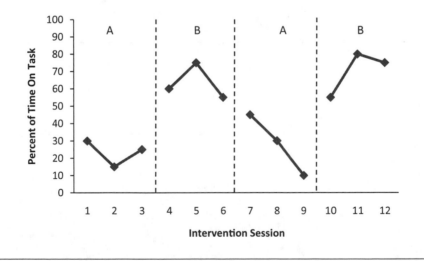

FIGURE 4.A. Initial intervention outcome data for Chelsea using an A-B-A-B design.

(continued)

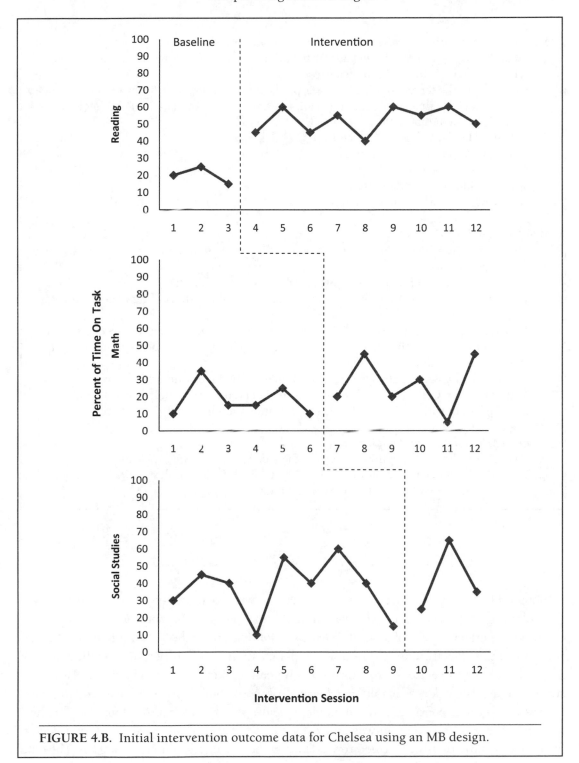

FIGURE 4.B. Initial intervention outcome data for Chelsea using an MB design.

Steps to a successful MB design (adapted from Tawney & Gast, 1984)
1. Clear description of the target, target behavior, and ecology (time, place, instructional activities, and all other relevant features).
2. Similarity in the targets in terms of their predicted functional relationship with the independent variable (intervention) with minimal threat of contamination of the intervention effect from one target to the next.
3. A defensible data collection method.
4. As frequent data collection as possible.
5. Sufficient baseline data (A).
6. Sufficient intervention data (B).
7. Sufficient lag between phase changes across participants, settings, or stimuli.

What an MB design can tell you
1. That there was a change in outcome data from the baseline to the intervention phases for the participant(s).
2. The specific nature of that change (e.g., level, trend, or variability).
3. The settings and/or stimuli for the participant(s) for which that change could be replicated.
4. That the change observed was due to the intervention. Or, in practical terms, that the intervention was effective. This assumes that all four phases of baseline logic are supported by the pattern of the outcome data.
5. That a lack of observed change suggests the intervention is not functionally related to the target behavior. Or, in practical terms, that the intervention was ineffective. This assumes that the baseline phase is verified across settings or stimuli.

What an MB design cannot tell you
1. That the results are generalizable beyond the participants, settings, or stimuli studied.
2. What the functional relationship is for an individual student unless data are compared across settings or stimuli for that particular student.

MULTIELEMENT DESIGN

Although the effectiveness of an intervention can be well documented with MB designs, it is difficult to use MB designs to compare different interventions. Data presented in Figure 4.4 examine the effectiveness of a word rehearsal intervention on the reading fluency of three students in the fourth grade. These students demonstrated difficulties with reading fluency in baseline, which may be improved through repeated practice (Therrien, 2004). However, students may also lack reading fluency because of motivational issues, which are often best addressed through contingent reinforcement (Daly, Witt, Martens, & Dool, 1997). Thus, a second phase of intervention was added for these three students in which they selected from a list of individually identified rewards when they reached a fluency criterion. The data for Tom and Wayne suggest that the word rehearsal method increased reading fluency, but adding a reward did not substantially improve the outcomes. However, data in the contingent reinforcement phase for Jim increased in level and slope as compared to both baseline and the word rehearsal phases.

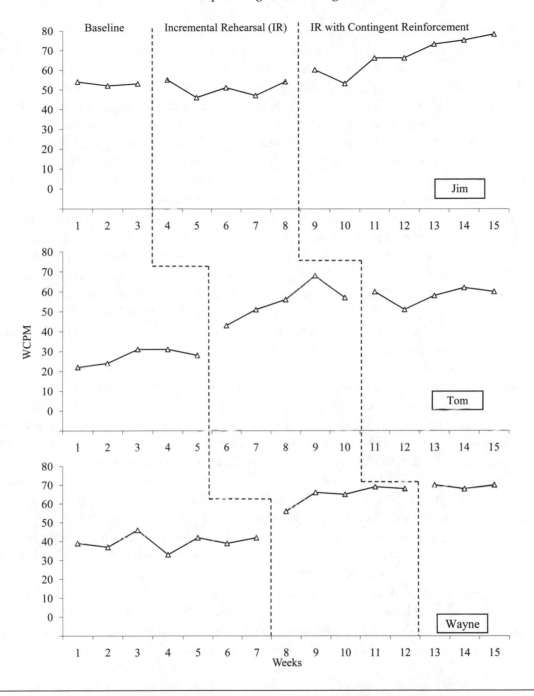

FIGURE 4.4. Example of an MB design across participants with two interventions.

Assuming adequate implementation integrity for all phases, experimental control for these three students was exhibited only for the combination of the two interventions, but those data may mask the idiosyncrasy of the student behavior. A plausible hypothesis could be that the rehearsal intervention was more appropriate for Tom and Wayne because they lacked sufficient skill, but Jim's deficit may have been more motivational in nature, which suggests the need for contingency reinforcement as the primary intervention. However, these data cannot address the skill-intervention match hypothesis with sufficient experimental control. Moreover, it could very well be that contingent reinforcement may have resulted in the same effect for Tom and Wayne as the word rehearsal intervention if it were attempted first, and would have been much simpler to implement.

The classic alternating treatment design is the approach that will likely result in the greatest internal validity for comparisons of intervention effectiveness. For example, a comparison of two interventions with a final return to baseline would be A-B-A-C-A-B-A-C-A, or A-B-A-C-A-C-A-B-A, or A-B-C-A-B-C-A, or A-B-C-A-C-B-A, and so on. These designs, and the advantage thereof, are discussed in the previous chapter, but one potential difficulty exists within an applied setting. Assuming a return to baseline is both desirable and possible, and that at least three to five data points are needed for each phase, it would probably involve nine phases for a total of at least 27 to 45 data points. That level of data collection may require too much time in an applied setting where rapidly made decisions are frequently needed. In this situation, a multielement (ME) design would perhaps be preferable.

ME designs share the same characteristics of classic A-B-A-B designs, but alternate between conditions at a much more rapid rate. The data presented in Figure 4.5 represent a comparison of three instructional conditions for three students with math difficulties. All three students exhibit difficulty with time on task during independent work in math. Using the criteria for instructional and frustration levels based on digits correct per minute (Burns, VanDerHeyden, & Jiban, 2006), the task difficulty for the classroom assignments represented a frustration level. Therefore, we compared three conditions, the typical classroom material (frustration level, which served as baseline), using easier material that represented an instructional level, and using easier material that represented an instructional level along with providing tangible reinforcement for time on task. The data in Figure 4.5 suggest that using easier material increased time on task for all three students, but adding contingent reinforcement did not substantially increase time on task over using instructional-level materials. A comparison of interventions occurred after approximately 15 data points, but two to three times as many data points would have been needed for an A-B-A-B design.

Number and Types of Data Points

As with MB designs, there is no hard or fast rule for the number of data points required for an ME design. Data should be collected for each condition until differentiation occurs. However, ME designs differ from MB designs in that there may not be a baseline condition. It is not unusual for ME designs to use two or more interventions as the conditions, or to use currently existing conditions as the baseline (Kennedy, 2005). The example in Figure 4.5 uses classroom materials as the baseline condition, which represents a frustration-level task.

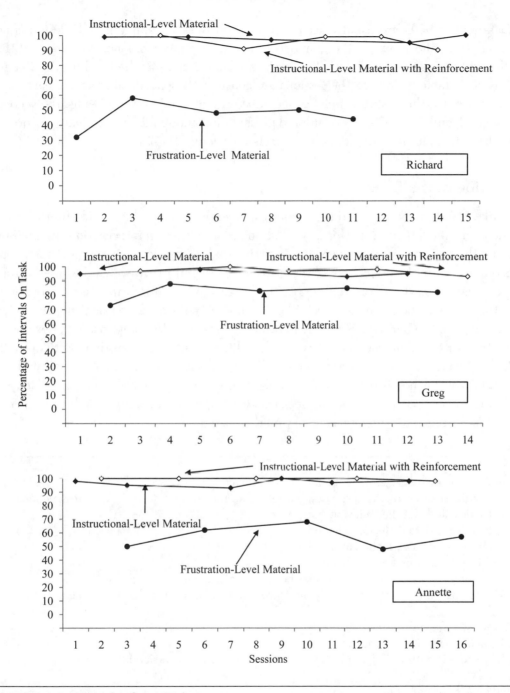

FIGURE 4.5. Example of an ME design.

Data within SCD are usually displayed in a time-series graph, and ME design is no exception. Thus, the *X*-axis of the graph should include some component of time and the data should be presented sequentially. Figure 4.5 uses sessions as the label for the *X*-axis, which is acceptable as long as the sessions are consistently spaced, such as one each day. More importantly, the first data point collected is presented first on the *X*-axis, the second one is second, and so on. This time-ordered presentation allows for a more clear interpretation of the data including potential order effects (Kennedy, 2005).

Replication of the Effect

Again, like MB designs, an ME design requires the effect to be replicated in order to demonstrate experimental control. This is most often accomplished in intervention research by repeating the design across participants. Experimental control for a single participant can be accomplished with replications across settings or stimuli. However, information from one set of data (e.g., data from the top panel in Figure 4.5) can inform decisions depending on the decisions being made. Much like the simple A-B design, decisions not requiring experimental control may be adequately informed by a single ME comparison. For example, if a practitioner is attempting to identify what condition would work best in a particular setting for a specific student in order to suggest an intervention, then a simple design without replication may be helpful. However, if student intervention response outcome data are then going to be used for important decisions (e.g., special education eligibility), then a higher standard for experimental control would be needed.

Steps to a successful ME design (adapted from Tawney & Gast, 1984)
1. Clear description of the target, target behavior, and ecology (time, place, instructional activities, and all other relevant features).
2. A defensible data collection method.
3. As frequent data collection as possible.
4. Sufficient data for each condition.
5. Rapid alternation between conditions in a random or counterbalanced order.
6. Use of interventions that distinctly differ from each other or from baseline practice.

What an ME design can tell you
1. Which intervention is the most effective.
2. The specific nature of that effectiveness (e.g., level, trend, or variability).

What an ME design cannot tell you
1. That the results are generalizable beyond the participants, settings, or stimuli studied.

REPEATED AND CUMULATIVE ACQUISITION DESIGNS

RTI has made the rate at which students learn skills an important variable in educational decision making. Thus, SCD should inform practitioners about slopes of student learning and should identify the intervention that led to the greatest growth. Boren (1963) proposed that repeated acquisition design (RAD) be used to examine how quickly skills are acquired under different conditions. In an RAD, two different conditions can be delivered in distinct sessions with equivalence within each condition, using an alternating treatment approach. The data presented in Figure 4.6 are from a 9-year-old male student with moderate mental retardation. We taught the student 30 sight words each week for 3 weeks using two conditions. Half of the words were taught with a high opportunity-to-respond model (OTR) in which he was presented each word as many as 81 times, and a moderate OTR model in which each word was presented 27 times. All 15 words for each condition were rehearsed daily in an alternating sequence, and were then followed by an assessment to determine which of the 15 words were correctly read within 2 seconds of presentation. As can be seen from the data, the student learned all 15 words by the end of each week for the high OTR condition, but only learned 7, 10, and 11 for the moderate OTR condition. The data presented for the first week indicate that within the high OTR condition, the student learned 3 words on the first day, correctly stated a total of 5 words on the second day (most likely he retained the previous 3 and learned 2 more), 11 on the third day, and 15 on the fourth day of the week.

Data within an RAD are interpreted somewhat differently than an A-B-A-B, MB, or MF design. The level and trend of the data are certainly compared, but it is the trend that usually matters most. For example, the rate of learning in Figure 4.6 was clearly higher for the high OTR condition than the moderate OTR condition. Therefore, the high OTR condition would be judged to be the more effective approach even though the difference in end result (e.g., learned 15 words rather than 10 or 11 in the final two sets) was not particularly large.

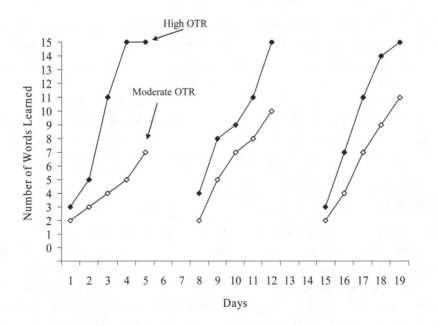

FIGURE 4.6. Example of an RAD.

A modification to the RAD has recently appeared in the research literature, stemming mostly from interest in instructional efficiency. As stated earlier, the rate at which students learn can be important data. Thus, recent studies have compared the rates at which students acquired reading skills and words for two or more conditions over a period of weeks, again using an alternative treatment paradigm. These new designs can be called a *cumulative acquisition design* (CAD), which involves graphing the data by plotting the total to that point for each point in time. Cates, Skinner, Watson, Smith, Weaver, and Jackson (2003) compared interspersing conditions when teaching spelling using instructional efficiency (i.e., the amount of time needed to learn the task) as the primary dependent variable. The results found that there was not much difference between the conditions when learning the spelling words, but that one condition clearly required less time. A similar approach was used by Nist and Joseph (2008) to demonstrate that one intervention may be the most effective, but it is not necessarily the most efficient. Thus, it seems that CADs have implications for instructional efficiency research, which has been accepted as a critical component of intervention decision making.

An example of a CAD is found in the simulated data presented in Figure 4.7. The data in the top panel are the cumulative rates at which the student acquired sight words with two instructional conditions. There was no clear differentiation between the two approaches. However, data presented in the bottom panel suggest that condition A required less time (a total of approximately 113 minutes over 20 days) than condition B (a total of approximately 174 minutes over 20 days), which suggested that A was the more efficient of the two. The movement toward instructional efficiency in intervention research will likely lead to CADs being more frequently used in research and practice.

Number and Types of Data Points

Unlike ME and MB designs, the number of data points collected is usually an a priori decision based on a practical criterion. The example in Figure 4.5 was conducted for a period of 5 days each, which required that each condition contain 5 data points before changing the stimulus set. Certainly the condition could be continued for 2 weeks (10 data points), but that would likely be determined before the data collection began rather than by responding to the data. Data collection in a CAD would continue until a clear differentiation occurs, with no predetermined length. Moreover, an RAD or CAD usually do not involve baseline data, but likely could use standard educational practice as one of the conditions.

Replication of the Effect

Replication in an RAD can be accomplished with multiple stimulus sets for one student. Thus, this approach has stronger internal validity for a single participant than an ME design, but the internal validity is enhanced for the RAD when it is replicated across subjects as well. Internal validity for the CAD would more likely be dependent on multiple participants. However, if a CAD is used as only one aspect of the decision-making framework, less internal validity would be needed. For example, if intervention effectiveness was examined

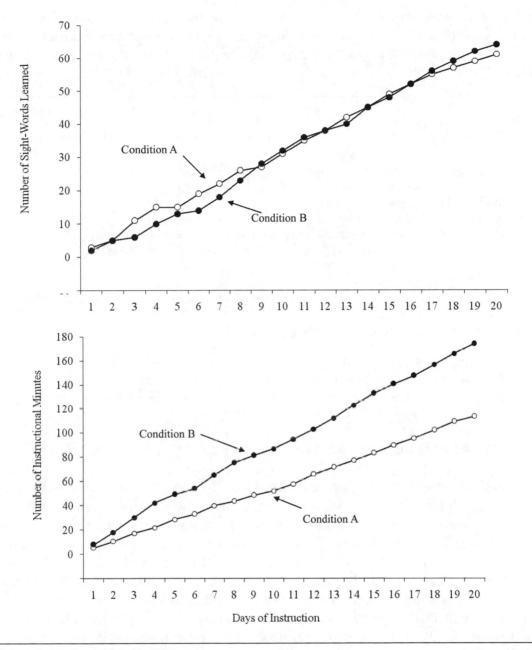

FIGURE 4.7. Example of a CAD.

with an ME across stimulus design, a CAD could be used to compare the efficiency of the two conditions. The ME across stimulus design would have sufficient internal validity to evaluate the effectiveness of the interventions, and the CAD could provide additional potentially useful data.

Steps to a successful RAD
1. Clear description of the target, target behavior, and ecology (time, place, instructional activities, and all other relevant features).
2. A defensible data collection method.
3. As frequent data collection as possible.
4. Sufficient data for each condition.
5. Alternation between conditions in a random or counterbalanced order.
6. Use of interventions that distinctly differ from each other or from baseline practice.
7. An a priori determined, practical, and meaningful phase length for an RAD.

What an RAD can tell you
1. That there was a difference in the rate with which behavior occurred (e.g., skills were acquired) between conditions.
2. The specific nature of that difference (e.g., level, trend, or variability).

What an RAD cannot tell you
1. That the results are generalizable beyond the participants, settings, or stimuli studied.

MAXIMIZING INTERNAL VALIDITY IN COMPLEX DESIGNS

Campbell and Stanley (1966) proposed what is now the nine commonly accepted threats to internal validity in research, selection bias, history effects, maturation, repeated testing, instrumentation, regression to the mean, experimental mortality, selection–maturation interaction, and experimenter bias. Many scholars have suggested that SCD adequately address common threats to internal validity (Kazdin, 1982; Kratochwill, 1985; Kratochwill, Mott, & Dodson, 1984; Shaughnessy, Zechmeister, & Zechmeister, 2003) and true experimentation is dependent on active manipulation of an independent variable, which is a hallmark of SCD. Kazdin (1982) recommended that the behavior of interest be observed continuously during the intervention period using objective sources of data, and that phases be alternated so that performance improves and reverts. Thus, complex designs may very well address threats to internal validity that simple A-B and A-B-A-B designs do not, but confidence in causal inferences cannot be attributed to a particular design as much as it is to the specific experimental procedure. Moreover, complex SCD are more susceptible to some of these threats to internal validity than others.

Given the extensive history of SCD, much of what is done in single-case research is proudly, rightly, and firmly steeped in tradition. However, as further discussed in Chapter 8 RTI calls for a higher standard for internal validity of applied research and data-based decisions. Thus, applied SCD researchers should consider current and future practices in light of the RTI movement. Perhaps the single issue that practitioners and researchers need to consider is the role of randomization in SCD research.

The current "gold standard" for traditional between-group studies is random assignment of participants to treatment or control groups. Randomly assigning participants prevents an interaction between selection bias and treatment effects, and greatly enhances the internal validity of the conclusions. Given that participants in SCD research serve as their own controls, random assignment seems irrelevant, but perhaps randomization of other aspects of an SCD could enhance the internal validity for these conclusions as well. Data collection in SCD is generally dependent on responding to the data. For example, data are usually collected until they are stable at which time a phase change generally occurs. However, a random order of condition sequence would evenly distribute the influence of order effects among the various conditions (Kennedy, 2005). Thus, practitioners could consider presenting treatments in an ME, RAD, or CAD design in a randomly determined order until the data differentiate between the conditions. Randomization of condition orders within SCD could address issues of history and maturation. In an ME design, the rapid alternation of conditions in rapid succession could result in an order effect because C would always follow B, and C could be susceptible to changes from maturation because it would be the final phase. Randomly determining the order would distribute the likelihood for order and maturation effects evenly across the conditions. Moreover, a counterbalanced order may also be beneficial, but still suggests an increased likelihood for maturation effects for one condition that is not possible for the others.

The order for conditions is predetermined for MB designs, but randomization could still be used to enhance internal validity by randomly determining the order in which the participants receive the intervention (Christ, 2007). For example, a researcher could randomly determine that Student B will have the fewest baseline data points and receive the intervention first, then Student A, and finally Student C. The order of presentation would be determined, but the exact number of baseline data points would still depend on the stability of the data.

Because intervention research is becoming so prevalent and important, and practitioners are more frequently using SCD for educational decision making, research about SCD methodology is ongoing. The result of critical and empirical reviews of SCD methods could result in either an endorsement of a new practice or validation of a current one, including the role of randomization. However, it seems that complex designs, such as MB, ME, and RAD, will remain an integral component of intervention research and applied data-based decision making.

5

Visual Analysis and Interpretation Strategies for Single-Case Design

The final stage of an RTI or problem-solving model is to formally analyze the outcome data to answer two basic questions. First, "Was there a change in the target behavior(s)?" Second, "Was any observed change the result of the attempted intervention(s)?" In Chapters 5 and 6 we review how that data should be graphed, and provide guidelines to aid in analysis and interpretation of assessment data used to monitor the effects of intervention implementation. Please note that all examples in this chapter use simulated data.

SUMMARIZING DATA THROUGH VISUAL PRESENTATION: CREATING THE LINE GRAPH

Although data may be summarized in many ways, visual formats (e.g., bar chart, scatterplot, line graph) are the most effective and efficient means of presentation (vs. a table or just a list of numbers). In particular, line graphs provide a simple way to review data collected over time, especially for monitoring student progress. The line graph, with a few standard elements (e.g., phase change lines), provides an excellent picture of the outcome data collected over time. Given that the goal of intervention monitoring in RTI is to observe change over time, visual analyses play an important role in any RTI model.

It is important to begin with a review of some basic SCD graphing guidelines. These guidelines are rather consistently adhered to in the literature, and make it easy for any knowledgeable reader to understand what is being represented in an SCD graph. Moreover, consistent adherence to these standards will assist practitioners in becoming more fluent with standard graphing protocol. The basic standards for an SCD graph are as follows:

1. Each target behavior should have its own series of data that use the same marker (e.g., ■, O, or ▲). Tawney and Gast (1984) suggest that no more than three target behaviors

be plotted on any single graph. It is our experience that every additional behavior on a graph makes interpretation more confusing. While this is not a concern with experienced consumers of SCD line graphs, this can be a significant issue in typical educational environments. As such, in an educational environment where consumers typically have limited experience (at least initially) with such data presentations, it is advisable to graph outcome behaviors on separate graphs unless there is a compelling reason to combine them into one presentation (e.g., graphing related behaviors like WCPM and errors).

2. Each series of data should have a line that connects data points. This process creates what is called a *data path*. There are several important conventions regarding data paths (Cooper et al., 2007).

    a. Data points should only be connected within a phase.

    b. If a significant amount of time has passed (see 5c below), the data points before and after the break should not be connected.

    c. If planned data are not available for any reason, the data points before and after the unavailable data should not be connected.

    d. Follow-up data (any data collected at a later date to check on the target behavior) that are not collected in the same interval as the initial data should not be connected with each other. For example, when A-B-A-B data are collected daily for 4 weeks and follow-up data are collected bimonthly for 2 months following the end of the initial design, the follow-up data should not be connected.

3. Phase changes should be noted on a line graph with a vertical line. The vertical line can be solid or dashed. We suggest use of a dashed line as it draws attention to the phase change and looks different than a data path.

4. The Y-axis (vertical axis) should be used to represent the outcome data values.

    a. The scale should be appropriate for the target behavior and use an equal interval.

    b. It is important to present the minimum and maximum values possible in the scale for the Y-axis (e.g., 0% on task to 100% on task). If the outcome data are not evenly distributed (e.g., ranging from 5 to 25%), it is acceptable to scale the graph partially (e.g., 0 to 50%), then place a scale break (//) in the Y-axis above the highest number in the selected scale (50% in this case), and then extend the scale to 100% immediately above the scale break.

5. The X-axis (horizontal axis) should be used to represent time.

    a. The earliest recording of the outcome data being place next to the Y-axis, and the most recent on the far right of the X-axis with an equal interval in between.

    b. The units should be a logical representation of the case. Thus, for a whole-day intervention "intervention day" could be used. However, if multiple intervention sessions occurred each day, it would be more appropriate to use "intervention session."

    c. If there is a gap in time (e.g., winter break), the X-axis should have a scale break (//) placed on the line between the last point before the break and the first point after the break. This informs the reader that there was an interruption in the phase.

6. It is suggested that in cases where 0 is the minimum possible score that 0 not be at the intersection of the X-axis and Y-axis. In such a case, 0 should be placed as the first option on the Y-axis.

7. Labels for both the X- and Y-axes should be utilized, and should briefly orient the reader to that axis.

8. Tawney and Gast (1984) suggest that the ideal ratio of the Y-axis to the X-axis is 2:3. They contend that this presentation minimizes visual distortion that can occur with a longer Y-axis (e.g., 3:3 ratio) or a longer X-axis (e.g., 2:4 ratio).

In this section we briefly review the process for developing A-B and MB line graphs including standard SCD graphing practices. Some readers will want to develop their SCD graphs using computer software. Software packages such as Microsoft Excel make it rather easy to develop professional-looking graphs. For those interested in this graphing method, see Appendix A at the end of the book for a step-by-step guide to developing SCD graphs using Microsoft Excel and Microsoft Word.*

Steps for Developing a Simple A-B Line Graph

1. Label the Y-axis (vertical) with behavior of interest (e.g., percentage of time on task or number of times a student calls out).
2. Select the scale for the Y-axis based on the data collected (e.g., 0 to 100% for percentage of time on task or percentage of intervals of out of seat, number of WCPM, number of aggressive acts per day, average daily rating, and so on).
3. Select the scale for and label the X-axis (horizontal) with observation intervals (e.g., day, period, week).
4. Separate preintervention (baseline) and intervention phase data with a vertical dashed line (e.g., 5 days of baseline data followed by 15 days of intervention).
5. Connect consecutive data points within phases to show progress. Do not connect lines across phases (i.e., preintervention to intervention), or across missing data. Break-in lines should represent missing data points or change in intervention conditions when accompanied with a vertical solid or dashed line.

Appendices 5.1–5.4 at the end of this chapter provide blank A-B graphs for your use.

In Figure 5.1, "calling-out" behavior (Y-axis) data were collected once a day for a total of 20 days (X-axis). A visual analysis reveals that the maximum number of calling-out behaviors reported in a day is 16 (scale set 0 to 20). (Note that the same scales should be used when comparing information across graphs in order to avoid inaccurate interpretation due to visual presentation.) The vertical dotted line separates the preintervention (baseline) period from the intervention phase and enables an evaluation of the effectiveness of an intervention. Consecutive data points within phases are connected.

---

*Microsoft Excel and Microsoft Word are registered trademarks or trademarks of Microsoft Corporation in the United States and/or other countries.

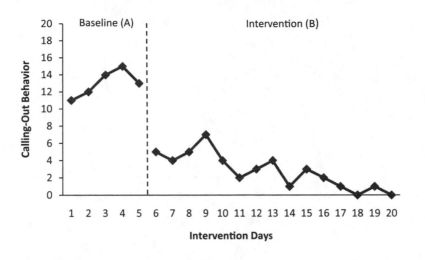

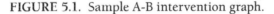

FIGURE 5.1. Sample A-B intervention graph.

Steps for Developing a MB Graph

1. Replicate the steps for an A-B graph for the first, second, and third target (e.g., behaviors, subjects, settings, or other).
2. Place the A-B graph where the intervention will be implemented first on the top.
3. Place the next A-B graph where the intervention will be implemented second under the first.
4. Place the final A-B graph under the second.
5. Connect the three intervention phases with a stair-step line.

Appendices 5.5 and 5.6 at the end of this chapter provide blank MB graphs for your use.

In Figure 5.2, calling-out behavior (*Y*-axis) was again collected once a day for a total of 20 days (*X*-axis). In this instance, however, the intervention was applied across three students in a varied presentation. The three A-B graphs are stacked with the student who receives the intervention first on top, followed by the student who receives the intervention second, and so on. As can be observed in Figure 5.2, the scale of each A-B graph is kept consistent to aid in visual analysis. The vertical dotted line separates the preintervention (baseline) period from the intervention phase and enables an evaluation of the effectiveness of an intervention. Consecutive data points within phases are connected. In order to represent an MB, these lines are connected in a step fashion. This stair-step line aids analysis as it allows for considering both the intervention effect for the first case and the continuation of baseline in the other cases. This can then be applied to the second case and so on.

CHANGE WITHIN A PHASE

Before addressing each method of visual analysis we should first consider the different levels in which to consider "change." Change can occur within a phase or between phases. As

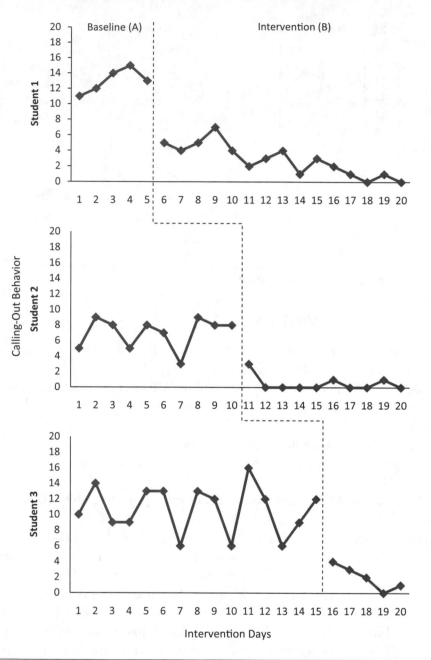

FIGURE 5.2. Sample MB intervention graph.

this book is specifically focused on SCD for the purpose of measuring a response to intervention, we focus primarily on between-phase analysis. Regardless, it is notable to consider that changes in the behavioral pattern within a phase can be important. For example, as we discuss later in this chapter, the trend in baseline can impact one's assessment of the effect of an intervention. In addition, changes within a phase, such as gradually increasing variability, can greatly decrease one's confidence in that data. Several of these issues are discussed below.

Within-phase change in the pattern of the target behavior inevitability leads to the question, "What caused the change?" It could be that the target behavior is simply variable. For example, it is not atypical for on-task behavior to range from close to 0% to close to 100% depending on changes in the ecology. On the other hand, it could be that some change in the ecology or child has occurred that impacted the target behavior. It is understood that any prediction statement based on a phase data path is known to have an expiration date (as reviewed in Chapter 2). Perhaps that date came sooner rather than later. This is particularly relevant in an educational environment where changes to curriculum, staff, and procedures occur all the time. The most general implication of changes in outcome data within a phase is that more data are needed within that phase before a defensible phase change can occur. The collection of additional outcome data will better allow for a fuller understanding of the target behavior. If the change was temporary, that will be documented with additional outcome data. Likewise, additional outcome data will show whether the change was permanent. Alternatively, if the outcome data were simply much more variable than predicted, the full behavioral pattern will become apparent with additional data. In the end, if you are not confident that you fully understand the pattern of the target behavior within a phase, collect more data. Our general rule of thumb for this, and most instances in practice, is when in doubt, collect data.

TWO STAGES FOR THE ANALYSIS OF SCD DATA

Once the outcome data have been graphed in an appropriate manner analysis can begin. For the remainder of this chapter, we consider basic visual analysis techniques and subsequent decisions. In Chapter 6, we consider more mathematically advanced (although not necessarily "better") methods of analysis. Before addressing visual analysis techniques, it is critical to consider the analytic process and the desired outcomes of analysis.

As previously noted, there are two basic questions that must be addressed when considering outcome data in a single-case format. The first is "To what degree was there a change in the target behavior(s) when the intervention was implemented (or removed)?" This question focuses on the idea of "response" in terms of the target behavior. At this stage, we are not overly concerned if this response was functionally related to the intervention, but simply, "Was there a documented change?" There are several types of changes that can be documented (e.g., change in level or change in variability), and thus there are a number of visual analysis strategies. The second question is a bit more complex—specifically, "Can we say that intervention was responsible for the observed change?" Clearly, the first question must be answered before addressing the second. Although, as discussed in Chapter 3, there are a number of designs that will never be able to reach the criteria of experimental (running B, A-B, and A-B-A, for example), even those that express each stage of baseline logic are dependent on the outcome data changing in a specific manner when the intervention is implemented (or removed). As such, we consider this a logical two-stage process similar to that proposed by Horner, Carr, Halle, McGee, Odom, and Wolery (2005).

Step 1. Was There a Change?: Strategies for Summarization and Analysis of Behavioral Data

We start with visual analysis as this is indeed the most typical manner in which SCD outcome data is considered and presented to stakeholders. As such, educational professionals should be fully prepared to guide untrained individuals (e.g., parents) through the process of effective visual analysis. Traditional visual analysis includes examining (1) level, (2) immediacy, (3) variability, and (4) trend. As we discuss later in this chapter, each of these methods of considering outcome data is more important in some situations than others. For example, with some reading interventions the effect might be an increase in rate of learning rather than an immediate change in behavior. Thus, it is important to carefully consider what the predicted change in outcome data is upon implementation of the intervention and select the analysis strategy, or strategies, that can document that effect.

Change in Level

The most basic way to interpret SCD outcome data is to compare the level of the data during the baseline phase with the level of the data in the intervention phase. Obviously, one of the main goals of an intervention is to substantially alter the target behavior after the intervention is implemented. These changes over a stream of outcome data should result in a change in the level between the phases. This change in level can then be considered in regard to the goal of the intervention. Specifically, was the change in level sufficient to meet the intervention goal? The mean or median of the data within a phase can be used to describe the level. For example, in Figure 5.1, the mean number of observed calling-out behavior in baseline was 13 times per day compared to 2.8 times per day during the intervention phase. This represents a large decrease in the total number of the target behaviors each day. Although an analysis of means suggests a dramatic decrease, the examination of intervention effectiveness using only means can provide an incomplete conclusion. In the example, not only is there a decrease in rate of calling-out behavior between phases, but during the intervention phase the rate is a decreasing trend. The focus on the mean number in the intervention phase might miss that in the final stages, the calling-out behavior is close to nonexistent (0.5 per day over the final four intervention sessions).

   Another concern with comparisons of means is the impact of a single-deviant data point on the mean. Technically, the mean is only a defensible measure of central tendency if the outcome data have a normal distribution. If, however, one or two of the data points are very high or low, the mean will be artificially "pulled" in that direction. In the example, if data for days 14 and 15 were actually 15 and 15, instead of 1 and 3, respectively, the intervention mean would increase from 2.8 to 4.5. These two days would be outliers in the phase, and thus the mean would be a bit misleading. This is particularly an issue with SCD analysis in that there tends to be a small amount of data, and thus the impact of outliers is magnified. One final consideration concerns the importance of the general phase level (mean) and the level at the end of the phase. If the final two to three data points are higher or lower than the general level of the phase, those final data points should receive additional consideration and use of the phase mean should be minimized.

Immediacy/Latency of Change

Visual analysis also involves an examination of data immediately after intervention is initiated. In an ideal situation an intervention changes the target behavior in such a manner that one can literally observe a "step" in the graph at the time of the intervention application. While this is not critical as many interventions are not expected to produce an immediate impact, it is ideal to observe such a change, particularly when we consider design adherence as we discuss later in this chapter. In Figure 5.3, the arrow indicates the point at which there is a large change in the level of the rate of behavior. If no changes are noted between phases, possible changes in trend at the time of intervention should be examined. Level changes within a phase might indicate the influence of an external factor to the intervention or instruction (either facilitating or interfering).

Latency of change refers to the amount of time for the intervention to have an impact on the behavior. Intervention effects can be immediate or delayed. This reality has a major implication in that, the more delayed the change in outcome data after the intervention has begun, the more difficult it is to attribute any change to the intervention. As noted above, a quick step change is much easier to interpret than a slowly developing alteration of the target behavior. An analysis of baseline and intervention data represented in Figure 5.4 suggests that impact of the intervention takes time to become evident. If this was predicted before the intervention was implemented, then a latent response is not concerning. If, how-

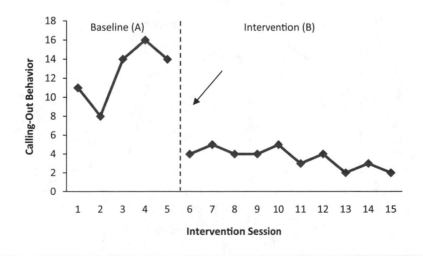

FIGURE 5.3. Sample intervention graph: Immediacy of change.

ever, there was no reason to believe that the response to intervention would take a good deal of time to manifest, it can be concerning when we start to consider if the observed change is functionally related to the intervention.

Change in Variability

Variability refers to the amount of variation in range and/or consistency in a set of data. It is not atypical, particularly with social behavior interventions, that the goal is simply to minimize the variability of the target behavior rather than to demonstrate some altogether new level. For example, even the most disengaged student will likely demonstrate on-task behavior at some point in time. Therefore, the goal is to reduce the rate of problematic off-task moments, and thus reduce the variability of the behavioral presentation. In Figure 5.5, a classwide intervention was implemented to decrease "out-of-seat" behavior. In the baseline phase, considerable variability can be observed (Note: Mean scores are not representative). However, after intervention, overall variability of problem behavior is decreased.

Presenting a high–low range is a simple manner of expressing variability of data within the phase. In this case, in the baseline phase out-of-seat behavior ranged from 2 to 16. In the intervention phase out-of-seat behavior ranged from two to six. A number of additional methods of computing estimates of variability are presented in Chapter 6.

A final variability consideration is the amount of overlap between phases. Ideally, there would be no overlap in behavior between the two phases: for example, if in the baseline phase on-task behavior ranged from 10 to 40%, while in the intervention phase on-task behavior ranged from 60 to 95%. In this case, the same level of behavior is not seen across phases. Or, in other words, a new range of the behavior was observed after the intervention was implemented. This idea, called *percent of nonoverlapping data* (PND), is more deeply discussed in Chapter 6, but the idea also impacts traditional visual analysis. Observing a new range of behavior after an intervention is implemented is strong evidence of an intervention effect.

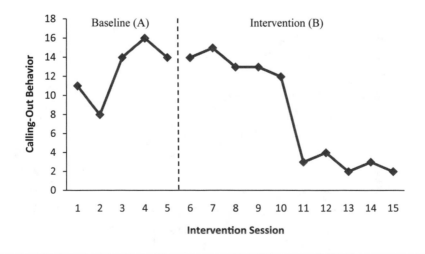

FIGURE 5.4. Sample intervention graph: Latency of change.

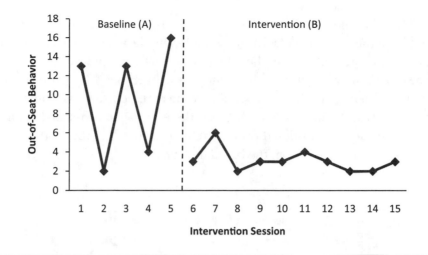

FIGURE 5.5. Sample intervention graph: Decreased variability.

As noted above, changes in variability within a phase can be quite important. One of the critical elements in SCD is that enough data are collected within a phase so that a summary statement can be made. Such a summary is only possible if the data are rather consistent throughout a phase. For example, it is acceptable if outcome data are consistently variable, or consistently stable. It would not be acceptable, however, if within a phase outcome data started with a stable pattern, and within the phase, became highly variable. As a result, it would be very difficult to make a statement as to what the data in that phase predicted. In such a case, it is critical to continue data collection within that phase until a defensible summary statement can be made.

Change in Trend

In addition to level and slope, it is critical to consider the trend of the outcome data. Generally, a stream of outcome data is increasing, decreasing, or remaining stable over time. The trend is the rate of change within a phase and is a critical component of the analysis package. Increasing the rate of learning, as documented by an increasing trend in the outcome variable, is often the very goal of an intervention. In such a case, an alteration in the trend of the outcome data postintervention, which predicts that a child will progress to a goal level over an acceptable period of time, is evidence of acceptable change. For example, in baseline a child might be increasing his/her rate of reading (measure by WCPM) by one each week. If this target behavior were to increase to four each week in the intervention phase, then there would be strong trend evidence as to the positive effect of the intervention. As discussed in Chapter 3, the analysis of trends can be critical in the withdrawal phases as well.

Even in cases where trend is not the primary mode of analysis, it is critical to document whether the trend of data in one phase would logically predict the observed data in a subsequent phase. In Figure 5.6 three examples of trends in the baseline phase are presented preceding the same outcome data in the intervention phase. In the first case, there is a generally neutral trend in the baseline phase. As a result, the observed intervention effect was not predicted from the baseline data. In the second example, where there is a positive trend in baseline data, the outcome data in the intervention phase are predictable, thus minimizing confidence in a "change." In the third example the exact opposite pattern is presented. In this case, there is a negative trend in baseline, which predicts that over time the behavior would keep decreasing (theoretically to 0). Thus, the increase in pro-social behavior in the intervention phase can be considered even more of a "change" as this pattern is the exact opposite of what was predicted from the baseline data.

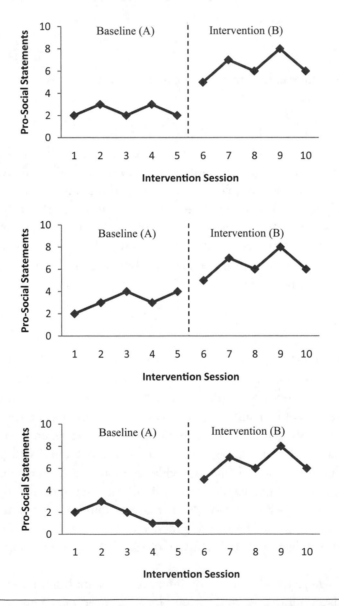

FIGURE 5.6. Sample intervention graph: Impact of trends in the baseline phase on the intervention phase.

Considering the Interaction of Level, Variability, and Trend

While basic visual analysis has typically been discussed as the analysis of level, trend, variability, and immediacy/latency, it is also critical to consider potential interactions (Horner, 2008). For example, we just reviewed the interaction of trend analysis on level analysis. As discussed the trend in baseline can minimize (in the case of an increasing baseline trend) or magnify (in the case of a decreasing baseline trend) an observed positive level change between baseline and intervention phases. What is critical to notice is that in all three of the cases presented in Figure 5.6 there is actually a change in the mean from the baseline to intervention conditions. This is not a surprise in the case of the level baseline (baseline mean of 2.4; intervention mean of 6.4) or the descending baseline (baseline mean of 1.8; intervention mean of 6.4). It is somewhat surprising that in the case of the increasing baseline there is still a rather large difference between the baseline mean (3.2) and the intervention mean (6.4). Focusing only on level data would not catch the predictability of the intervention data from the baseline data. This is not simply an issue of trend impacting level. Variability in the outcome data can, for example, minimize the importance of a level change, or decreased variability can make a small level change more important. The take-home message is that all of the aspects of visual analysis must be considered as a package rather than in isolation.

Step 2. Was the Documented Change Functionally Related to the Intervention?: Reconsidering Baseline Logic during Analysis

While it is tempting to get rather excited about changes in the target behavior after the application of an intervention, there is a critical step that must follow if the change is to be attributed to the intervention. In this final step, we must consider whether the changes that have been observed are consistent with those predicted at the time of design selection. If we see the pattern as predicted, then we can be more confident that we have high levels of experimental control. Experimental control is only documented with a SCD, which allows for the full expression of baseline logic (e.g., A-B-A-B or an MB design) and whether we see the pattern as predicted. If both criteria are met, then we can be more confident that the intervention is responsible for the change in behavior. As discussed previously, this statement becomes more and more critical as the stakes are raised in an RTI model.

A-B-A-B Design

Remember that in an A-B-A-B design, the assumption is that an intervention effect would not only be observed in the A-B (**A-B**-A-B) phase, but that some return to baseline would occur in the first B-A (A-**B-A**-B) phase. Finally, there was a prediction that in the final A-B (A-B-**A-B**) phase we would again see an intervention effect. Let's consider two cases.

In Figure 5.7 we have an intervention case using an A-B-A-B design. In this case, a slightly descending baseline suggests that on-task behavior is becoming somewhat more problematic. When the intervention is implemented, we see an immediate level change, no overlap in the behavior, as well as the trend shifting from descending to one that is

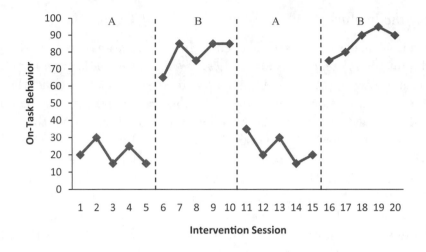

FIGURE 5.7. A-B-A-B graph suggesting experimental control.

ascending. This is considerable evidence of a change in the target behavior. In regard to the issue of "Was it the intervention that caused the change in the outcome data?" we must go beyond documentation of change in the target behavior. In the case of an A-B-A-B the next step is the removal of the intervention so that the baseline phase can be verified. Finally, the intervention is again implemented to replicate the intervention effect or document replication by affirmation of the consequent. In the current example, after the intervention is withdrawn, visual analysis shows an immediate level and trend change in the predicted direction. In addition, the outcome data in the second A phase return to the same range they were in during the initial baseline phase. This is a textbook example of verification. In the final phase, when the intervention is applied a second time, the initial intervention effect is replicated with an immediate change in level and trend. This full documentation of baseline logic through visual analysis allows for a confident statement that there was indeed a "response to the intervention."

The data in Figure 5.8 are also displayed with an A-B-A-B design, but the predicted pattern is not followed. Notably, there was no return to baseline. Unfortunately, because the return to baseline stage (verification) is not realized, we have no real understanding of why the observed change occurred as there is simply too much chance that some other variable is controlling the outcome data. Although the outcome behavior has changed in Figure 5.8 (an immediate change in level and trend with no overlap), this case presents us with a particular challenge in both research and practice. For the researcher, the lack of experimental control is a fatal flaw if the goal is to document that the outcome data is functionally related to the intervention. The researcher must consider what other variables were not considered and then return to the experimentation stage.

An educational practitioner is in a more difficult situation because the stage of analysis is critical in terms of the course of action. If this is a low-stakes case, the lack of experimental control is probably not a real problem. In the end, the child is behaving in the desired manner. It is still uncomfortable that the reason for the change in behavior is essentially

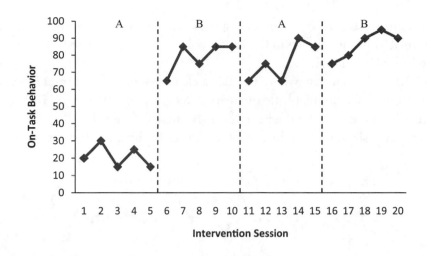

FIGURE 5.8. A-B-A-B graph not suggesting experimental control.

unknown. The most significant impact at the low-stakes level is that the practitioner would not be able to confidently suggest a course of action if the behavior returns to problematic levels. If this were a high-stakes case, we would have a larger issue because we know the child responded to something, but not necessarily the intervention. This is a scary place because we would likely use these data to suggest that the child does not need more intensive services, but without knowing why the child is responding, the effect could be short term.

MB Design

Let's now look at the same issue with an MB design. Baseline logic is documented in an MB design across the three targets rather than within a single target. See Figure 5.9 for an example of an MB across settings design where experimental control is observed. In Setting 1 the intervention effect can be observed across A-B phases. Specifically, visual analysis shows a large change in level that occurred immediately after the intervention was applied. Baseline data was actually descending, the opposite direction of the level change, which magnifies the intervention effect. Finally, while the data is somewhat variable, there is no overlap between the two phases. In sum, this is strong evidence of an intervention effect. In regard to the issue of "Was it the intervention that caused the change in the outcome data?" we must again go beyond documentation of change in the target behavior and consider the pattern in reference to the current design. In the case of an MB design it is essential that there is no change in the baseline phase for the other two settings when the intervention is applied in Setting 1. This continuation of the baseline provides verification of the original baseline statement in Setting 1. When the intervention is later applied in Setting 2, the intervention effect is replicated thus completing the full baseline logic statement. In this example, Setting 3 is also included to provide verification (in the case of the baseline in Setting 2) and later a final replication of the intervention effect. In sum, the MB design presented in Figure 5.9 is an excellent example of evidence that the intervention is indeed functionally related to the change in the target behavior. In other words, there was a clear "response to the intervention."

Figure 5.10 presents a case where there is a clear change in the target behavior in the three settings, but unfortunately little evidence for experimental control. In Setting 1, the intervention effect is documented across the A-B phases. Again, level, trend, immediacy, and variability analysis point to a documented change in the outcome data at the time the

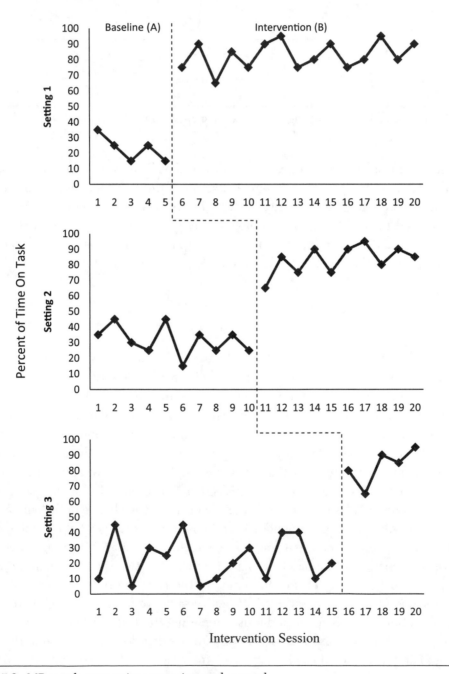

FIGURE 5.9. MB graph suggesting experimental control.

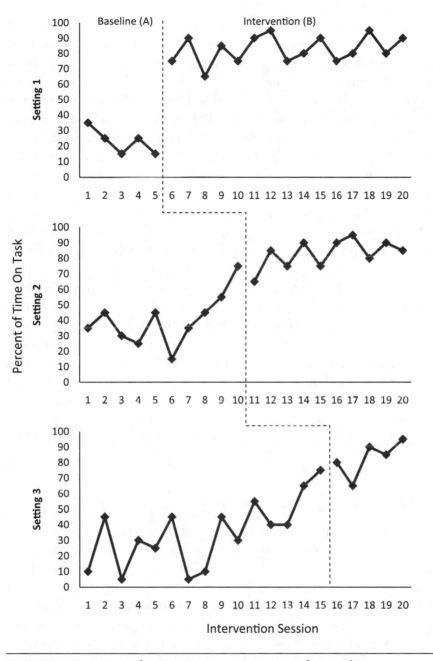

FIGURE 5.10. MB graph not suggesting experimental control.

intervention was implemented. In this case, however, looking at all three settings in the MB design, we can see that each step of baseline logic is not present. In Setting 2, the baseline starts to increase in trend at the same time the intervention is applied in Setting 1. In addition, there is no replication of the intervention effect in Setting 2. This same ascending baseline and lack of a defensible intervention effect can be observed in Setting 3. Whereas in Setting 1 a prediction statement and the initial affirmation of the consequent is observed, verification and replication are not documented.

As in the A-B-A-B case presented in Figure 5.8, the current MB example (Figure 5.10) is also a difficult situation as there is clearly a change in the target behavior but without a full documentation of baseline logic, this change cannot be defensibly tied to the intervention. For a researcher, this threat to internal validity could be explored in subsequent cases. For the practitioner, however, the next step would be based on the type of decisions being considered. If this was a low-stakes case (Tier 1 or 2) then the situation could simply be monitored, and the lack of a documented functional relationship could be tolerated. If, however, this was a high-stakes case (Tier 3), particularly if eligibility decisions were to be made, this would not be acceptable evidence of either an RTI, or a lack thereof, and future analysis would be critical.

On a side note, it should be clear to the reader at this point (if not earlier) just how critical the design selection stage is. If one is implementing an intervention in which a child would not be predicted to return to baseline (such as a learned behavior), or it would be unethical to attempt a return to baseline, then an A-B-A-B design is an illogical choice. Simply put, in such a case it would be inevitable that the design utility would end at the A-B stage, and an obvious problem would lay ahead if experimental control, or a true documentation of response to a specific intervention were a goal when selecting the SCD. As such, it is critical that both researchers and educational professionals consider the expected data path pattern at the time of design selection so that the full line of baseline logic can be documented if necessary. In addition, the need for the documentation of a functional relationship should be carefully considered because that may result in a much more complex case. If the current case (e.g., lower-stakes Tier 1 and Tier 2 cases) only requires the documentation of change in a target behavior, then a more basic design (e.g., A-B) is advisable.

Alternative Method of Documenting Experimental Control

One alternative to using baseline logic is a method suggested by Horner et al. (2005) that looks for three demonstrations of the predicted change in outcome data when the intervention is manipulated (applied or removed). Horner and his colleagues call these demonstrations *experimental effects* and technically define them as the predicted change in the dependent variable that covaries with a manipulation of the independent variable. The change in the dependent variable can be a change in level, trend, or variability (or combination thereof) that is the logical result of the manipulation of the independent variable. Reaching the level of experimental control requires three demonstrations of the experimental effect. This quick method is attractive in that it provides a simple rule for when an SCD reaches the level where one can claim the documentation of a response to intervention. While this is similar in theory to baseline logic, there are several differences that should be highlighted. In an attempt to simplify the documentation of experimental control, Horner and colleagues make the intervention effect (A-B) and the return to baseline (B-A) equivalents as each is considered an experimental effect. In addition, this method does not require the verification stage of baseline logic. As a result, when using this heuristic, it is critical to have a fully defensible initial baseline.

MOVING FROM SUMMARIZATION AND ANALYSIS TO DECISION MAKING

After data are summarized and described, decisions related to a number of questions can be made. For example, it would then be possible to ask, "Is the intervention working?" "Should we change the intervention?" or "Do we need a new intervention?" Before directly addressing these questions, the first step when interpreting data within the context of the assessment situation is to determine whether the data are adequate to answer the questions. Adequacy is determined by considering what data should and have been collected, what method was used to collect the data, whether the method was used appropriately, and so on. Additional questions to ask regarding your data are presented in Table 5.1 (adapted from Merrell, 2003). If the collected data can appropriately answer the intended questions, interpretation of the data patterns can continue.

Developing and Making Decisions with a Goal Line

Effective monitoring of intervention effects also requires specific decisions that will often utilize a *goal line* to determine current intervention effectiveness. Goal lines are useful for interpretation of intervention effectiveness (see Figure 5.11), and are based on an intervention team's determination of where the behavior should be at the end of a specified period of time. This goal and a goal line can be specifically used to consider changes in level, variability, trend, and immediacy/latency by providing a visual aid on the graph. A goal line is developed by comparing the goal of the intervention to a documented baseline level of the target behavior on a line graph that has an extended X-axis to capture the scope of the goal timeline (e.g., 4 weeks or 4 months). The result is a line graph indicating the current level of the target behavior, the goal, and the time frame for this goal to be realized. This behavior goal is expressed on the graph using the following steps:

1. Find the median (middle value) of the last three baseline data points on the Y-axis.
2. Place a point on the graph where $x =$ the middle point of the baseline data, and $y =$ the median value identified in Step 1.
3. Determine the level at which the behavior is desired at the end of the intervention period, as well as the length of the period.

TABLE 5.1. Questions to Ask When Interpreting Your Data

- Do the data confirm the identified problem?
- What additional information do the data provide?
- How can we use the data to answer the referral questions?
- Are there other factors that appear to be contributing to the problem?
- Are any data missing (and if so, how will I collect those data)?

Note. From Chafouleas, Riley-Tillman, and Sugai (2007; based in part on Merrell, 2003). Copyright 2007 by The Guilford Press. Reprinted by permission.

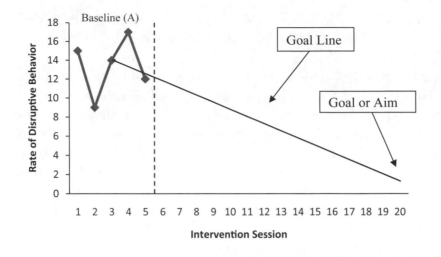

FIGURE 5.11. Sample intervention graph with goal line.

4. Extend the *X*-axis out over the entire intervention period.
5. Place a point on the graph where *x* = the last day of the intervention period, and *y* = the level at which the behavior is expected to be if the goal is met.
6. Draw the goal line between the baseline median and the goal point.

In Table 5.2, types of decisions that can be made based on data analysis using a goal line are presented; interpretation ("If . . . " column) corresponds to intervention action plan ("Then . . . " column). Consider whether, in the example involving disruptive behavior (see Figure 5.12), analysis of the data after intervention implementation suggests improvement in "out-of-seat" behavior in accordance with the goal line. If agreement is reached that the goal has been met, a decision can be made to (1) continue the intervention as is, (2) discontinue the intervention outright, or (3) institute procedures to fade the use of the intervention. In this case, for example, a decision could involve continuing the intervention, but changing the target behavior to another that the intervention would logically functionally relate to (e.g., on-task behavior). If this were the decision, a new graph, goal, and goal date would be developed, and data collection and monitoring would continue on the new target behavior.

To provide additional guidance in decision making, the *three-point decision rule* can be applied. Using the three-point decision rule, the last three intervention data points are examined to determine whether they fall (1) well below (deceleration target) or above (acceleration target) the goal line (good progress), or (2) around the goal line (adequate progress toward goal). If good progress is being made, decisions might be made to modify the intervention for efficiency and maintenance of effects. In Figure 5.13, examples of the use of the three-point decision rule are presented. The solid line represents the goal, and a decrease in behavior is desired. The pattern in the top line of intervention data does not suggest that the goal will be obtained in the time allotted; thus, a change to the intervention should be considered. The middle line of data appears to fall around the goal line, which suggests that the goal is likely to be met in the time allotted and that the intervention should continue as planned. Finally, the bottom line of intervention data suggests that the goal will be obtained

TABLE 5.2. Possible Intervention Decisions Based on Collected Data

If . . .	Then . . .	Description
Student is making sufficient progress toward a goal.	Make no change.	Continue to monitor progress, but make no changes to the current intervention program.
It does not look like the student will achieve his/her goal in the allotted amount of time, but you feel that the intervention is appropriate and is having positive effects.	Change the goal date.	Push back the date by which you expect the student to achieve the goal.
The student has been successful with some part of the behavior/skill, but is not making progress overall.	Slice back.	Slice back the behavior/skill to a more manageable level. For academic behaviors, perhaps focus on only one type of problem at a time. For social behaviors, perhaps reduce the behavioral goal (e.g., aim for 60% on task rather than 80%).
The current work is simply too difficult for the student to be successful.	Step back.	Step back to teach and review an earlier skill in order to ensure that the student possesses the prerequisite skills.
You believe that the goal that is in place is appropriate for the student, but he/she is not making sufficient progress.	Try a different instructional procedure.	Make a change to either the antecedent conditions (e.g., try a different method of teaching a skill in the case of academic behavior), or consequent conditions (e.g., ignore problem behaviors rather than reprimanding the student in the case of social behavior).
The student's progress seems to have reached a sufficient plateau (started off progressing at an adequate rate, but then flattened out or dropped off at 80%).	Move on to a new phase of learning.	Although the student is performing the behavior accurately, he/she may now need to work on building fluency. It may be necessary to provide more time to practice the skill or additional incentives for improving fluency.
The student has met his/her goal more quickly than expected (and the behavior is observed across settings to be both accurate and fluent).	Move on to a new skill.	Establish a new goal for the student. This could be accomplished by either setting a higher goal for the same behavior or moving on to an entirely new skill/behavior.
You believe that the goal that is in place is appropriate for the student and he/she is already receiving adequate assistance to meet the goal, but he/she is not making progress.	Begin compliance training.	It may be necessary to work on improving the student's responsiveness to teacher directives.

Note. From Chafouleas, Riley-Tillman, and Sugai (2007; based in part on Wolery, Bailey, & Sugai, 1988). Copyright 2007 by The Guilford Press. Reprinted by permission.

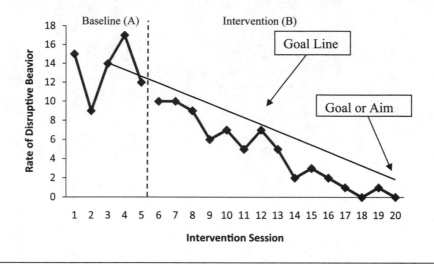

FIGURE 5.12. Sample intervention graph with goal line and outcome data.

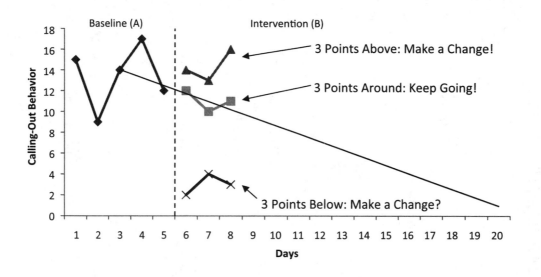

FIGURE 5.13. Sample intervention graph: Three-point decision rule.

more quickly than expected and perhaps some changes to the intervention could be considered.

The three-point decision rule does have some significant limitations. Specifically, such a heuristic is acceptable for Tier 1 and some Tier 2 decisions, but this is not an acceptable method in Tier 3 when educational placement or disability diagnostic decisions are being considered because the resulting decisions are too unreliable (Burns & Scholin, 2008). Moreover, the steepness of the aim line is too heavily influenced by the time allotted and baseline skill level. It is quite possible that the data for students who make more progress than others may be judged as negative while the progress for their less successful peers is deemed acceptable. In addition, it is critical to consider if a specific intervention is expected to have a steady trend to a goal, or if a different pattern is predictable. For example, if an intervention includes removing a reinforcer for a problematic behavior, it is expected that the problematic behavior will increase (called an *extinction burst*) immediately after the reinforcer is removed before decreasing. This is an understood behavioral pattern that poses a problem to the simple three-point decision rule. As such, in that case, this method would not be appropriate. Despite these limitations, the three-point decision rule is a nice starting point for many lower-stakes intervention cases.

CONCLUDING COMMENTS

In summary, many options for summarization and analysis of behavioral data are available, and typically several of those options are used in combination. Strategies for visual analysis have a long history and are widely accepted and easy to use. It is important to note, however, that visual analysis of outcome data in SCD is not without drawbacks. Gresham (2005) summarized three widely noted potential drawbacks of relying exclusively on visual inspection. First, there is often a lack of a clear standard for deciding if a change in outcome data is educationally significant. Second, exclusive reliance on visual analysis can result in an increased potential for rejecting an intervention effect when one is actually present (Type 1 error). Finally, there are difficulties associated with the interpretation of autocorrelated time series data. In partial response to these limitations, as we will see in Chapter 6, options for the further "quantification" of intervention effects are becoming more widespread.

NOTE

Sections of this chapter were adapted from Chafouleas, Riley-Tillman, and Sugai (2007). Copyright 2007 by The Guilford Press. Adapted by permission.

CASE EXAMPLE 5.1: MR. GREENWOOD

During the previous summer Mr. Greenwood participated in his school's RTI training program, which focused on heavily on intervention, data collection, data analysis, and design. When he left the training, he was excited and ready to implement this technology in his third-grade classroom. Mr. Greenwood conducted a number of interventions over the course of the first half of the year, most of which used an A-B design. While the summer RTI training program was motivating, and taught Mr. Greenwood a good deal about the topic, he did not feel fully competent in terms of outcome data analysis. Luckily, the intervention team that conducted the training anticipated the need for follow-up training and had offered follow-up consultation. In this case, Mr. Greenwood requested that Ms. Wilson, a fellow teacher with several years of experience on the intervention team, help him look at two intervention cases using A-B designs he had conducted in his class for advice on how to analyze the outcome data. In each case he felt he had an example of a successful intervention, but was having difficulty expressing the success in terms of analysis.

Andy

The first student, Andy, was having difficulty with calling-out behavior early in the year. As suggested in the training, Mr. Greenwood began collecting baseline data using DBR, which required him to rate Andy's disruptive behavior each day on a 0–10 scale (0: no disruptive behavior; 10: 10+ disruptive behavior events in the observation period). After a few weeks it was clear that Andy's behavior was consistently problematic. Mr. Greenwood noticed that Andy's disruptive behavior in the baseline phase tended to result in him increasing attention to Andy. As a result, he decided to conduct an intervention where he would ignore Andy's disruptive behavior, and at the same time reinforce Andy (attention and praise) several times an hour when he was behaving appropriately. The resulting outcome data are presented in Figure 5.A Ms. Wilson noted that examining the level of outcome data would be most appropriate given the goal of reducing the behavior. The level as described by a mean was

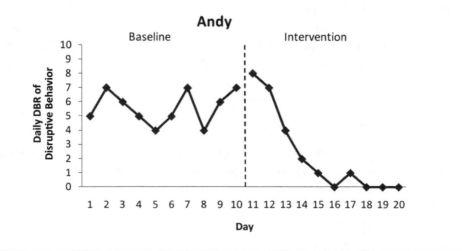

FIGURE 5.A. Intervention outcome data for Andy using an A-B design.

(continued)

5.6 in the baseline phase and 2.3 in the intervention phase. In addition, Ms. Wilson thought that the trend of the data should be considered as it was flat in baseline, descending in the first half of the intervention, and flat in the second half of the intervention. Thus, while the mean is an accurate description of level in baseline, it was an overestimate of the level in the final stages of the intervention phase. Thus, Ms. Wilson quickly computed the mean for the final week, which was 0.2. Using this combination of level and trend, Mr. Greenwood had an excellent manner to describe this effective intervention.

Webster

The second student, Webster, also was behaving in a problematic manner. He was typically on task but would have days where he was simply off task all day long. Mr. Greenwood collected baseline data on Webster, using DBR of academic engagement (0: fully off task; 10: fully on task), for 2 weeks. Webster was rated an 8, 9, or 10 for 7 of the 10 days in baseline. Unfortunately, the other 3 days he was rated a 1 or 2. Mr. Greenwood learned from a conversation with Webster's parents that his off-task days occurred after having difficulties with other students on the school bus. Mr. Greenwood talked to the bus driver, principal, and school psychologist in an attempt to end the problems on the bus, and set up a "pit stop" for Webster where he could talk to someone if conflict did occur. Over the course of the intervention phase, Webster utilized the "pit stop" once for a minor incident and indicated that the conflict had ended. The classroom results of this intervention are presented in Figure 5.B. After looking at the outcome data Ms. Wilson suggested that the best way to describe the effectiveness of the intervention was to focus on the reduction of variability through the removal of the problematic days observed in the baseline phase. Looking at the high–low range in baseline phase (1–10) and intervention phase (8–10) was an ideal way to describe the dataset in a manner that spoke to the effectiveness of the intervention. Mr. Greenwood was able to present this information to Webster's parents at their next meeting.

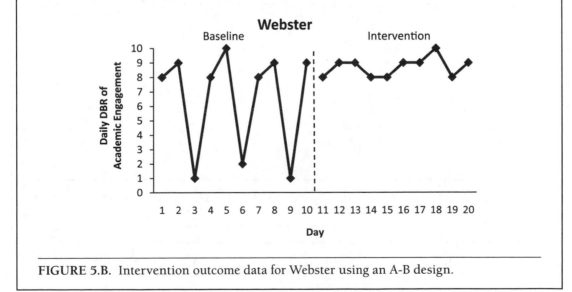

FIGURE 5.B. Intervention outcome data for Webster using an A-B design.

Intervention Graph (Percent)

Student Name: _____   Interventionist: _____

Dates: _____   Setting: _____

Intervention: _____

_____

Outcome Data: _____

_____

Intervention Goal: _____

_____

Comments: _____

_____

Intervention Graph (Percent with 0 above *X*-Axis)

Student Name: _____   Interventionist: _____

Dates: _____   Setting: _____

Intervention: _____

_____

Outcome Data: _____

_____

Intervention Goal: _____

_____

Comments: _____

_____

Intervention Graph (Frequency Count)

Student Name: _____ Interventionist: _____

Dates: _____ Setting: _____

Intervention: _____

_____

Outcome Data: _____

_____

Intervention Goal: _____

_____

Comments: _____

_____

Intervention Graph
(Frequency Count with 0 above *X*-Axis)

Student Name: _____ Interventionist: _____

Dates: _____ Setting: _____

Intervention: _____

_____

Outcome Data: _____

_____

Intervention Goal: _____

_____

Comments: _____

_____

Multiple-Baseline Across-Targets Intervention Graph

Student Name: _____   Interventionist: _____

Dates: _____   Setting: _____

Intervention: _____

_____

Outcome Data: _____

_____

Intervention Goal: _____

_____

Multiple-Baseline Targets: _____

_____

_____

(continued)

Multiple-Baseline Across-Targets Intervention Graph (Frequency Count)

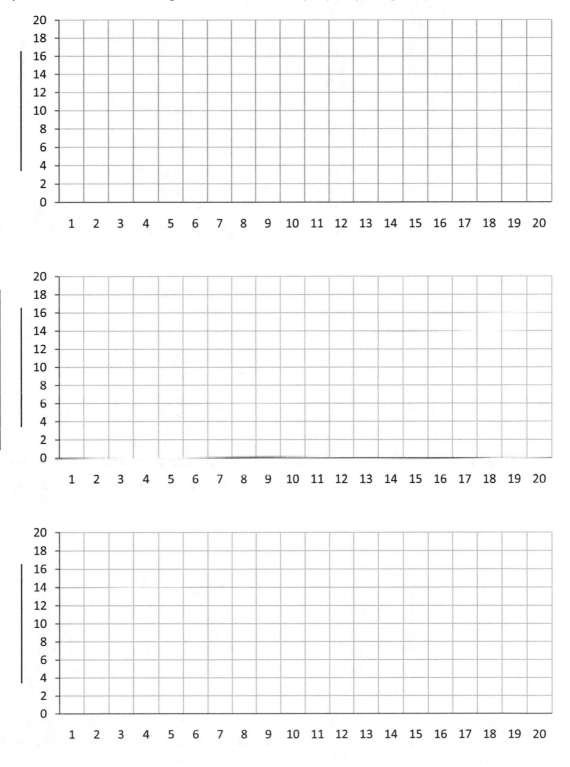

Multiple-Baseline Across-Targets Intervention Graph (Percent)

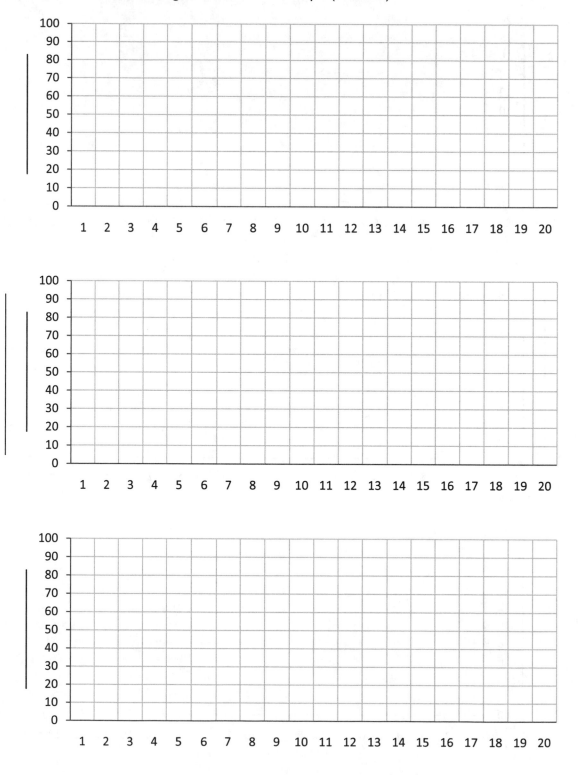

APPENDIX 5.6

Multiple-Baseline Across-Targets Intervention Graph (with 0 above *X*-Axis)

Student Name: ____________________ Interventionist: ____________________

Dates: ____________________ Setting: ____________________

Intervention: ____

____

Outcome Data: ____

____

Intervention Goal: ____

____

Multiple-Baseline Targets: ____

____

____

Multiple-Baseline Across-Targets Intervention Graph (Frequency Count)

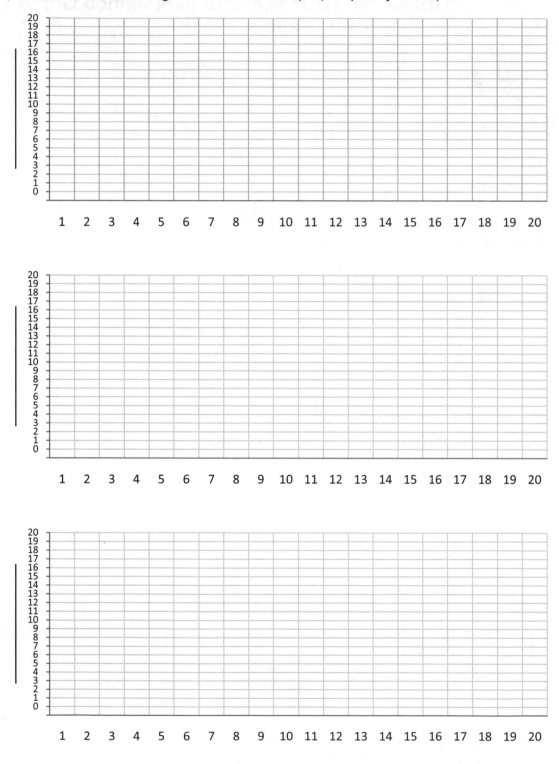

Multiple-Baseline Across-Targets Intervention Graph (Percent)

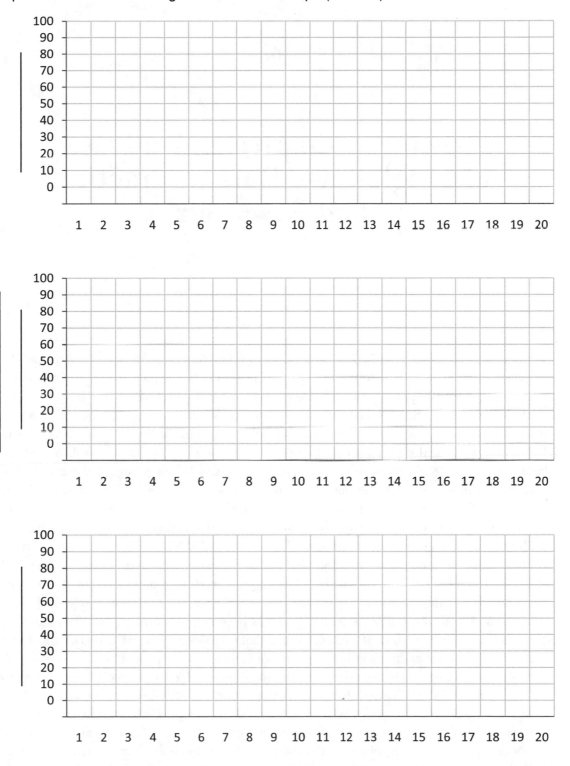

6

Advanced Empirical Analyses
of Single-Case Data in Practice
and Research

Despite how frequently individuals claim not to be a "numbers person," Americans like empirical data. Social scientists have always worked within the empirical domain, but thanks to No Child Left Behind (NCLB), educators now have a heightened interest in empirically evaluating student progress. However, there is no consensus as to what types of data will meet the needs of scientists, educators, and public consumers. For decades, researchers focused on statistical significance, but more recently the implications of significance have been questioned (Kirk, 1996). SCD researchers emphasized clinical importance over statistical significance well before the general science community, but did so through visual interpretations of slope, level, and trend. However, using empirical estimates of effects within SCD research could enhance objectivity, precision, dependability, and general acceptability by the science community (Parker & Hagan-Burke, 2007a). The evidence-based intervention (EBI) movement in education also increased interest in quantitative estimates of effects (Parker & Hagan-Burke, 2007b), and the importance of meta-analytic procedures in educational policy decisions suggests the need to report effect sizes for research (Kavale & Forness, 2000). The interest in effect sizes has become so prominent that the American Psychological Association (2001) has indicated that p values are not estimates of effect and encouraged researchers to include more suitable empirical indices of effect.

Meta-analytic procedures and effect-size data have had a dramatic effect on interventions and intervention research. Glass (1976) developed the meta-analytic approach, which is the systematic examining of a body of research through a presumably exhaustive search with well-established inclusion/exclusion criteria to examine the effect of variables on the phenomenon of interest. A primary difference between meta-analyses and narrative reviews is that meta-analyses include the reporting of an empirically derived effect size (Cooper, Valentine, & Charlton, 2000) such as Cohen's d (1988). The d statistic represents the difference between an experimental group and a control group in pooled standard deviation units, and is frequently interpreted as 0.80 being a large effect, 0.50 a moderate effect, and 0.20 a small effect. Although these criteria were suggested by Cohen (1988), they were somewhat arbitrarily determined.

Research syntheses that employ the meta-analytic approach are potentially advantageous over narrative reviews for policy decisions because they use quantitative methods to organize and extract information, eliminate study selection bias, detect interactions, and attempt to provide more objective general conclusions (Kavale & Forness, 2000). One of the first applications of a meta-analysis was the somewhat famous examination of special education research that resulted in a negative effect size and questioned the effectiveness of special education (Kavale & Glass, 1981).

In addition to challenging traditional special education practices, meta-analytic research has identified shortcomings in several commonly used interventions within special education. For example, in the 1960s and 1970s interventions for struggling learners focused on matching instruction to a child's preferred modality (i.e., visual, auditory, or kinesthetic), psycholinguistic training, and perceptual–motor training. Each of these interventions was well researched with results that were significant to .05 and .01. However, a meta-analysis of these approaches for students with learning disabilities (LD) resulted in mean effect sizes (d) of 0.14, 0.39, and 0.08, respectively (Kavale & Forness, 2000). Clearly these were unimpressive data, especially when compared to other more effective yet less popular interventions such as direct instruction ($d = 0.84$), formative evaluation ($d = 0.70$), and mnemonic strategies ($d = 1.62$) (Kavale & Forness, 2000). A recent national survey of special education teachers by Burns and Ysseldyke (in press) found that 89.6% of the respondents reported using direct instruction at least on a weekly basis (83.3% almost every day), 70.5% regularly use formative evaluation, and 62.1% reported at least weekly use of mnemonic strategies. These compare favorably to the formerly dominant interventions such as perceptual–motor training (30.6% at least weekly) and psycholinguistic training (40.2% at least weekly). Although modality instruction seems more resistant to a lack of research base (79.9% at least weekly use), clearly the emphasis on effect size over significance in intervention research has influenced practice.

EFFECT SIZES AND SCD RESEARCH

Although meta-analytic research should be used to inform policy decisions (Kavale & Forness, 2000) and seems particularly useful for the research-synthesizing role for school psychologists (Keith, 2002), less than 2% of articles in school psychology journals were meta-analyses and there were 22.7 times as many narrative reviews as meta-analyses (Burns et al., 2007). The infrequent use of meta-analytic research in school psychology could be related to the current focus on intervention research, which tends to employ SCD (Winn, Skinner, Allin, & Hawkins, 2004), especially given that only one meta-analysis of solely single-subject research (Maughan, Cristiansen, Jenson, Olympia, & Clark, 2005) was found in a recent reviews of school psychology journals (Burns et al., 2007).

Some argue that meta-analyses of SCD do not capture patterns across time, could miss idiosyncrasies in the data, are too significantly affected by atypical baseline data, and may lead to misrepresenting conclusions (Salzberg, Strain, & Baer, 1987; White, 1987). More-over, there are no accepted methods for conducting meta-analytic studies for SCD and commonly used effect sizes may not adequately apply to data about individual research participants (Baron & Derenne, 2000). For example, Cohen's d is not an appropriate metric to use because it examines differences between groups rather than within subjects. Thus, different metrics such as a no-assumptions effect size (Busk & Serlin, 1992), percentage nonoverlapping data (Scruggs, Mastropieri, & Casto, 1987), R^2 (Cohen & Cohen, 1983), and percentage of all nonoverlapping data points (Parker, Hagan-Burke, & Vannest, 2007) were developed and recommended. Several meta-analytic researchers have endorsed the percentage of nonoverlapping data (Kavale, Mathur, Forness, Quinn, & Rutherford, 2000), which is by far the most commonly used effect size within meta-analyses of SCD research (Scruggs & Mastropieri, 2001). However, the percentage of nonoverlapping data (PND) has its critics as well (Parker et al., 2007), as do all effect sizes used within SCD research. Below is a concise description of the four effect sizes listed above.

No-Assumptions Effect Size

The no-assumptions effect size (Busk & Serlin, 1992) results in a d statistic much like Cohen's (1988) commonly used d. A no-assumptions effect size (NAES) is computed by subtracting the mean of the baseline from the mean of the intervention data and dividing by the standard deviation of the baseline. Although NAES makes some intuitive sense, there are potential difficulties. First, there is no clear interpretive scheme. Cohen (1988) suggests that effect sizes of 0.80 are large, 0.50 are medium, and 0.20 are small, but those criteria do not seem to apply to an NAES d because they were developed for effect sizes based on between-group analyses and effect sizes for SCD research often exceed 2.00. A recent meta-analysis of SCD intervention research found a mean NAES of 2.87 for interventions identified as effective (Burns & Wagner, 2008), but those criteria require additional research before they can be used with confidence. Swanson and Sachse-Lee (2000) suggested using Rosenthal's (1994) formula to put the NAES d on the same scale as Cohen's (1988) d statistic.

$$d = (X_{\text{intervention}} - X_{\text{baseline}})/[SD_{\text{pooled}}/\sqrt{2(1 - r)}]$$

The above formula represents the mean of the baseline data being subtracted from the mean of the intervention data, and that product is divided by the second half of the formula. Thus, within the denominator, SD_{pooled} is the standard deviation of the baseline and intervention data pooled and r is the correlation between baseline and intervention data. This formula puts the data on a more commonly used interpretative scheme, but does not overcome other difficulties associated with NAES.

Perhaps more important than the lack of an interpretive scheme is that the NAES violates many assumptions for parametric analyses. In order for a d statistic to be interpretable, the data within the baseline and intervention phases would have to be independently normally distributed (Van den Noortgate & Onghena, 2003), which given the nature of SCD research is rarely if ever the case. The term *no assumptions* implies that the assumptions for parametric analyses are not considered. Thus, it would be more accurate to call the d statistic for SCD an *ignored assumptions* effect size. In addition, data within a time-series graph are autocorrelated. A review of SCD studies found that for 80% of the data sets, the correlation among the data ranged from .10 to .49 (Busk & Marascuilo, 1988) and data sets with serial dependency of .09 to .42 had a large effect on statistical interpretations of SCD data (Brossart, Parker, Olson, & Mahadevan, 2006). The Rosenthal (1994) formula may assist in interpreting *d*, but does not address the issue of autocorrelation. These are significant limitations of the NAES that should be strongly considered before use.

Percentage of Nonoverlapping Data

The percentage of nonoverlapping data (Scruggs et al., 1987) is perhaps the most straightforward and easy to compute of all the SCD effect sizes. First, the most extreme positive baseline data point (highest if the desired effect is an increase, such as reading fluency, and lowest if the desired effect is a reduction, such as incidence of self-injurious behavior) is identified and a straight line from that point is drawn through the intervention data as shown in Figure 6.1. The number of data points above or below the line, depending on the direction of the desired effect, is divided by the total number of intervention data points. The example in Figure 6.1 contains 10 intervention points, seven of which are above the highest baseline point of 38 WCPM. Because the desired effect is increased WCPM, intervention points that exceed the value of the highest baseline point are considered nonoverlapping. Thus, the PND for Figure 6.1 is 70%.

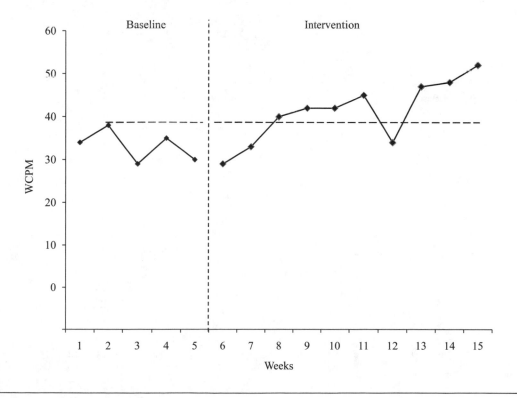

FIGURE 6.1. Sample data to compute the PND.

Scruggs and Mastropieri (1998) recommended a PND of at least 80% for a large effect. The mean PND of oral reading fluency interventions identified as effective within a recent meta-analysis was 81.83% (*SD* = 31.27%) (Burns & Wagner, 2008), which supported the 80% recommendation. However, these data are not conclusive and additional research is needed. Moreover, PND have a ceiling effect that makes comparisons between interventions difficult to do (Parker et al., 2007). For example, the simulated data in Figure 6.2 include two different interventions for two different children, both addressing oral reading

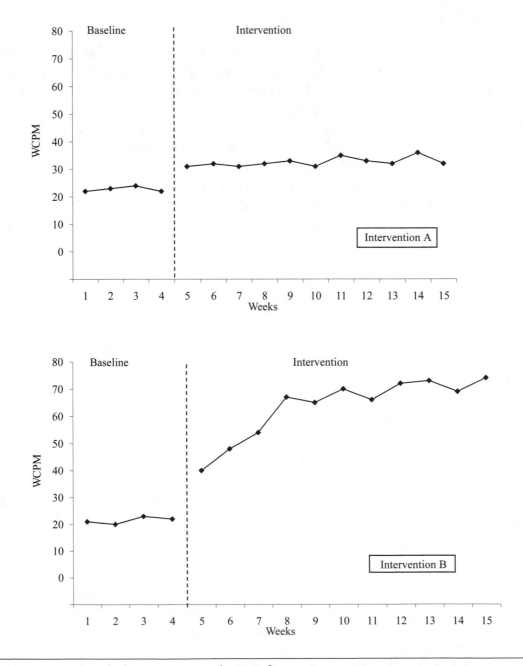

FIGURE 6.2. Sample data to compare the PND for two interventions.

fluency. Clearly there was a larger effect for intervention B, but both resulted in a PND of 100%.

The intuitive appeal of PND is clear. It is easy to understand, applies to any SCD, is quite easy to compute, and is consistent with the logic of visual analysis. Moreover, an empirical review of PND data found that results were both practically meaningful and consistent with the original research (Scruggs & Mastropieri, 1998). Although PND is the most commonly used effect size by SCD researchers (Scruggs & Mastropieri, 2001) there are difficulties inherent to the PND approach other than the ceiling effect discussed above. First, there is no known sampling distribution and the reliability of the statistic is unknown, which makes it impossible to compute confidence intervals. In addition, PND is also based on only one baseline data point, which could be an outlier and certainly is less reliable than a group of data.

Percentage of All Nonoverlapping Data Points

The percentage of all nonoverlapping data points (PAND) is a relative newcomer to the SCD effect-size debate, but is one with particular promise. PAND was described by Parker et al. (2007) as a nonparametric approach that alleviates many of the difficulties associated with PND. Based on Cohen's (1988) description of the relationship between effect sizes and percentage of data nonoverlap (Parker et al., 2007), PAND converts nonoverlapping data to more useful and commonly accepted ϕ and ϕ^2 coefficients. Moreover, ϕ and ϕ^2 can be converted to Cohen's d with the formula below.

$$d = \frac{2\phi}{\sqrt{1 - \phi^2}}$$

PAND and ϕ are computed by completing a 2 × 2 table as shown in Table 6.1 using data from Figure 6.3. Student A had three baseline data points and 12 intervention data points, two of which overlap with the highest baseline data point of 28. Student B had six baseline data points and eight intervention points, none of which overlap with the highest baseline data point of 29 WCPM. Finally, Student C had eight baseline data points and six intervention points, one of which overlapped with the highest baseline data point of 36 WCPM. Thus, there was a total of 42 data points, 17 of which were baseline and 25 of which

TABLE 6.1. 2 × 2 Table for PAND Computation

	Intervention	Baseline	Total
Higher	37.0 *Cell a*	3.5 *Cell b*	40.5
Lower	3.5 *Cell c*	56.0 *Cell d*	59.5
Total	40.5	59.5	100

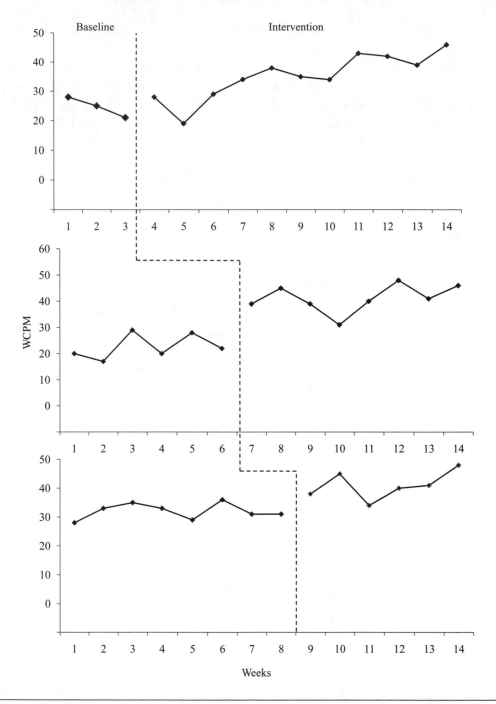

FIGURE 6.3. Sample data to compute the PAND.

were intervention. This relatively equal distribution is necessary to complete a PAND calculation. A total of three intervention points overlapped with baseline, which was a total of 7.1% of the data. That percentage is then divided into cells c and b (c = 3.5% and b = 3.5%). The percentage of overlapping data split into the two cells (3.5%) is then subtracted from the percentage of baseline (17/42 = 40.5%) and intervention (25/42 = 59.5%) data points, to equal 37.0% and 56.0% respectively. These data are then put into cells a and d as shown in Table 6.1. The PAND is simply 100% − 7.1% = 92.9%, which is reflected in the total of cells a and d in Table 6.1 (Parker & Hagan-Burke, 2007a). Moreover, the data in Table 6.1 can be used to compute a ϕ with the following formula $[a/(a + c)] − [b/(b + d)]$, or $[37.0/(37.0 + 3.5)] − [3.5/(3.5 + 56.0)] = 0.855$, which could also be derived by multiplying PAND by 2 and subtracting 1 from the total (Parker et al., 2007).

PAND offers several advantages over PND including the ability to convert it to ϕ and compute confidence intervals, and the use of all data rather than one potentially extreme data point. Moreover, the coefficient is computed for all sets of data within an MB design (e.g., three sets in Figure 6.3) considered together rather than three individual scores averaged. Although PAND is not affected by autocorrelation, ϕ and PAND cannot be computed with fewer than 20 data points with at least five in each cell (Parker et al., 2007). Moreover, PAND has a similar ceiling effect as does PND and probably does not substantially differentiate between effective interventions.

R^2

The oldest and mostly widely accepted effect size used with SCD studies is R^2. This statistic is different than the others discussed here because it relies on regression, which is the basis for all univariate analyses (Cohen & Cohen, 1983). R^2 is easily computed with most spreadsheets including Microsoft Excel 2007. After creating the line graph, as usually used within SCD, simply right click on the line and select "Add trend line." Next, select the "Display R-squared value on chart" option and click "Close."

An R^2 effect size can be interpreted with Cohen's (1988) recommendation of 0.25 as large, 0.09 as moderate, and 0.01 as small effects. The data presented in Figure 6.3 resulted in R^2 scores of 0.84 for Student A, 0.71 for Student B, and 0.94 for Student C, or an average of R^2 = 0.83, which is a large effect. However, Brossart et al. (2006) found that R^2 effect sizes for data judged to demonstrate a very effective intervention ranged from 0.034 to 0.895 (median = 0.528), and data from interventions judged as not effective ranged from −0.022 to 0.649 (median = 0.360). Thus, the usefulness of Cohen's (1988) interpretive scheme is somewhat questionable for R^2 data derived from SCD research.

Perhaps the most notable shortcoming of the R^2 effect size, and all effect sizes in the R^2 family, is that most data within SCD research do not meet the assumptions for parametric analyses; most notably the autocorrelation of the data. Advanced researchers can correct for autocorrelation through statistical methods, but to do so exceeds the skills of most researchers and certainly of a vast majority of practitioners, and most data series do not provide the necessary 34 to 40 data points to do so (Brossart et al., 2006).

Comparison of SCD Effect Sizes

Data presented within Figure 6.3 resulted in a ϕ coefficient of 0.86 and a PAND of 92.9%, a d of 6.36 (converted from ϕ), an average PND of 88.4%, and an average R^2 of 0.83. Thus, the conclusion of a large effect was reached for all four approaches to computing effect sizes. This is not surprising given that PND and PAND correlate at $r = .85$, PND and R^2 at $r = .78$, and PAND to R^2 equals $r = .87$. However, the magnitude within the designation of a large effect is limited by the ceiling effects of PND, PAND, ϕ, and R^2, and the lack of an interpretive scheme and sufficiently meeting parametric assumptions for d. For example, if a comparison of two interventions resulted in PAND of 90% and 94%, and d values of 4.80 and 7.80, respectively, both interventions would be judged as effective, but these data do not adequately state which was *more* effective.

The commonly used effect sizes discussed here seem most applicable to A-B designs, but the utility for designs with equally strong implications for internal validity (e.g., ME designs, A-B-A-B, and A-B-A-C-A-D) is mostly unknown or limited. For example, ME designs frequently compare two interventions without baseline. If the study included baseline data, then an effect size could be computed for both interventions. However, a lack of baseline data suggests the need to compute an effect size with the two sets of intervention data. Certainly one could compute a PAND or PND by comparing the two trend lines, but comparing data derived from two interventions is clearly and meaningfully different than comparing data to a baseline trend. Moreover, data collected in a simultaneous manner do not lend themselves to R^2 interpretations.

Another shortcoming of SCD effect sizes is that they do not fully take into account all interpretive approaches for SCD data. For example, the data presented in Figure 6.4 show a clear linear trend between baseline and intervention. These data suggest little experimental control and little confidence that the intervention led to the effect, but the PND would be a perfect 100%. Thus, most recommendations for the use of effect sizes within SCD suggest that they be used as a supplemental analysis that could enhance an objective understanding of the intervention strength, put intervention strength on a continuous rather than dichotomous scale, assist in interpreting results that are small and less obvious, and provide a means to compare the effectiveness of interventions (Parker & Hagan-Burke, 2007b). However, research questions within SCD should be primarily answered through visual analysis rather than effect sizes, and researchers should resist the temptation to reverse the order of importance.

In order to understand the need for effect sizes, one must also consider the trend from which they became commonly used. Researchers previously depended on the finding of a significant result as the interpretive gold standard, but significant findings from large sample sizes actually masked small effects. Thus, clinical importance should also be considered when interpreting data (Kirk, 1996), which is usually done by reporting effect sizes. As a result, the American Psychological Association (2001) recommended that effect sizes be reported in research articles. However, SCD researchers have long been concerned with clinical importance and do not rely on inferential statistics to interpret data. Although effect sizes allow for data to be synthesized meta-analytically, the strength of SCD research is

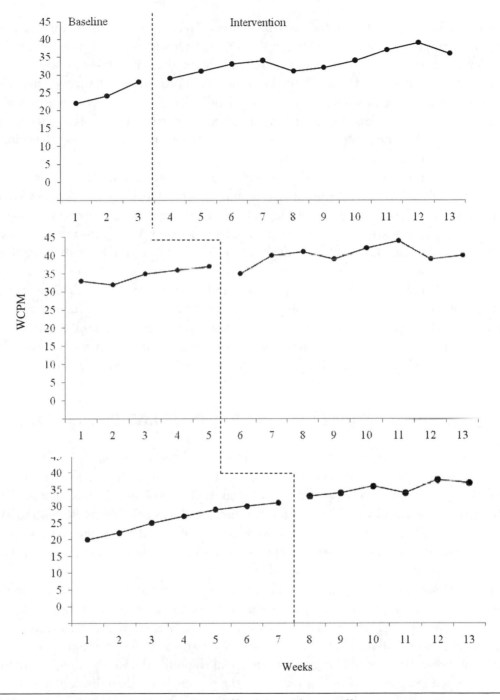

FIGURE 6.4. Sample data to demonstrate difficulties with SCD effect sizes.

strong internal validity with limited external validity. Thus, it may be more appropriate to answer a research question by following up SCD research with a between-group analysis with a large sample size and random assignment, rather than a meta-analytical study of SCD research. Parker and Hagan-Burke's (2007a, 2007b) assertions that reporting effect sizes within SCD research would enhance acceptability by the science community and be more consistent with the EBI movement in education are correct, but are those acceptable reasons to modify practice? Moreover, additional research is needed regarding the suitability of SCD research for meta-analytic study.

There are additional approaches to computing effect sizes that are not discussed here but could be promising in the future. For example, a hierarchical linear model could be a useful approach (Van den Noortgate & Onghena, 2003), as could clinical outcomes such as success rate difference, relative success rate, relative success rate improvement, and odds ratio (Parker & Hagan-Burke, 2007b). Fortunately, The Institute for Educational Science recently funded a center to develop and refine methodology for meta-analyses in SCD research (Shadish, 2007), which will hopefully soon inform our practice. Until then, SCD researchers are encouraged to cautiously consider effect sizes, to base conclusions on visual analyses and to treat effect sizes as subordinate, to use effects sizes that most closely suit the data conversation, and to not rely on any existing interpretive scheme. In essence, no effect-size metric can or should replace thinking when interpreting intervention data.

EMPIRICAL INTERPRETATION OF SCD EFFECT IN PRACTICE

The effect-size debate within SCD research centers mostly on which one is best to use, but the debate among practitioners should be more along the line of *if* rather than *how*. SCD are extremely useful when internal validity is essential. In Tier 3 of an RTI model, it is necessary to identify the causal variable of a student difficulty (Burns & Gibbons, 2008), and well-implemented SCD can lead to considerable confidence in causality conclusions. However, the causal conclusions should come from visual analysis of the data; effect sizes do little to enhance the identification of a causal variable.

The PND and PAND estimates of effect provide succinct and easily understood data that could be useful to practitioners because of their ease to compute and they could help inform decisions when clear causality is not evident. However, empirical interpretations of data in practice would likely center around numerical estimates of slope value.

Recent research within RTI suggests that special eligibility decisions should result from a lack of student progress in Tier 3 as judged by the presence of a dual discrepancy (Fuchs, 2003). For example, if a student's reading fluency scores after an intervention fall below a particular criterion (e.g., 20th percentile or DIBELS standards) and the rate of growth is more than one standard deviation below the average growth rate for the general population, then that student would be considered eligible for special education. Conversely, if a student's progress falls within an acceptable range but the amount of resources required to maintain that level of growth are so intense that they cannot be successfully implemented without the resource allocation of special education, then that student would also be identified as LD.

The reason the dual discrepancy (DD) approach is used to identify significant nonresponse, rather than simply finding three data points below an aim line, is because the aim line approach is used to judge effectiveness of interventions and does not result in sufficiently consistent conclusions for important entitlement decisions such as special education eligibility (Burns, Scholin, Koscielek, & Livingston, 2008). There are no studies that examine the validity of entitlement decisions based on aim line comparisons. However, there are several studies that suggest DD data significantly differentiate reading skills of children at risk for reading failure with and without a DD profile (Burns & Senesac, 2005; Speece & Case, 2001; Speece, Case, & Molloy, 2003), and result in a decrease in ethnic biases in identifying students for intense intervention (Burns & Senesac, 2005). Moreover, the slope of the aim line is dependent on how low the student's scores were to begin with and how much time elapses between baseline and target score. For example, a student whose median baseline score in January is 20 WCPM and whose end-of-the-year goal (May) is 60 WCPM would have a much steeper aim line than a student with a baseline score of 30 in which the intervention started in September. The former student would need to improve by 2.22 WCPM each week to stay on target, but the latter would only need to progress by 0.83 WCPM per week. Thus, the first student may make significantly more progress than the latter student, but still be three points below the aim line. Comparisons to aim lines can be very useful for instructional decisions within Tier 3, but entitlement decisions, such as special education eligibility, should be made with the psychometrically more rigorous DD model.

The importance of measuring student growth within special education eligibility decisions cannot be overstated. In fact, Fletcher (personal communication, 2008) noted that "the construct of [learning disabilities] has no meaning in the absence of an assessment of instructional response. None. Nada. Nil." Thus, empirical analyses of SCD data in RTI practice generally involve presenting a numerical value for slope. The slope of student learning represents the increase (or decrease) of behavior over a period of time. For example, a slope of 1.55 for oral reading fluency suggests that the student increased an average of 1.55 WCPM for every unit of time in which the data were gathered and computed. The unit of time is usually divided into weeks, as opposed to days or months.

A classic process for determining a trend is the split-middle technique (Kazdin, 1982). This method is applied to data sets within phases and as a result produces within-phase trends. The steps for determining a split-middle trend line for each phase are as follows (see Figure 6.5; Chafouleas, Riley-Tillman, & Sugai, 2007):

1. Split data within each phase in half. In the example, baseline data are split into two groups of three points, and the intervention phase data are split into two groups of seven points. If an odd number of data points, make the split at the middle data point (i.e., point three of five), and do not include this point in the remaining steps.
2. Within each half of each phase, identify the point where the middle value on the X-axis meets the middle value on the Y-axis. On the X-axis, the median value will always be the middle day or session. On the Y-axis, the median value is identified. For example, in Figure 6.5, the middle day on the first half of baseline data would be the second day (the median of 1, 2, and 3) on the X-axis (days) and the third data point (which is 50, or the middle of 35, 50, and 54) on the Y-axis (percent of time on

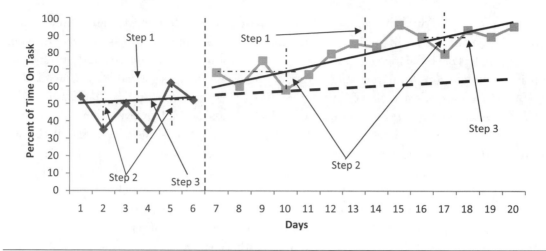

FIGURE 6.5. Split-middle technique step by step. Adapted from Chafouleas, Riley-Tillman, and Sugai (2007). Copyright 2007 by The Guilford Press. Adapted by permission.

task). A line is drawn vertically through the *X*-axis median and horizontally through the *Y*-axis data point so an intersection is indicated.

3. Connect the two points formed by the median values for each half to form the trend line for those data of that phase. The same procedure is applied to the intervention data to determine a second trend line.

4. Describe the trend lines within and between phases with respect to direction and change. By extending the trend line beyond the data used to draw the initial line, a tentative prediction of future behavior is indicated and can be used to analyze current behavior patterns (e.g., intervention effects vs. predicted performance if baseline had been continued).

The simulated data in Figure 6.5 show a slightly accelerating trend in the baseline phase with some variability. In the intervention phase an increase in the accelerating trend and a small initial increase in level are observed. The extension of the baseline phase trend line into the intervention can be used to consider the intervention effect. Comparing this to the intervention trend line, the positive effect of the intervention is apparent. Specifically, the positive trend of on-task behavior accelerated after the intervention was implemented.

Trend lines are an excellent tool to visualize goal development and aid with decision making. The following steps (from Chafouleas et al., 2007) provide an example using Figure 6.5:

1. Identify the points on the trend line corresponding to the first and last day of the phase (e.g., day 1 and 6 in baseline) and determine the *Y* values (percent of time on task). On day 1 in the example, the trend line is at 50% of time on task. On day 5, the trend line is at 52% of time on task. In the intervention phase, on day 14 the trend line is at 83% and 93% 5 days later (day 18).

2. Divide the larger value by the smaller value. In this case, 52/50 results in 1.04, which means that during baseline the percentage of time on task increased 0.04%

over the course of 5 days, which would be a long time before substantial change might be realized. In the intervention phase, on the other hand, 93/83 results in 1.13, indicating an increase of 13% over the same period of 5 days.

One of the primary benefits of computing behavioral change numerically is to predict the length of time before a target goal will be reached. In the current example, the goal stipulated that the child would increase on-task behavior by 40%. The baseline trend line predicted that it would take 100 school weeks to make this gain (assuming no change in ecology). The intervention trend line documented that the goal was obtained in less than 3 weeks. Clearly, in terms of immediacy of goal attainment, the intervention in this case was much more effective than the ecology in the baseline condition.

Computing the slope for data is also easily done with basic spreadsheet programs such as Microsoft Excel. Say, for example, a student's reading progress was monitored on a weekly basis with curriculum-based measures of oral reading fluency. The first five data points were collected in the baseline phase and the remaining eight points were collected during the intervention phase, for a total of 13 weeks of data. The resulting data would be week 1 = 20 WCPM, week 2 = 24 WCPM, week 3 = 18 WCPM, week 4 = 21 WCPM, week 5 = 22 WCPM, week 6 = 27 WCPM, week 7 = 29 WCPM, week 8 = 26 WCPM, week 9 = 33 WCPM, week 10 = 30 WCPM, week 11 = 36 WCPM, week 12 = 34 WCPM, and week 13 = 35 WCPM. These data are graphed in Figure 6.6 and clearly show a change in level, trend, and slope. A practitioner may examine this single case of an A-B design and conclude that the intervention was successful. This would be further evaluated by arranging the data in one row of a Microsoft Excel spreadsheet and the weeks in the second row as shown in Figure 6.7 (see Appendix B at the end of the book for a step-by-step guide to computing

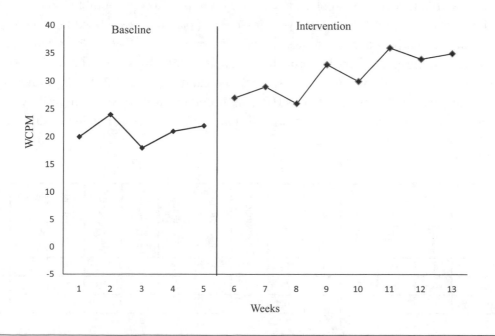

FIGURE 6.6. Sample data to compute slope.

slope). In this example, the slope value for the baseline phase is 0.10 WCPM (virtually no increase per week) and for the intervention phase, the slope value is 3.20, which represents an average increase of 3.20 WCPM per week.

The advantage of computing slope in this manner is that the rate of student growth can then be interpreted by comparing it to the average for the student's respective grade and/or class. To determine a classwide mean slope value, simply set up the data as shown in Figure 6.8. The numbers in the first three columns (A, B, and C) are the data for each student's benchmark reading assessment. For example, the first student (row 2) read 7 WCPM during the fall benchmark assessment, 10 WCPM during the winter assessment, and 31 WCPM at the spring benchmark assessment. Entered into columns E, F, and G are the numbers that represent the weeks. The first assessment occurred during the second week of the school year, the second was 16 weeks later, or the 18th week of the year, and the final one was an additional 16 weeks after that (34th week of the year). The weeks of the year can be dragged into the subsequent cells by highlighting all three boxes and dragging them into the cells below. After doing so, simply insert the slope function in the empty column in H, use the data in cells A, B, and C as the dependent data (Y) and the data in columns E, F, and G as the independent (X) variables. Finally, drag the slope formula into the desired cells and the slope value for the entire classroom, grade, or school can be computed quite quickly and easily.

If our student in Figures 6.6 and 6.7 was a member of this class, the postintervention slope of 3.20 would exceed that of the classwide mean and suggest a strong rate of growth. There are many potential ways to interpret slope data, none of which have been empirically identified as superior to the others. A comparison to class- or grade-level mean growth would require a cross-cohort comparison because it is not possible to compute an annual rate of growth midyear. Cross-cohort comparisons are probably acceptable if data are gathered for a period of 3 to 5 years, but a year-to-year comparison is questionable. A potentially interesting alternative could be to use the average rate of growth from a national sample, such as the one presented by Hasbrouck and Tindal (2006), in which the 50th percentile for first grade was 1.9 (from winter to spring), second grade was 1.2, third grade was 1.1, fourth grade was 0.90, fifth grade was 0.90, sixth grade was 0.70, seventh grade was 0.70, and eighth grade was 0.60. Those data are all slope values representing an average increase in WCPM per week.

	Baseline	Baseline	Baseline	Baseline	Baseline	Intervention	Intervention	Intervention	Intervention	Intervention	Intervention	Intervention	Intervention
WCPM	10	14	8	11	12	17	19	15	25	30	36	34	35
Weeks	1	2	3	4	5	6	7	8	9	10	11	12	13
Slope value					0.10								3.20

FIGURE 6.7. Setting up data within Microsoft Excel to compute slope for an individual.

	A	B	C	D	E	F	G	H
1	Fall	Winter	Spring		Week	Week	Week	Slope
2	7	10	31		2	18	34	0.75
3	4	7	8		2	18	34	0.125
4	9	17	13		2	18	34	0.125
5	13	16	18		2	18	34	0.1563
6	5	6	19		2	18	34	0.4375
7	13	29	71		2	18	34	1.8125
8	24	71	82		2	18	34	1.8125
9	6	35	65		2	18	34	1.8438
10	10	67	84		2	18	34	2.3125
11	10	14	38		2	18	34	0.875
12	11	12	27		2	18	34	0.5
13	23	60	74		2	18	34	1.5938
14	31	45	61		2	18	34	0.9375
15	5	8	16		2	18	34	0.3438
16	14	25	55		2	18	34	1.2813
17	30	88	105		2	18	34	2.3438
18	19	32	65		2	18	34	1.4375
19	24	52	82		2	18	34	1.8125
20	25	59	78		2	18	34	1.6563
21	26	60	67		2	18	34	1.2813
22	15.45	35.65	52.95					1.17

FIGURE 6.8. Setting up data within Microsoft Excel to compute slope for a group.

Perhaps the most defensible and useful model for computing slope standards is the approach used by the St. Croix River Education District in Minnesota. Reading fluency data are compared to a local norm and those who fall at or below the 7th percentile are considered below the fluency standard as part of the DD model (Silberglitt & Gibbons, 2005). However, rates of growth are evaluated by correlating scores at the three benchmarks with state accountability test scores and deriving target scores with receiver operating characteristics curves that can be used to compute a target slope. For example, in third grade the fall target is 72, while the spring target is 107. There are 34 weeks between the fall and spring benchmark assessments, which results in a slope of 1.03. Finally, a confidence interval around this criterion is computed and students below this confidence interval are considered significantly below criterion (to assist in eligibility decisions), and students above the confidence interval are considered significantly above criterion (to assist in decisions about exiting students from special education services). Thus, interventions that resulted in a postintervention level that fell below the 7th percentile and a slope of learning that fell below the confidence interval around the criterion for their grade level were considered unsuccessful (Silberglitt & Gibbons, 2005). Again, this approach appears to be quite promising but more sophisticated statistical analysis skills are required.

Although research has found consistent decision making with DD that led to reduced ethnic biases, other psychometric issues regarding slope values should be considered. Christ

(2006) found that under what would likely be typical assessment conditions, the standard error of the estimate for slope values can be $\pm$ 1.00 or greater (as high as $\pm$ 9.19) until data are collected for 9 weeks. In other words, collecting data twice each week for 8 weeks and computing a slope of 1.80 would actually mean that the true slope falls between 0.71 and 2.89. Clearly those are difficult data to interpret. Using optimal assessment conditions can reduce the standard error of the estimate to as low as $\pm$0.53 to $\pm$0.27 after 7 weeks, but typical conditions require approximately 8 to 10 weeks to find slope estimates that are sufficiently stable over time. Thus, empirical interpretations of SCD that lead to valid decisions are once again dependent on sound methodology.

CONCLUDING COMMENTS

Although including advanced empirical interpretations of SCD data may add information to the decision-making process, how and when that should happen is not yet clear. Researchers have many accepted effect sizes from which to choose, but all include some level of difficulty. Practitioners can apply slope data to a DD, but only if those data are collected with sound assessment procedures for a period of at least 8 weeks. Moreover, both empirical applications are limited to A-B designs.

There is quite a bit of current interest in the empirical interpretation of SCD data. Thus, it is possible that more definite answers are forthcoming. However, for now, researchers and practitioners are encouraged to note the limitations of the analyses they may use and to couple them with visual analyses.

7

Brief Experimental Analysis

What is the purpose of educational assessment? The focus of data collection efforts in schools frequently tends to be the evaluation of current practice. In other words, we collect data to make sure the instruction and practice is working. However, assessment data should also suggest what needs to be taught and how to best teach it, which is assessment for learning rather than assessment of learning (Stiggins, 2005). SCD assist in the assessment-for-learning approach by testing the effectiveness of interventions for specific students with specific settings or stimuli. Doing so allows practitioners to select an intervention that will likely be successful to implement over an extended period.

In addition to the use of A-B-A-B and complex designs for identifying interventions, recent researchers have proposed and examined the use of brief experimental analysis (BEA) to quickly test the relative effects of two or more interventions on a target behavior such as oral reading fluency (Daly et al., 1997). Witt, Daly, and Noell (2000) refer to such procedures as an opportunity for an intervention test drive. Developed from applied behavior analysis and SCD methodologies, a BEA manipulates environmental or instructional variables by implementing a series of interventions and assessing the immediate effect on a particular outcome. The intervention or combination of multiple interventions that leads to the largest gains in the target skill is then implemented over an extended period. In an RTI service delivery model, BEA is an ideal step to maximize the match between the intervention and the student's needs, the teacher preference, and the realities of the natural environment (Riley-Tillman, Chafouleas, & McGrath, 2004).

The primary benefit of BEA is the opportunity to initially evaluate the effectiveness of intervention strategies before investing significant time in implementation. A secondary benefit of BEA is that upfront testing of interventions allows for consideration of the ease of implementation of several different interventions without fully implementing any of them (Martens, Eckert, Bradley, & Ardoin, 1999). In the end, BEA could increase the understanding of both the effectiveness of the intervention and the likelihood that implementation will be feasible (Riley-Tillman et al., 2004). Even if an intervention is appropriate, if it is too complex, too time-consuming, or simply a poor fit for a particular setting, then it is unlikely to be implemented with fidelity. BEA can pinpoint which intervention components are essential and feasible. This allows educational practitioners to discover *realistic* solutions to those problems.

There is a decade of published BEA research in the applied behavior analysis and school psychology literature supporting that BEA is both consistent with a behavioral framework and assists in directly linking assessment to intervention (Martens et al., 1999). Moreover, the use of BEA to identify potential interventions has consistently led to positive effects for reading fluency (Burns & Wagner, 2008), math (Carson & Eckert, 2003), spelling (McComas, Wacker, Cooper, Asmus, Richman, & Stoner, 1996), writing (Duhon, Noell, Witt, Freeland, DuFrene, & Gilbertson, 2004), and behavior problems (Carter, Devlin, Doggett, Harber, & Barr, 2004; Wacker, Berg, Harding, & Cooper-Brown, 2004). These positive data are encouraging, especially given that BEA procedures require approximately the same amount of time to complete as would standardized measures of achievement (Jones & Wickstrom, 2002). Considering the prevalence of standardized assessment, this is an intriguing resource comparison considering the potential value of BEA.

Although BEA has become somewhat prevalent in intervention research, its use in practice is unknown. One study found that BEA was as acceptable to school psychologists as norm-referenced assessment (Chafouleas, Riley-Tillman, & Eckert, 2003). However, that same study found low levels of reported training in BEA with 70% of responding school psychologists indicating little or no training. Moreover, the literature does not contain a detailed explanation of BEA other than method sections of intervention studies, chapters on brief analysis (e.g., Kennedy, 2005), and brief reviews (Riley-Tillman et al., 2004). Therefore, the procedures for conducting a BEA in a school setting as described below include approaches for selecting interventions to attempt as well as the SCD procedures.

PROCEDURES FOR CONDUCTING BEA

The process for conducting BEA is rather straightforward. Figure 7.1 provides a checklist of each required step. In the first step, the interventions are selected. The intervention selection stage is obviously critical for BEA, but it is also critical that each intervention is implemented correctly. Thus, a step-by-step protocol should be developed to assist with intervention implementation. After interventions have been selected and protocols developed, baseline data on the target behavior must be collected. Next, each intervention is briefly administered in a predetermined order to gauge both its effectiveness and allow the interventionist an opportunity to try out administration (Noell, Freeland, Witt, & Gansle, 2001; VanAuken, Chafouleas, Bradley, & Martens, 2002).

The order of implementation for the interventions is based on ease of implementation or a conceptual framework. The actual process requires SCD procedures, which are reviewed in more depth later in this chapter. The resulting data are then used to select a final intervention based on both student performance and reported feasibility by the individual ultimately responsible for implementation. This intervention would then be used in a more extensive trial. While the BEA process is rather straightforward, the intervention selection and SCD phase can be quite complex. As such, the remainder of this chapter focuses on these stages of BEA.

- ☐ Review all initial data and consider appropriate goals.

- ☐ Select the intervention-s to be tested based on the suspected cause of the student's difficulty.

- ☐ Design a protocol (i.e., the specific procedures) for implementing each intervention.

- ☐ Choose the order of implementation for the interventions based on ease of implementation or a conceptual framework such as the five common reasons for student failure.

- ☐ Determine an outcome measure and prepare all necessary materials.

- ☐ Collect baseline data using the outcome measure to determine current level of performance.

- ☐ Reevaluate goal based on baseline data.

- ☐ Implement interventions in the predetermined order. Administer an outcome measure after each intervention is completed.

- ☐ Analyze data.
  - Compile the information into an easy-to-read format.
  - Compare performance during each intervention with the baseline and other interventions.

- ☐ Select the intervention that demonstrates the best results and is also reasonable to implement.

FIGURE 7.1. Summary checklist of procedures for conducting BEA. Adapted from Riley-Tillman, Chafouleas, and McGrath (2004). Copyright 2004 by the National Association of School Psychologists. Adapted with permission in T. Chris Riley-Tillman and Matthew K. Burns. Permission to photocopy this figure is granted to purchasers of this book for personal use only (see copyright page for details).

INTERVENTION SELECTION

Although BEA can test the relative effectiveness of any intervention or combination of intervention components, the system with which they are selected is an important aspect of the analysis. BEA is only useful if the interventions tested are evidence based and logically functionally related to the target behavior. Thus, it is suggested that interventions attempted within a BEA be selected a priori using a conceptual system such as the instructional hierarchy (Haring, Lovitt, Eaton, & Hansen, 1978), skill versus performance deficit (Lentz, 1988), or the five hypotheses for student difficulty (Daly et al., 1997). The five hypotheses presented by Daly and colleagues (1997) are (1) insufficient motivation, (2) insufficient practice, (3) insufficient feedback and assistance, (4) insufficient modeling, and (5) materials that are too difficult. Instructional variables and interventions are developed according to one or more of these hypotheses. Examples of interventions based on these hypotheses for reading fluency would be a contingent reward for insufficient motivation, repeated readings for insufficient practice, immediate error correction for insufficient feedback and help, listening passage preview for insufficient modeling, and using materials that represent an instructional level for materials that are too difficult.

The results of BEA will suggest which intervention is most effective and this in turn can give insight into what the root of the difficulty is. For example, if immediate error correction leads to the largest effect, then it could reasonably be concluded that the student's academic difficulties were at least contributed to by a lack of adequate feedback regarding the academic task. This is in the end a dynamic recursive model (see Figure 7.2) with the conceptual system driving which interventions are attempted and then outcome data decid-

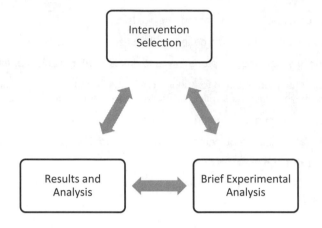

FIGURE 7.2. Dynamic recursive model of BEA.

ing which one is most successful (and thus ultimately implemented). This outcome data in turn can be used as additional evidence in future intervention selection stages.

SCD PROCEDURES

Experimental control in a BEA is demonstrated by using an ME design (Eckert, Ardoin, Daisey, & Scarola, 2000; Eckert, Ardoin, Daly, & Martens, 2002; Noell et al., 2001), or a brief ME design followed by a mini-reversal with baseline or the least successful intervention (according to the BEA procedure) to strengthen the design (Daly et al., 1998; Daly et al., 1999). However, a true functional relationship cannot be demonstrated with this direct replication because the analysis is usually too brief and does not contain a sufficient number of repeated conditions. Moreover, BEA is consistent with the ME approach, but is not truly an ME design. For example, the top panel of Figure 4.5 (an example of an ME design) from Chapter 4 looks very much like a BEA with a few exceptions. First, there are probably more data points collected in each condition than what would be used in a BEA. If the data from Figure 4.5 were used for a BEA, then likely only the first three data points would have been collected. In this example, the decision would have remained the same in that the data for the instructional-level material suggested a potential intervention, but the data did not differentiate from the condition that included a contingent reward. While the inability to document a causal relationship using BEA is important to note, given that this procedure is seen as a precursor to more extended analysis, this is not a critical limitation of appropriate use.

The second major difference between a BEA and pure ME design is more fundamental than the number of data points. A BEA is very much an assessment, which means the data are collected in a controlled environment in a short time period (e.g., 45 to 60 minutes). However, ME designs attempt to more closely replicate or directly sample the setting to which the behavior would generalize. For example, an ME design that compares two interventions for learning letter sounds would likely involve conducting those interventions with fidelity in the classroom and collecting data on a daily or weekly basis. A BEA regarding the same topic would conduct a baseline measure of letter–sound correspondence knowledge, implement the first intervention, repeat the measure or an equivalent one, conduct the second intervention, repeat the measure or an equivalent one, conduct a baseline probe, and repeat the two conditions in reverse order. Thus, a BEA is a much smaller sample of behavior that less directly represents the target setting.

BEA CASE STUDY

The simulated data within Figure 7.3 were based on a BEA conducted with a second-grade male who demonstrated significant writing difficulties (Burns, Ganuza, & London, in press). Information presented by the classroom teacher and review of existing writing samples suggested that letter formation was an important goal to address within the BEA. Thus, the common reasons for failure given by Daly et al. (1997) were used to test the effectiveness of letter-formation interventions within one 45-minute session. The procedures for the writing BEA involved (1) conducting a baseline assessment, (2) implementing each intervention with a return to baseline between each, (3) repeating the two intervention conditions that led to the greatest increase in a reversed order, and (4) finishing with a final return to baseline. It should be noted that BEA for reading and math often use the same stimulus (i.e., same reading probe or set of math problems) for the baseline condition and at least one of the interventions. Multiple probes are also conducted with high content overlap passages

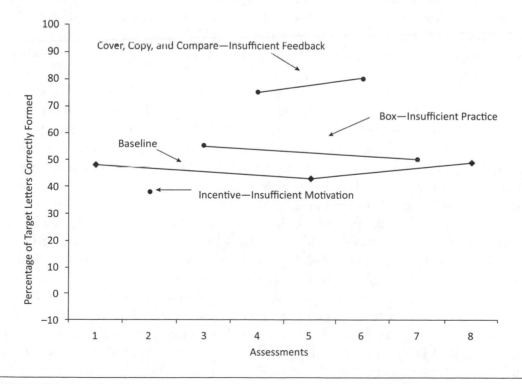

FIGURE 7.3. Sample BEA data.

for reading (Daly et al., 1998; 1999; Daly, Murdoch, Lillenstein, Webber, & Lentz, 2002) or math probes containing the same type of problems.

The incentive intervention in the current writing BEA addressed a potential lack of motivation by providing a student-selected reward if he wrote 30% more correctly formed letters in a writing sample than the baseline condition. A box intervention addressed the possibility that the student had not had enough practice writing by placing his writing paper over large-box graph paper that was taped to the student's desk. The graph paper showed through the top sheet of writing paper and provided a visual cue for writing, and he practiced writing letters that were incorrectly formed during baseline by writing them five times each using the graph-paper cue. Finally, the hypothesis that the student required more feedback was tested by using a cover–copy–compare (Skinner, McLaughlin, & Logan, 1997) procedure in which he traced the letters, wrote them from memory, and then compared the freehand letters to the original model. If the freehand letter closely approximated the model, then he wrote them five additional times with the model in his view.

Data were collected during the assessment using a short 3-minute writing probe. The student was provided a grade-appropriate story starter and asked to write for 3 minutes. After completing the writing, the percentage of the target letters that were correctly formed served as the dependent variable for analysis. The same story starter was then used to assess the formation of the target letters for each condition. The first baseline data were collected with one story starter, then the incentive condition was conducted with the same story starter, followed by the cover–copy–compare (CCC) and box conditions with the same story starter administered two different times. Thus, the same story starter was used a total of four times, and was replaced with a second story starter for the second baseline probe and the two conditions that were repeated. Finally, a third story starter was used for the final baseline probe. Certainly a different story starter could be used for each writing assessment, but we chose to use only three to control for potential differences in interest between story starters.

Many BEA include a return to baseline and a mini-reversal to support the effectiveness of the intervention that was shown to be most successful. If the effect is replicated, then the most effective intervention is implemented for a period of time, referred to as the *extended analysis* or *implementation phase*, which is similar to the classroom-based intervention (Noell et al., 2001; Wilber & Cushman, 2006). During extended implementation, progress monitoring of student performance is conducted using the same assessment format and metric as in the BEA in order to measure the effectiveness of the intervention over time (Noell et al., 2001). The data presented in Figure 7.3 suggest that the CCC intervention was the most effective for this student. Thus, it could be suggested that a functional relationship existed between the amount of feedback the student received and his writing difficulties. Given the limited amount of data and the single replication of effect, the internal validity of the conclusion is somewhat questionable. However, the decision made from this 45-minute assessment was simply which intervention to try for the extended period. In this case, a lower standard for experimental control in this applied setting is probably acceptable. The result of this BEA was that the CCC intervention was implemented for a period of approximately 10 weeks and was evaluated with an MB across-stimuli design. A strong effect was found for all three data sets, which suggested a functional relationship and convergence with the BEA.

AMOUNT AND TYPES OF DATA

As almost always, more data are better than less data. However, the purpose of a BEA is to collect enough data to make a decision in as little time as possible, which is why most BEA are limited to approximately two data points per condition. Often the least effective intervention in the first round of treatment implementation is not replicated, which means that it is possible that some conditions may be assessed with a single data point. As repeatedly stated, that is not enough replication to claim experimental control, but is likely enough for differentiation to suggest an intervention with a high likelihood for success.

BEA begin with information from other sources (e.g., the classroom teacher, review of permanent products) to identify the specific target behavior. Next, equivalent assessment probes for that behavior are developed in order to collect baseline data and measure the effectiveness of the treatments. Curriculum-based measurement (Deno, 1985) is often used for this purpose because it leads to data that are reliable for use over time and exist in multiple, yet equivalent forms to facilitate repeated measurement (Wilber & Cushman, 2006). However, systematic direct observations may also be used for behavioral questions within a BEA, as would any data collection system that results in data sensitive enough to demonstrate an immediate change.

Most BEA include a baseline condition in addition to data for the various conditions. The inclusion of baseline data is necessary because the intervention should be more effective than other interventions, but should also lead to a large effect as compared to baseline behavior. Moreover, a return to baseline between conditions, or between the first implementation of conditions and the replications, increases confidence in conclusions from the data. Finally, not all BEA include a mini-reversal of the two most effective interventions, but we suggest this as standard practice because although true experimental control cannot be established in the brief format, reversing the conditions enhances the degree of confidence in the conclusions. Internal validity is not a binomial standard in that varying degrees can exist.

HOW LARGE OF AN EFFECT IS NEEDED?

One potentially important area of inconsistency in BEA research is the criteria with which a successful intervention is identified. Some researchers relied on post-hoc visual analysis (Wilber & Cushman, 2006), some tested interventions selected a priori until clear differentiation was shown between two adjacent conditions (e.g., Daly et al., 1999), and others set a priori criteria such as a 20% or greater increase over baseline or over the immediately preceding condition (Jones & Wickstrom, 2002; Noell et al., 2001). However, there was little justification provided for any of these approaches within the studies. A recent meta-analysis found that interventions identified as effective within a BEA resulted in an average of 80% nonoverlapping data points as compared to other interventions (Burns & Wagner, 2008). Moreover, an average score increase of 73% over the median baseline score was also found. Thus, effective interventions within a BEA should probably result in a substantial increase in performance (e.g., approximately 70 to 75%) with few overlapping data with the other interventions. It should be noted that these data were obtained with reading interventions, but the data presented in Figure 7.3 resulted in a 127% increase between the median baseline point and the lowest data point from the most effective intervention, with 100% nonoverlapping data.

CONCLUDING COMMENTS

A relatively large and ever-growing literature supports the use of BEA of academic performance and brief analyses in general. BEA seems especially useful for identifying interventions for students with the most severe needs (Barnett, Daly, Jones, & Lentz, 2004). Certainly not every struggling learner requires the high level of individualization that comes from conducting BEA, and many would respond well to common "first-line" interventions such as repeated reading, flashcards, mnemonic strategies, and so on. However, as a student progresses through the RTI tiers and the stakes of response to intervention increase, BEA is an essential tool. This is particularly the case in educational environments with schoolwide problem-solving models. In such settings, wasting time on interventions that are bound to fail can be fatal to the whole-school service delivery model. The effective use of BEA can maximize the effectiveness of the whole-school problem-solving process. In addition, some students present enigmas to the dedicated staff who attempt to provide necessary assistance, and the first step to answering any difficult question should always be data collection. This is especially true if the data do more than just describe current functioning or evaluate instructional programming. The data should suggest what to teach and how to teach it, and a BEA could be a critical component in that process.

8

A Response-to-Intervention Model Incorporating Experimental Design

Throughout the first seven chapters of this book, there is a direct and indirect focus on the general topic of "response to intervention." At this point, though, we explicitly consider the role of SCD in a fully implemented RTI service delivery model. More accurately, we consider a fully developed model of RTI that includes SCD as its methodological backbone. In comparison to other schoolwide problem-solving models, the most unique facet of an RTI model is that a student can be deemed eligible for educational services within the model. While this aspect of an RTI model is probably part of the model's attractiveness to educational professionals, it should be carefully considered in terms of what standards must be required to make a high-stakes decision. There is a considerable amount of literature that focuses on the importance of the intervention (Burns, 2007), assessment tools (Christ, 2006), and the general process of decision making for an RTI service delivery model (Burns & Senesac, 2005; Fuchs, 2003). Unfortunately, there has been little focus on the need for higher levels of experimental control as the stakes of the decision start to amplify.

While experimental control is of course positively influenced by using an effective intervention implemented with integrity, defensible outcome data, and sound decision-making practices, it is sound methodology (SCD) that is most critical when making defensible high-stakes decisions. In this chapter we provide an overview of an RTI model that includes all of these elements, and then consider the implications of the addition of SCD into it. Note that the purpose of this chapter is not a comprehensive guide to implementation of an RTI model, but rather a conceptual guide to incorporation of SCD into an RTI framework. There are a number of excellent resources available for those looking for a comprehensive guide to implementation of an RTI model (e.g., Brown-Chidsey & Steege, 2005; Burns & Gibbons, 2008; Jimerson, Burns, & VanDerHeyden, 2007; Wright, 2007).

RTI AND INTERVENTION

While no one part of an RTI model is any more essential than the others, the logical starting point is to focus on the "intervention." What is considered a defensible intervention will change throughout the three tiers, but the one constant is that it must be evidence based. By evidence based we do not only mean that a series of empirical studies has shown that the intervention is effective, but that is it also used for the purpose for which it was validated. It is important to remember that any evidence-based intervention (EBI) has been validated for a specific purpose, not simply generally validated. As such, it is assumed that EBIs will be used appropriately. In addition, it is assumed that the EBI is implemented as it is validated. This issue, often referred to as *treatment fidelity*, is a critical issue in that there is no reason to expect that an EBI implemented poorly will be effective. When playing golf, simply picking up the right club does not result in a good shot; one must also swing the club effectively. Based on this concept of an EBI, we proceed to talk about versions at each tier (see Figure 8.1).

Intervention at the Tier 1 Level

While we tend to think of intervention as something we do in response to a problem, in reality intervention begins the minute a child walks into a school. The first series of interventions that a student receives (unless he/she enters the system as a student with a disability) is the school's standard academic and social behavior curriculum for the student's respec-

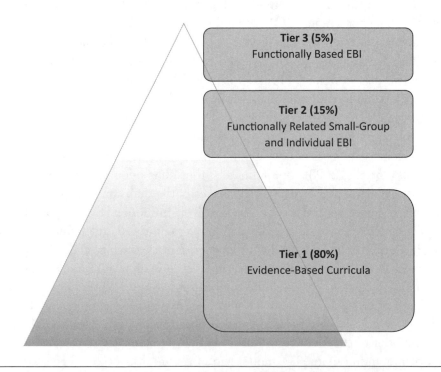

FIGURE 8.1. RTI model with minimum acceptable intervention in each tier.

tive grade. The effectiveness of the intervention in the first tier is essential as this success determines the number of referrals into Tier 2 and subsequently Tier 3. Obviously, a highly effective academic curriculum maximizes student success and conversely minimizes the number of academic problems. On the other hand, schools that utilize suspect academic curricula experience increased numbers of referrals into Tier 2 and Tier 3. Simply put, such a situation is bound for failure as it is unlikely that any school will have the resources for 30–40% of the population to be serviced individually.

In a situation where more than 20% of the student body is not successful in the general education curriculum, then it may be more efficient to bring the intervention to the classrooms than to take students to an intervention. VanDerHeyden and colleagues (VanDerHeyden & Burns, 2005; VanDerHeyden, Witt, & Naquin, 2003) discuss a classwide problem in which too many of the students experience a difficulty for a Tier 2 intervention to be successful. Specifically, when a classwide problem is moved to a Tier 2 level, the RTI system can become overwhelmed and at the same time the reality that the problem exists in the classroom rather than with any specific child can be missed. In such a case, a classwide intervention, such as the Peer Assisted Learning Strategies (Fuchs, Fuchs, & Burish, 2000), is implemented until a sufficient number of students demonstrate adequate proficiency. In the end, it is critical to use either schoolwide or classwide EBIs to successfully service the mass majority of students.

Intervention at the Tier 2 Level

Assuming that an effective package of academic and social behavior interventions was utilized in Tier 1, Tier 2 interventions are now able to focus on small groups of children who have difficulty with the standard curriculum. The difficulties that arise in each school should follow some pattern based on the student body, the Tier 1 curriculum, and the staff. For example, if a school does not focus sufficiently on early phonics instruction, then a large group of the children who experience failure in Tier 1 will likely require services that focus on early phonics. Moreover, reading and mathematical difficulties tend to follow developmental patterns. For the most part, Tier 2 interventions should be efficient, small-group EBIs that address these clusters of academic and social behavior problems. Thus, this is the first stage where the idea of tailoring the intervention to the specific problem occurs. While at this stage, the idea of functional-based EBI is looser than we see in Tier 3. However, it is still essential to match the Tier 2 intervention with the specific deficit that is at the core of the target student's difficulty.

There are a number of resources for educational professionals searching for evidence-based group interventions. The What Works Clearinghouse (*ies.ed.gov/ncee/wwc*) includes a number of group interventions in their database. Another excellent Internet resource for intervention suggestions is Intervention Central (*www.interventioncentral.com*). This website was created and is maintained by Jim Wright and provides a large number of intervention options with quick practice guides. The Florida Center for Reading Research website (*www.fcrr.org*) also lists, categorizes, and rates various small-group and individual interventions for reading. Finally, there are a number of published resources (e.g., Bowen, Jenson, &

Clark, 2003; Daly et al., 2005; Joseph, 2006; Murphy & Duncan, 2007; Rathvon, 2008) and intervention-focused journals (e.g., *Intervention in School and Clinic*, *Journal of Applied School Psychology*, and *Journal of Evidence-Based Practices for Schools*) that should be considered.

Intervention at the Tier 3 Level

In Tier 3, the intervention component becomes much more individualized and focused on the hypothesized reasons for academic or social behavior failure. In this stage of the RTI process, individualized interventions conducted with the highest levels of fidelity are essential. There is no room for loosely implemented interventions or interventions that are somewhat relevant for a target student but are altered for a larger group of children. In addition, it is critical that the intervention team take the time to consider the function of the problem behavior, or the likely reason for academic difficulty.

While we address the issue of determining the likely function of the problem in the assessment section below, the focus on function requires that the impact of the intervention (what it addresses) is fully understood. The most significant implication of this is that focused interventions that address a single problem, or a small number of problems, are implemented rather than a "shotgun" intervention approach. For example, repeated readings interventions address the common academic problem that the child has not had enough practice, but repeated readings will do little good if a child requires additional instruction in the skill or is unable to generalize the skill to different stimuli. By comparison, a phrase-drill intervention (see Daly et al., 2005 for more information) will assist a child who is still learning word recognition, but will do little to enhance the proficiency of a student with strong but dysfluent recognition skills. While both of these practices are defensible, the differences should be understood so that when a child responds, or does not respond, to the intervention the implications are apparent.

RTI AND ASSESSMENT

While intervention may be the engine in an RTI model, assessment provides the data that fuels the system. Without defensible academic and social behavior assessment it would be impossible to know who to service, how to best intervene, or whether the interventions are effective. Thus, an effective schoolwide RTI model requires that assessment methods for screening, prescriptive decisions, and progress monitoring must be available. In addition, these assessment methods need to be defensible (result in reliable and valid data for the application) and highly efficient considering the number of intervention cases at any given time. The balance between efficiency and effectiveness follows a logical pattern with feasibility being highlighted in Tier 1 and defensibility being highlighted in Tier 3. The focus of Tier 2 is efficiency, but a defensible assessment protocol is needed.

Regardless if the deficit is academic or behavioral, assessment data need to be more frequently collected and precise as students progress through the tiers of intervention. For example, general outcome data can be collected three times each year for Tier 1, but in Tier 2 data are collected perhaps weekly and include more specific measures, such as phonics or phonemic awareness, rather than just an outcome measure. Finally, in Tier 3, data are continuously collected (perhaps twice each week) and need to be quite precise. For example, in Tier 2 we may collect data about how well a student can sound out words, but in Tier 3 we assess exactly which letters, letter combinations, and so on, for which the student can correctly state the corresponding sounds. See Figures 8.2 and 8.3 for the minimal acceptable academic and social behavior assessment strategies by tier, respectively.

Assessment at the Tier 1 Level

As with intervention, assessment must start with the regular education classroom and schoolwide screening. It is in this tier that early identification occurs in order to identify students who are not responding to schoolwide instruction. Thus, it is critical that early screening via direct academic methods (e.g., curriculum-based measurement [CBM] or Dynamic Indicators of Basic Educational Literacy Skills [DIBELS]) are incorporated to quickly identify children as at risk for academic failure. Extant data sources such as office discipline referrals (ODR) could also provide a wealth of information for formative applications.

Universal screening and progress monitoring of all students are the hallmarks of Tier 1. Thus, incredibly efficient assessment tools are needed to provide adequate data for all students. There is a large set of instructionally useful assessment tools that are not appropriate

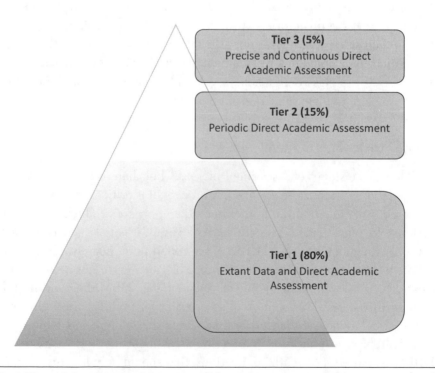

FIGURE 8.2. RTI model with minimum acceptable academic assessment strategy in each tier.

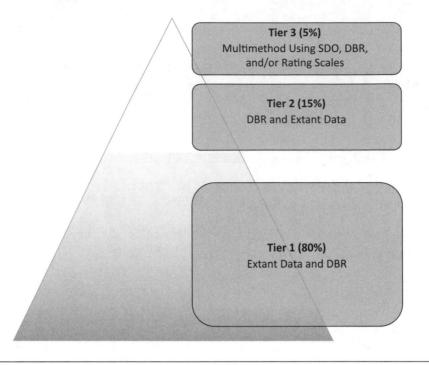

FIGURE 8.3. RTI model with minimum acceptable social behavior assessment strategy in each tier.

for Tier 1. For example, many classroom teachers positively report about the instructional utility of informal reading inventories. However, many of those tools require approximately 20 minutes for each student, which is not efficient enough to screen and they generally do not result in data reliable enough for placement decisions. That is not to say that other types of data are not useful to classroom teachers, it simply means that the data are not efficient and defensible enough to include in a resource allocation model.

Assessment at the Tier 2 Level

At the Tier 2 level, the stakes of assessment increase, but there is still a significant percentage of the population that must be serviced. Moreover, it is critical that a stream of outcome data be collected over time in order to monitor student progress. Thus, assessment methods must be defensible, feasible, and repeatable. As a result, it is not surprising that academic assessment tools such as CBM and DIBELS are relied upon heavily. Unfortunately, there is some debate as to the availability of a full range of Tier 2 (and Tier 3) assessment tools for RTI applications. While direct academic assessment (e.g., CBM) for reading fluency has a significant literature base, development of assessment for middle and high school applications, and social behavior have lagged behind. Regardless, there has been a considerable amount of research on a number of interesting assessment methods (e.g., direct behavior ratings [DBR] and early CBM math applications) that should help fill this void.

Assessment data within Tier 1 are used primarily to screen students for academic and behavioral difficulties, but data in Tier 2 also need to identify the category of the deficit.

Thus, Tier 2 assessments need to include defensible and repeatable measures of component skills such as phonemic awareness, phonics, reading fluency, and comprehension for reading. For example, subskill mastery measures (e.g., two-digit addition, three-digit by two-digit multiplication, basic algebraic equations, etc.) are important for identifying areas of remediation within a Tier 2 intervention for math.

Assessment at the Tier 3 Level

In Tier 3, as the stakes of decisions increase, the need for the most defensible of outcome data becomes paramount. To accomplish this, the general guide is to use multiple methods. In addition, the number of cases should be considerably smaller due to success in Tiers 1 and 2, which make more cumbersome methods feasible. On the academic side, direct academic assessment and standardized assessment are clear options. On the social behavior side, extant data and DBR can be augmented by systematic direct observation (SDO) to create a powerful package of social behavior assessment. In addition some use of behavior ratings scales for both summative and screening purposes may prove beneficial. It may be surprising to some that we list traditional standardized tests and behavior rating scales in Tier 3 as fully defensible assessment methods. As we discuss below, in some cases traditional psychoeducational assessment may become necessary and what constitutes a comprehensive evaluation always has been and always should be determined by the discretion of the evaluation team.

As stated above, precise data are needed in Tier 3. Not only are specific skills and skill sets assessed, but so are the different types of functioning within each. For example, and as stated above, Tier 3 data may determine what items are known and unknown. However, Tier 3 assessments also have to examine where in the learning hierarchy (Haring & Eaton, 1978) the student is currently functioning. To do so, the accuracy and rate with which the child can complete given tasks and items are both assessed. Students who can complete tasks with low accuracy and low rate require a different intervention than those with high accuracy but low rate. Thus, the assessment model within Tier 3 needs to include both pieces of information.

RTI AND SCD

Experimental methods are the final piece in a defensible RTI model. The introduction of functionally relevant EBI and defensible assessment methods so that outcome data are available present the opportunity to actually ask the question: "Did the child respond to intervention?" This question is obviously at the heart of the RTI model. As such, the statement that a child is "responding" or that a child is "not responding" has critical implications in terms of his/her educational future. It should be clear after reading this book that there is a substantial technology available so that this question can be legitimately answered. The effective application of intervention, assessment, and SCD allows for fully defensible statements as to a child's response to the intervention. Considering that such a sound answer is possible, education as a field should ask an important additional question: "How serious are we about measuring a child's response to intervention?" Are we willing to make somewhat cavalier statements about a child's response to intervention considering that such a statement, in this model of service delivery, has substantial educational implications?

Noell and Gansle (2006) likened decisions made within an RTI model without data supporting that the model was actually implemented to convening an evaluation review team to decide which assessments to administer for a special education eligibility evaluation, and then later convening an individualized educational planning team to identify the child as having a disability *without* ever administering any of the assessments identified in the evaluation review. In our perspective, making important decisions based on student response without appropriate and sufficient experimental control is the same situation described by Noell and Gansle. Obviously this is not something that should be taken lightly, and considering that the technology is available to proceed in a defensible manner, it would be unethical to do otherwise. That being said, it is probably not essential to utilize a fully experimental approach in Tier 1 or even Tier 2. Tier 1 could be called *response to instruction* and by definition refers to a cluster of intervention procedures. However, it is essential that high-stakes decisions incorporate experimental methods in addition to EBI and psychometrically sound assessment tools. As with any other feature of an RTI model, the required rigor is defined by the tier. In Tier 1 with a whole-school focus experimental control will not be the focus; rather, feasibility will be highlighted. In contrast, in Tier 3, experimental control is critical, and thus SCD methods that incorporate each step of baseline logic will be needed. As such, at that point we consider what level of experimental design is defensible at each tier. Figure 8.4 presents what we consider to be the minimum acceptable SCD method in each tier.

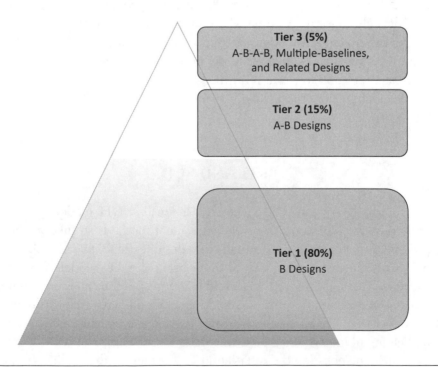

FIGURE 8.4. RTI model with minimum acceptable SCD method in each tier.

SCD at the Tier 1 Level

It is unrealistic to use complex SCD in Tier 1, but B and A-B designs are appropriate. General target behaviors and highly efficient assessment methods are the norm with this application of SCD. Causality is not a focus of Tier 1 practice, which makes B designs appropriate for all students. In addition, appropriate analysis should be conducted on essentially every student in a manner similar to the dashboard of a car. If everything is working, nothing alarming is noted and an indicator of effective functioning (miles per hour) is monitored. If something goes wrong, the check-engine light is illuminated and the driver knows to proceed to the nearest automotive mechanic. This quick-detection system, in a car on in a school, allows for intervention before any serious damage occurs.

There are some cases in Tier 1 where a more intense approach is required. In such cases A-B designs will prove appropriate. The use of an A-B design allows for a clear statement as to any change in the target behavior after an intervention is implemented. It is not a significant concern that causality cannot be documented as there will be ample opportunity in Tiers 2 and 3. The application of SCD and analysis in Tier 1 can best be described as a "feasible attempt."

SCD at the Tier 2 Level

A large number of students with a diverse range of problems are serviced in Tier 2. It is unlikely that any school environment will have the resources to conduct fully experimental designs with all Tier 2 cases. Thus, SCD in Tier 2 should be a mix of highly feasible nonexperimental designs (e.g., B and A-B) and more resource-intensive experimental designs (e.g., A-B-A-B and MB) as needed. For less severe cases, B and A-B designs will prove useful in monitoring the individual child's response to small-group interventions. For more severe cases, it is suggested that rigorously documenting a child's response to functionally based EBI is advisable, as this information will assist in the intervention process. In addition, it is in Tier 2 that BEA is likely to appear. The effective use of BEA can increase the effectiveness of the system to work with at-risk children by minimizing the use of interventions that are less likely to be effective. In addition, the opportunity to test drive the intervention should increase fidelity.

The primary analysis within Tier 2 is to identify the category of the deficit. Thus, students are placed into small groups based on skills with which they struggle, which is a decision that can be made with little experimental control. However, the more information collected on a struggling learner, the more quickly you can intervene effectively. Fully experimental designs provide critical information as to the effectiveness of an intervention in a timely manner so that the system can be adjusted accordingly. In addition, if the child does progress into Tier 3, this information will prove very useful.

SCD at the Tier 3 Level

SCD and baseline logic seem especially critical and well suited for Tier 3 decisions. An RTI model essentially increases precise and frequent measurement to address specific problems (Burns & Gibbons, 2008). Tier 3 could best be conceptualized as a systematic analysis of precise instructional variables in order to isolate target skill deficits and identify interventions for individual students, which is best accomplished through SCD analyses (Barnett et al., 2004). Thus, an A-B-A-B design, MB, and other full expressions of baseline logic provide the best paths to measuring a student's RTI. In the case of a lack of RTI, an A-B-A model is reasonably defensible. The primary analysis task within Tier 3 is to identify a causal relationship between deficit and intervention in order to develop appropriate interventions. A causal (or functional) relationship cannot be documented without baseline logic.

The use of SCD with the potential for causality attributions is even more imperative when eligibility for special education services and the corresponding label is being considered. While it may seem a daunting task to incorporate this level of experimental methodology into educational practices, we are discussing the most at-risk population in an educational system. Children at this level of risk, for whom RTI practices result in high-stakes decisions, deserve this level of service. In addition, this application of the RTI model is based on the ability to determine functional relationships between intervention and critical outcome data. Without this ability, the high-stakes decisions made in Tier 3 are simply not possible.

EDUCATIONAL DECISIONS

When an RTI model incorporates effective intervention, assessment, and SCD at each tier, the full potential of the model is finally accessed. Specifically, the opportunity arises for highly defensible educational decisions to be made at any stage. Figure 8.5 provides an overview of assessment, intervention, and SCD in a three-tier model. Assuming these standards have been met, the following four possibilities exist in any case.

Effective Intervention

The first possibility is that an effective intervention is identified and verified. For most students, this is the typical outcome in that the regular education curriculum is effective in maintaining acceptable educational and social behavior progress. This is the preferred possibility for all students, and schools should maximize the number of children who are best served at Tier 1. To maximize the likelihood of this possibility it is critical that evidence-based academic and social behavior curricula are implemented. In addition, it is critical that defensible outcome data are collected and a B design is utilized so that if minor problems arise, they can be addressed quickly.

Effective Intervention Not Successful

The second possibility is that an effective intervention is identified and verified, but the target child or group still remains in the at-risk range. It is likely that the results of Tiers 2 and 3 will produce a group of children for whom the most appropriate intervention is

	Decision making		Assessment		Intervention		Design		
	General focus	Decision rules	Academic	Social behavior	Acceptable evidence-based intervention	Fidelity requirements	Acceptable SCD	Required confidence in causality
Tier 1	Schoolwide progress while minimizing referrals		Permanent products and direct academic assessment	Permanent products, direct behavior ratings	Research-based curriculum and classwide intervention	Low to medium	Running B	No functional relationship consideration
Tier 2	Focused efficient intervention	Three-point	Direct academic assessment	Direct behavior ratings	Categorically functionally related, research-based, small-group and individual interventions	Medium to high	A-B	Some functional relationship consideration (low level—categorical, such as fluency, phonics, positive behavior support)
Tier 3	Focused intervention with the possibility for special education eligibility determination	Dual discrepancy or traditional	Multimethod using direct academic assessment and standardized assessment	Multimethod using systematic direct observation, direct behavior ratings, and/or rating scales	Functionally related individual interventions	High	A-B-A-B, MB	Documentation of functional relationship is critical, particularly when eligibility for special education is considered

FIGURE 8.5. Assessment, intervention, and SCD in a three-tier RTI model.

From T. Chris Riley-Tillman and Matthew K. Burns. Copyright 2009 by The Guilford Press. Permission to photocopy this figure is granted to purchasers of this book for personal use only (see copyright page for details).

clear, but either that intervention needs to be continued for an extended amount of time to remove risk, or the results of the intervention keep the child in the at-risk range. While it is not appropriate with this population to label the child as *disabled*, it is critical to continue the intervention with fidelity, collect appropriate formative assessment outcome data, and monitor the progress of the child using B or A-B designs. The results of this intervention and progress monitoring will range from the eventual removal of the at-risk status (the first possibility above) or to the eventual conclusion that more resources are needed to provide services (the third possibility below). Any experienced educational professional will also recognize that there will be a group of children who remain in this at-risk range throughout their education. This issue is not unique to an RTI model. Rather, children who are informally considered *slow learners* or formally considered *at risk* exist in any service delivery system. In addition, children with special circumstances (e.g., students who speak English as a second language) could likely fall within this possibility. Clearly intervention services are needed, but the child is unlikely to be legitimately considered disabled. As such, any model needs to have a plan to continue educational services for this population in the absence of eligibility for special education services.

Effective Intervention with Intense Resources

The third possibility is that an effective intervention is identified and verified with one critical caveat: The intervention requires intense levels of resources. This is a unique case in that an RTI model allows for the consideration of categorizing that child as specific learning disabled and thus eligible for services as a special education student. If that label and those services allow for the continuation of the intervention at the intensity required, then this is a defensible pathway. In fact, this is the desirably pathway to special education eligibility within an RTI model because RTI is a search for an intervention to help a struggling learner, not a search for pathology. However, it is critical that there is a defensible case that it was the intervention(s) that caused the success. This case can only be built with the implementation of EBI with fidelity, the collection of defensible outcome data, and the use of appropriate SCD.

Effective Intervention Not Identified

The final possibility is that an effective intervention was not identified/verified that either removes, or has the potential to remove, the dual discrepancy. It is critical in this case that you are confident that the student truly did not respond to interventions. Specifically, it is critical to be able to rule out that external factors were not depressing the effectiveness of what would have been effective interventions. This confidence can only be established though the implementation of EBI with fidelity, the collection of defensible outcome data, and the use of appropriate SCD. Assuming that each of these requirements has been meet, then two steps should be taken. First, it is time to consider special education services. Second, it is time to consider other pathways to understand the target student's academic or social behavior problems. It is essential in cases where an RTI approach does not identify effective methods to address the student's needs that the full assessment arsenal is accessed.

IMPLICATIONS FOR PRACTITIONERS AND CONCLUDING COMMENTS

While this is not rocket science, educational intervention is science and may be a challenge to implement in most educational environments. We are both heavily invested in the implementation of RTI in our respective states (North Carolina and Minnesota) and across the country. We clearly understand the uphill battle in changing a school culture and that the topic of including fully experimental methods may be met with a good deal of resistance. However, there *are* schoolwide problem-solving models that have had tremendous success in changing the school culture to one that embraces scientific methodology (Sugai & Horner, 2006; Sugai & Horner, 2008). For example, Positive Behavior Support (PBS) has been adopted in over 7,000 schools (*www.pbis.org*, May, 2008). Over 3,500 of these schools utilize the School-Wide Information System (SWIS) (*www.swis.org*, May, 2008) to store and analyze the outcome data collected in the environment. While PBS does not currently incorporate a fully experimental methodology in determining RTI, it is an example of how a problem-solving model can be highly successful in both implementation and student outcomes. It is also not surprising that we both anecdotally find that schools that have adopted a PBS model are often the schools where RTI implementation is most successful. RTI and PBS have much in common in that they are both extensions of the same construct (data-based decision making; Burns, 2007), and those of us interested in RTI implementation can learn a great deal from those who have implemented PBS.

Pragmatically, as with the rest of the RTI model, it will take a good deal of training to increase the capacity of the typical educational professional so that he/she can utilize SCD in his/her educational practice. Ideally, this training will begin with a significant amount of support from one or two individuals in the school trained in SCD. With a good deal of initial training and support an educational professional should be able to implement increasingly complex SCD and analysis strategies in his/her daily practice. Another ideal dissemination method is the intervention (or problem-solving) team. If you consider the significant amount of training and support that is required to implement SCD in most schools, starting with a small group is a logical first step. Once the team has been trained in the benefits and use of SCD, they can help with both dissemination and the workload that supporting new users will require. Training and support is of course not a new issue. Schools adopting an RTI model typically need a significant amount of training and support in the general model, intervention selection and implementation, and assessment. Experimental methodology must also be added to this list.

Regardless of the challenge, RTI or any problem-solving model has been developed with the same general idea of making education more scientific. Science is of course rigorous, and as such, there are correct and incorrect methods. Experimental design is the very basis of the scientific method, and thus the logical basis of any truly scientific model of education.

Thus, in order to fully realize the vast potential of an RTI model, or any problem-solving model in education, rigorous experimental design must be embraced. We are past the point as a field where it is acceptable to ignore the benefits of a fully scientific approach to education, which is especially true with children who are failing. Problem-solving approaches that incorporate EBI, formative assessment, and experimental methods are not going away. As parents ourselves, the thought of children being served in an educational model that ignores the technologies available to maximize success is maddening, particularly when that technology is so readily available. It is our hope that this book will be one small step in the direction of schools finally embracing a complete scientific approach to education, and thus committing to the highest standards of educational practice.

Summarizing Data through Visual Presentation with Microsoft Excel

While some prefer to graph by hand, software such as Microsoft® Excel can be used with ease to present professional-looking outcome graphs. While the process of graphing with software takes some time to learn, it is an excellent alternative to graphing by hand. In this section we present a step-by-step guide to creating A-B, A-B-A-B, and multiple-baseline (MB) graphs using Microsoft Excel 2007. Please note that some computer experience is required to complete these tasks. While this appendix has been developed with detailed step-by-step directions, it is assumed that the reader understands basic functions in Microsoft® Windows (opening a program, minimizing a window, and so on).

CREATING A BASIC A-B GRAPH

1. Enter data into the worksheet as shown in Screenshot A.1. The data should be entered vertically in column A, with the name of the student in cell A1.

SCREENSHOT A.1. Creating an A-B graph: Data entry.

2. Highlight the data by placing the pointer on the A1 cell (with the name of the student) then press the left button on the mouse, hold it down, and move the pointer to the bottom of the data and release the left button. Then, move the pointer to the "Insert" tab and press the left mouse button. Next, move the pointer to the "Line" button and press the left mouse button. Finally, select the first graph option as seen in Screenshot A.2 by aiming the pointer at that icon, and click the left mouse button.

SCREENSHOT A.2. Creating an A-B graph: Inserting a line graph using selected data.

3. After Step 2, a graph appears, as shown in Screenshot A.3. By quickly double clicking the left button with the pointer on the graph in any place without text or a line (e.g., the upper right corner) the "Chart Tools" toolbar will open at the top of Excel. When that toolbar opens, look at the "Chart Layouts" section and aim the pointer at the bottom arrow on the right side and press the left mouse button. This sequence opens the options menu as shown in Screenshot A.3. In order to allow for all of the necessary options in the A-B graph, select "Layout 10."

SCREENSHOT A.3. Creating an A-B graph: Selecting a new layout.

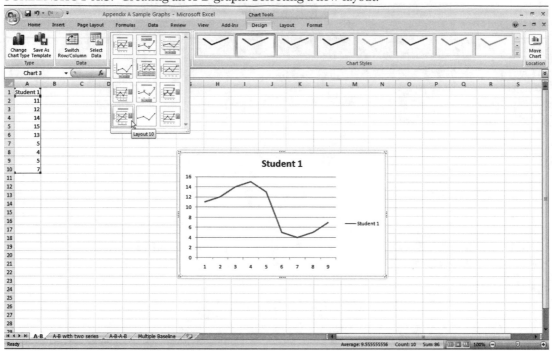

4. After Step 3 is completed, the graph now has an *X*- and *Y*-axis title label (see Screenshot A.4). The next step is to delete extraneous information (e.g., the data label). By placing the pointer on the label and pressing the right mouse button, a menu opens. On this menu, select the "Delete" option. This is accomplished by aiming the pointer at the "Delete" option, which highlights it, then press the left mouse button.

SCREENSHOT A.4. Creating an A-B graph: Deleting extraneous information.

5. It is also standard convention to remove the horizontal lines in the plot area. This is accomplished by aiming the pointer at any of the lines and pressing the left mouse button. Once the lines are selected, press the right button, which opens the menu as shown in Screenshot A.5. Select the "Delete" option. You may also simply press the delete button on the keyboard after the lines are selected.

SCREENSHOT A.5. Creating an A-B graph: Deleting extraneous lines.

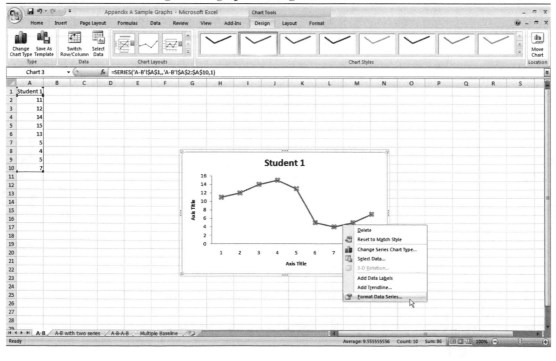

6. It is typical for each data point to be represented by a marker in SCD A-B graphs. To add data point markers in Excel, aim the pointer at the line, and right click on the mouse. This opens a menu (see Screenshot A.6) and allows for the option of "Format Data Series." Select that option.

SCREENSHOT A.6. Creating an A-B graph: Adding data markers I.

7. After selecting the "Format Data Series" option, the menu in Screenshot A.7 opens. On the left side of the menu, select the "Marker Options" tab. Next, click the "Automatic" option as shown in Screenshot A.7. Finally, select the "Close" button on the bottom right.

SCREENSHOT A.7. Creating an A-B graph: Adding data markers II.

8. It is important in SCD A-B graphs that there is a line break between phases. To remove the line just between two points (e.g., the end of phase A and the beginning of Phase B), aim the pointer at the section of line you want to remove and press the left mouse button twice. The first press selects all of the data, the second press selects only the data point to the right of the section you want to remove, as shown in Screenshot A.8. At this point, press the left mouse button to open the menu, and select "Format Data Point."

SCREENSHOT A.8. Creating an A-B graph: Creating a phase break I.

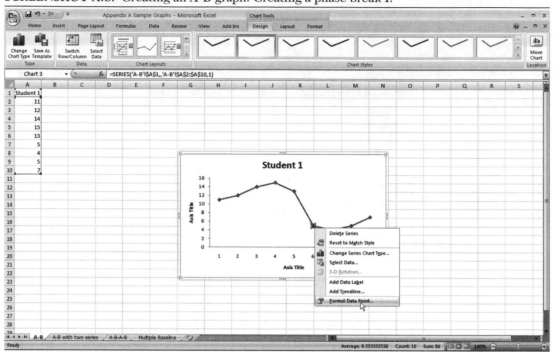

9. After selecting the "Format Data Point" option, the menu in Screenshot A.9 opens. On the left side of the menu, select the "Line Color" tab. Next, click the "No Line" option as shown in Screenshot A.9. Finally, select the "Close" button on the bottom right. The line between the two phases should now be removed.

SCREENSHOT A.9. Creating an A-B graph: Creating a phase break II.

10. It is important to place a dashed line between conditions to demonstrate a phase change. To accomplish this, move the pointer to the "Insert" tab and press the left mouse button. Then, move the pointer to the "Shapes" button and press the left mouse button. Finally, select the "Line" option as shown in Screenshot A.10 by aiming the pointer at that icon, and click the left mouse button.

SCREENSHOT A.10. Creating an A-B graph: Inserting a phase-change line I.

11. Step 10 results in the pointer being turned into a cross. Aim the cross at the top or bottom of where you want the line and press and hold the left mouse button (see Screenshot A.11). Next, drag the cross down to the bottom of the graph and release the button. This process creates the line and opens a new set of toolbar options as shown in Screenshot A.12.

SCREENSHOT A.11. Creating an A-B graph: Inserting a phase-change line II.

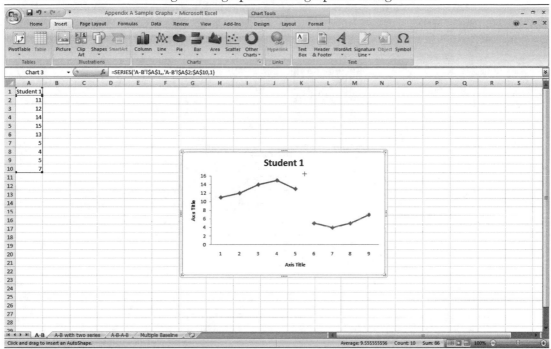

SCREENSHOT A.12. Creating an A-B graph: Inserting a phase-change line III.

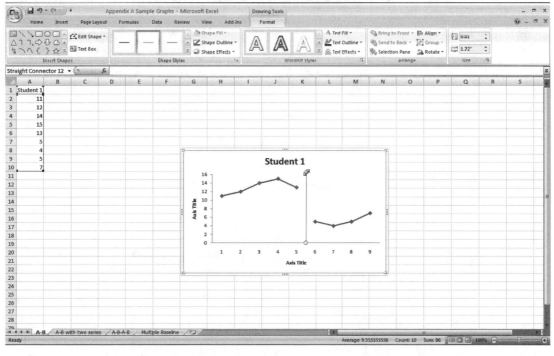

12. In order to make the phase-change line dashed, aim the pointer at the line and press the left mouse button. Next, select the "Shape Outline" option on the toolbar. Then, select the "Dashes" option. Finally, select the dashed line as shown in Screenshot A.13.

SCREENSHOT A.13. Creating an A-B graph: Inserting a phase-change line IV.

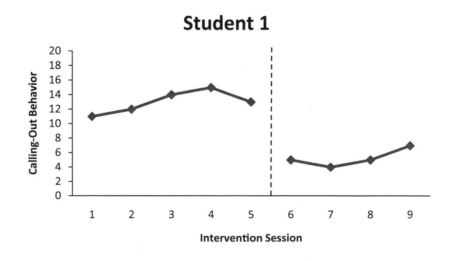

13. Finally, to change the axis titles so that they are appropriate labels, place the pointer on the axis label and press the left mouse button twice. This allows you to type in whatever label is appropriate, as shown in Screenshot A.14. This completes the process of creating an A-B graph (see Figure A.1). This graph can now be moved into other programs or simply printed out for a variety of uses.

Student 1

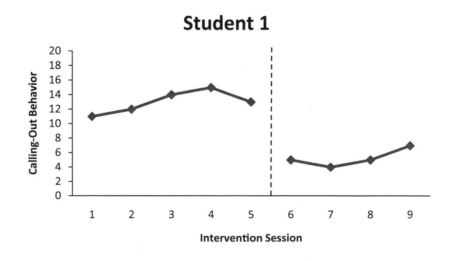

FIGURE A.1. Final A-B graph.

SCREENSHOT A.14. Creating an A-B graph: Editing the axis labels.

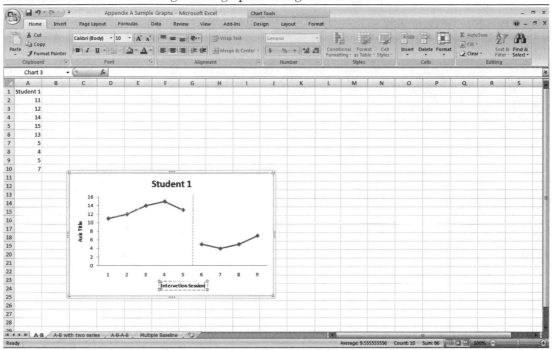

A-B Graph Options: Altering the *X*-Axis Data

1. In some cases it is important to use unique information for the *X*-axis. For example, you may want to note that each data point represents several sessions, specific dates, or show that there is some discontinuity in the data collection. To accomplish this using Microsoft Excel, you must add an additional column of data that will be utilized for the *X*-axis. To accomplish this, aim the pointer at the "A" at the top of the A column and press the right mouse button. This opens the menu shown in Screenshot A.15. Select the "Insert" option to create a new column.

SCREENSHOT A.15. A-B graph options: Altering the *X*-axis data I.

2. The result of Step 1 is the creation of a new column. In this column you can place the data to be used for the *X*-axis. In Screenshot A.16, dates have been added. It is important to put the information related to a specific data point to the immediate left of that data point. For example, on January 11th the target child called out 14 times.

SCREENSHOT A.16. A-B graph options: Altering the *X*-axis data II.

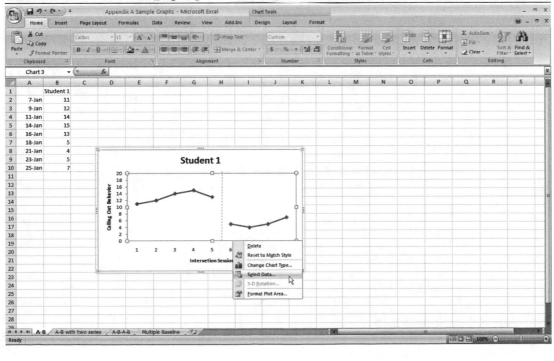

3. After the new column has been created and the new data for the *X*-axis entered appropriately, the chart can be altered. To accomplish this, aim the pointer at the *X*-axis and press the right mouse button. This opens the menu shown in Screenshot A.17. Choose the "Select Data" option.

SCREENSHOT A.17. A-B graph options: Altering the *X*-axis data III.

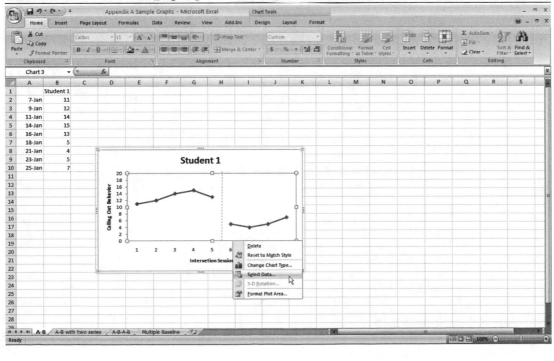

4. Successfully completing Step 3 opens the "Select Data Source" menu box. Notice that there are two places in which information can be entered. To alter the *X*-axis data, press the "Edit" button below "Horizontal (Category) Axis Labels" (see Screenshot A.18). This process opens the "Axis Labels" menu box shown in Screenshot A.19. At this point, select the new data (cells A2 to A10 in this example) as done in Step 2 of the "Creating a Basic A-B Graph" in this appendix. Then, press the "OK" button in the lower right corner of the "Axis Labels" menu box, and finally, click the "OK" button in the "Select Data Source" menu box (see Screenshot A.20).

SCREENSHOT A.18. A-B graph options: Altering the *X*-axis data IV.

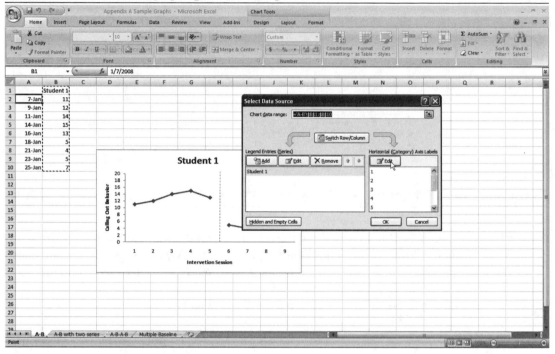

SCREENSHOT A.19. A-B graph options: Altering the *X*-axis data V.

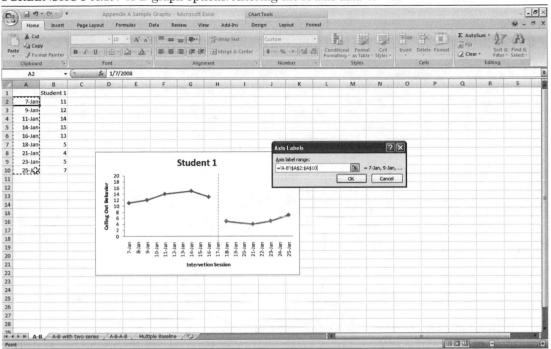

SCREENSHOT A.20. A-B graph options: Altering the *X*-axis data VI.

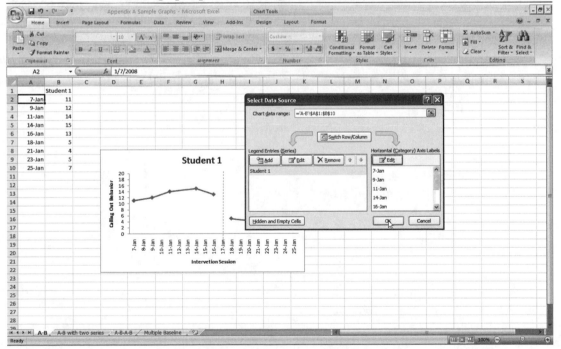

5. The successful completion of Step 4 changes the *X*-axis so that dates are now utilized rather than simply 1 to 7 as before. In many cases, the program alters the dates, though, and additional editing may be required. To edit the *X*-axis, aim the pointer at the axis and press the right mouse

button. This process opens the menu as shown in Screenshot A.21. Select the "Format Axis" option.

SCREENSHOT A.21. A-B graph options: Altering the *X*-axis data VII.

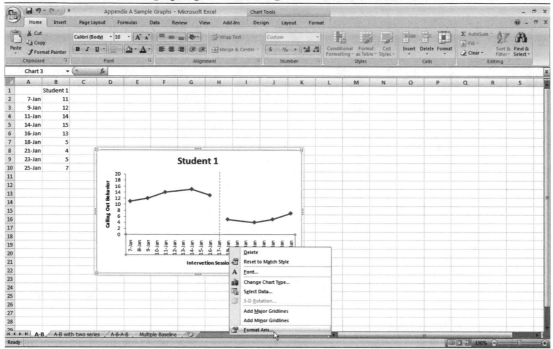

6. Step 5 opens the "Format Axis" menu box as shown in Screenshot A.22. To remove the added dates, select the "Text axis" option. Notice that a number of options can be altered in this menu box. To finalize the change(s), click the "Close" button in the lower right corner.

SCREENSHOT A.22. A-B graph options: Altering the *X*-axis data VIII.

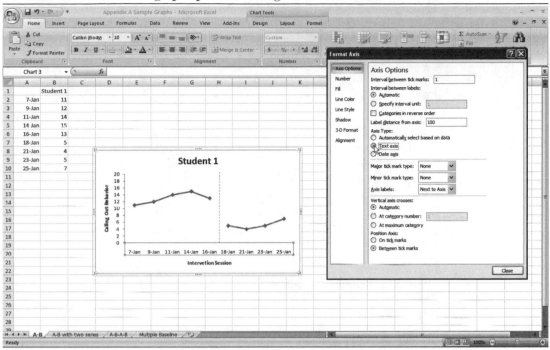

A-B Graph Options: Changing the Scale

1. At times it is desirable to change the scale on the *Y*-axis. To accomplish this, aim the pointer at the numbers on the *Y*-axis that you want to alter and press the right mouse button to open the menu options shown in Screenshot A.23. Select the "Format Axis" option.

SCREENSHOT A.23. A-B graph options: Changing the scale I.

2. After selecting the "Format Axis" option, the menu in Screenshot A.24 opens. On the left side, select the "Axis Options" tab. In order to change the maximum value on the scale, for example, click the "Fixed" option in the "Maximum" row as shown in Screenshot A.24. Then, in the text box input the maximum value that you want to select. You can also change the minimum value, major unit (the jump in scale from the lowest to highest number), as well as many other options. Another change than can be made using this menu is the value where the X- and Y-axes intersect. By selecting the "Axis value" option in the "Horizontal axis crosses" section and inputting–1 in the text box, the value of 0 will be placed above the X-axis. When you are finished changing the axis, select the "Close" button on the bottom right.

SCREENSHOT A.24. A-B graph options: Changing the scale II.

A-B Graph Options: Two Data Series on a Single A-B Graph

1. In some situations it is desirable to present two data series on the same A-B graph. Note, it is important that these series of outcome data are on the same scale (e.g., direct behavior ratings [DBR] of on-task and disruptive behavior, or frequency counts of calling out and throwing objects). To accomplish this, start back at Step 1 in "Creating a Basic A-B Graph." Rather than using one series of data, input two data series as shown in Screenshot A.25. Follow Step 1 and Step 2 as you would to create a basic A-B graph.

SCREENSHOT A.25. A-B graph options: Two data series on a single A-B graph I.

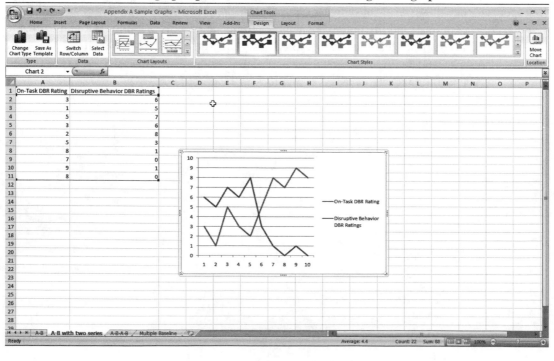

2. The result of Step 1 produces the graph shown in Screenshot A.26. This graph can be altered in the same manner as a basic A-B graph.

SCREENSHOT A.26. A-B graph options: Two data series on a single A-B graph II.

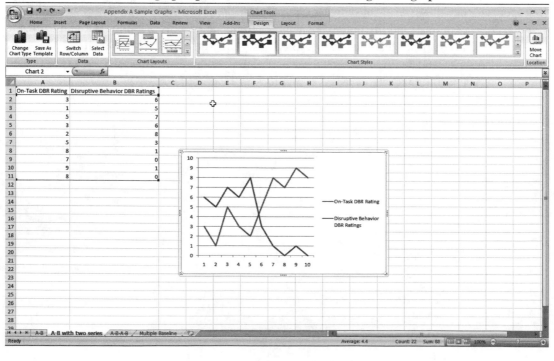

CREATING AN A-B-A-B GRAPH

1. The steps to creating an A-B-A-B graph are the same as "Creating a Basic A-B Graph," but with a bit more complexity. As shown in Screenshot A.27, the data should be entered vertically in column A, with the name of the student in cell A1. Note that all four phases are in column A.

SCREENSHOT A.27. Creating an A-B-A-B graph: Data entry.

2. Follow Steps 2–4 of "Creating a Basic A-B Graph." This creates a graph as shown in Screenshot A.28. As you can see, the A-B-A-B data series is now presented in a line graph format.

SCREENSHOT A.28. Creating an A-B-A-B graph: Basic line graph.

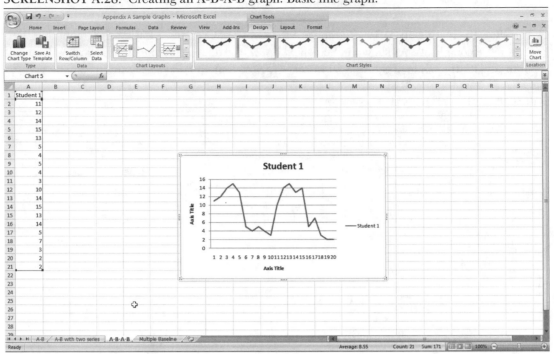

3. Follow Steps 5–7 of "Creating a Basic A-B Graph." At this point you are ready to remove the line between the phases. The only difference in this step for an A-B-A-B graph as compared to the basic A-B graph (Steps 8 and 9) is that three lines need to be removed. Follow these steps for the three-phase change. This creates a graph as shown in Screenshot A.29.

SCREENSHOT A.29. Creating an A-B-A-B graph: Graph with data markers and phase breaks.

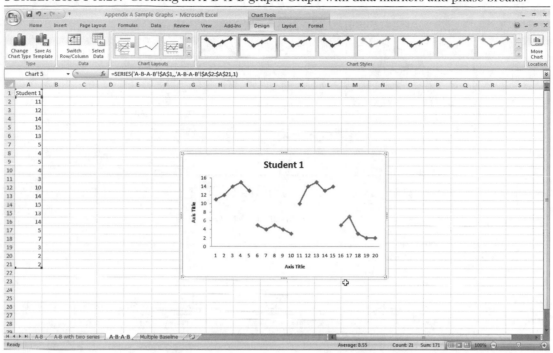

4. As with the line-removal step, the dashed vertical line creation process (Steps 10–12 in "Creating a Basic A-B Graph") must be repeated three times for each phase change. One shortcut to assist in this process is to "cut and paste" the second and third lines after the first dashed line has been created. This is accomplished by pointing the pointer at the line and pressing the left mouse button (which selects the line). Then press the "Ctrl" and "C" buttons on the keyboard simultaneously to copy the line. Next, press the "Ctrl" and "V" buttons on the keyboard simultaneously to paste the line. This process creates an exact replica of the first line. Next, move the pointer to the new line and press and hold the left mouse button. You can now drag (by moving the mouse) the new line to the appropriate location. If you want to make minor adjustments to the placement of the line, use the arrow keys on the keyboard while the line is selected. This will "nudge" the line slightly in the selected direction. Repeat for the final dashed line demarcating a phase change. The final product is shown in Screenshot A.30. At this point you can alter as with a basic A-B graph. This completes the process of creating an A-B-A-B graph (see Figure A.2). This graph can now be moved into other programs or simply printed out for a variety of uses.

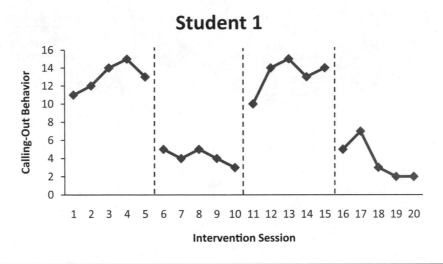

FIGURE A.2. Final A-B-A-B graph.

SCREENSHOT A.30. Creating an A-B-A-B graph: Graph with phase-change dashed lines.

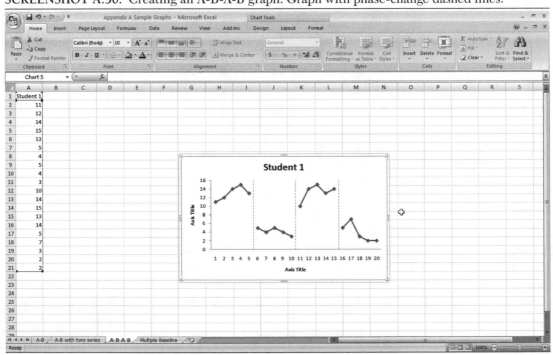

CREATING A MULTIPLE-BASELINE GRAPH

1. To create an MB graph begin by creating multiple A-B graphs in roughly the same manner as presented previously. A few general issues need to be noted. First, the A-B graph that presents the case where the intervention is applied first should be placed at the top. This should be followed by the A-B graph presenting the case where the intervention is applied second and so on.

will aid in the process of transferring the graphs to Microsoft Word. Second, the scale for each of the A-B graphs should be the same (this is not mandatory, but suggested). To accomplish this, follow the steps in the "A-B Graph Options: Changing the Scale" sections. Third, you will not want an *X*-axis for any of the A-B graphs that will be used in the MB graph. While one would think that in the bottom graph you would want the axis label, it will actually change the size of the final A-B graph causing it to be smaller than the other A-B graphs in the full MB graph. Finally, rather than labeling the *Y*-axis as the outcome variable, use that axis label to put in the student or condition number. In the end, you should have a spreadsheet that looks like Screenshot A.31.

SCREENSHOT A.31. Creating an MB graph: Data entry and three A-B graphs.

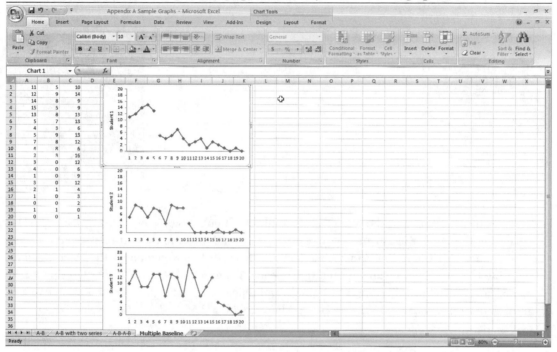

2. The next step is to move the graphs to a program like Microsoft Word for formatting. To accomplish this using Microsoft Word, begin by opening a new document. Once opened, minimize this program and go back to Microsoft Excel, and "copy" the first A-B graph by aiming the pointer at the edge of the graph and pressing the left mouse button. Next, press the "Ctrl" and "C" buttons on the keyboard simultaneously to copy the graph. Now, go back to the Word document and paste the A-B graph in by pressing the "Ctrl" and "V" buttons on the keyboard simultaneously. This results in the A-B graph being copied into the Word document. Repeat this process with the second and third A-B graphs. Screenshot A.32 shows the results of this sequence.

SCREENSHOT A.32. Creating an MB graph: Three A-B graphs in Microsoft Word.

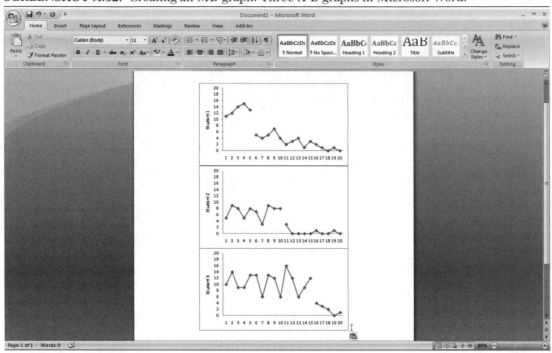

3. Next, each A-B graph must be resized so that all will fit on a single page. This is accomplished by aiming the pointer at any of the three A-B graphs and pressing the left mouse button. This action opens the "Chart Tools" toolbar. Select the "Format" tab, which opens the "Size" toolbar. By using that toolbar you can alter the size of each A-B graph. Alter (it is suggested that a 2.5″ × 4.5″ size is used in a three-part MB graph) and repeat the process for the remaining two A-B graphs. In Screenshot A.33, this process is shown, with a 2.5″ × 4.5″ graph selected for each A-B graph.

SCREENSHOT A.33. Creating an MB graph: Resizing the A-B graphs.

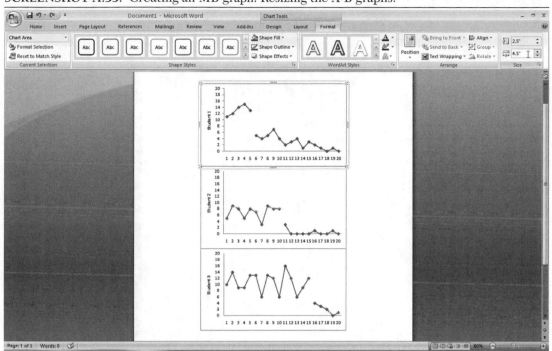

4. Next, the border around each A-B graph needs to be removed. Aim the pointer at the border of the first A-B graph and press the left mouse button. This selects the border and opens the "Chart Tools" toolbar. Select the "Format" tab and then "Shape Outline" and finally, "No Outline." This process, shown in Screenshot A.34, removes the border. Repeat this process for each A-B graph in the MB design. Screenshot A.35 shows the result of the entire sequence.

SCREENSHOT A.34. Creating an MB graph: Removing the borders of the A-B graphs.

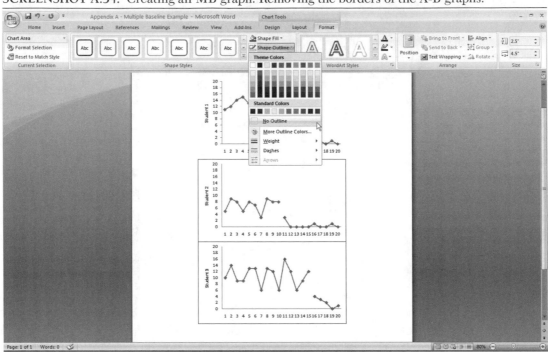

SCREENSHOT A.35. Creating an MB graph: A-B graphs with borders removed.

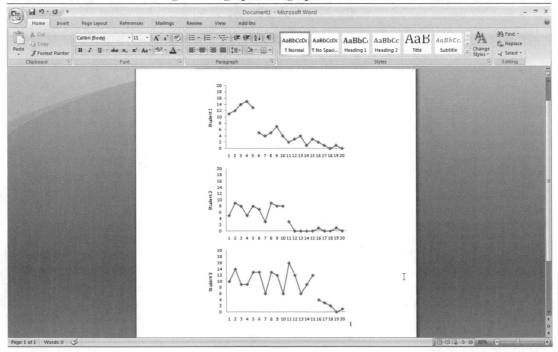

5. Screenshots A.36–A.40 show the process of adding a phase-change line in the standard MB format. The process is similar to that used in a simple A-B graph (Steps 10–12 in "Creating a Basic A-B Graph"). Begin by moving the pointer to the "Insert" tab and press the left mouse button.

Then, move the pointer to the "Shapes" button and press the left mouse button. Finally, under "Lines" select the "Elbow Connector" option shown in Screenshot A.36 by aiming the pointer at that icon, and clicking the left mouse button.

SCREENSHOT A.36. Creating an MB graph: Inserting a phase-change line I.

6. Step 5 results in the pointer changing into a cross. Place the cross at the top of the first A-B graph where the phase-change line should be placed, then press and hold the left mouse button. Next, while holding down the left mouse button, drag the cross straight down, and then to the right. The result of these actions is the creation of a stair-step line. Continue this motion to the bottom of the second A-B graph in between the phase change for that condition (see Screenshot A.37). Once you release the left mouse button, you will notice that three diamonds appear (a green diamond at the top and bottom of the line, and a yellow diamond in the middle of the stair). By aiming the pointer at either of the green diamonds, and pressing/holding the left mouse button, you can move just that segment of the three-part line. If you do the same action with the yellow diamond on the stair, you can move that stair up or down (see Screenshot A.38). Using these functions, you can alter the stair as needed.

SCREENSHOT A.37. Creating an MB graph: Inserting a phase-change line II.

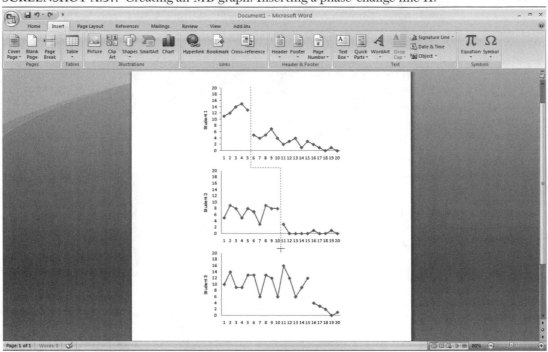

SCREENSHOT A.38. Creating an MB graph: Inserting a phase-change line III.

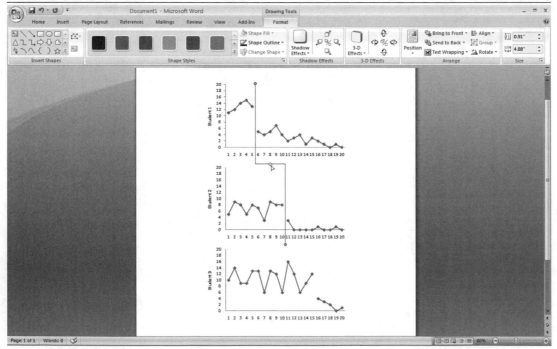

7. Next, repeat Steps 5 and 6 to produce the second stair (see Screenshot A.39). Make sure to line up the second line with the first elbow connector.

SCREENSHOT A.39. Creating an MB graph: Inserting a phase-change line IV.

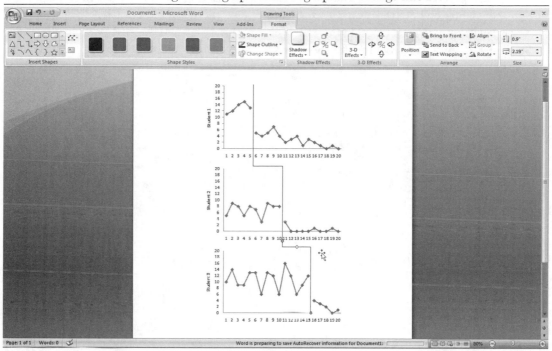

8. Finally, make the two elbow connector lines dashed. To do so, aim the pointer at one of the lines and press the left mouse button. Next, select the "Shape Outline" option on the toolbar. Then, select the "Dashes" option. Finally, select the dashed line option as shown in Screenshot A.40.

SCREENSHOT A.40. Creating an MB graph: Inserting a phase-change line V.

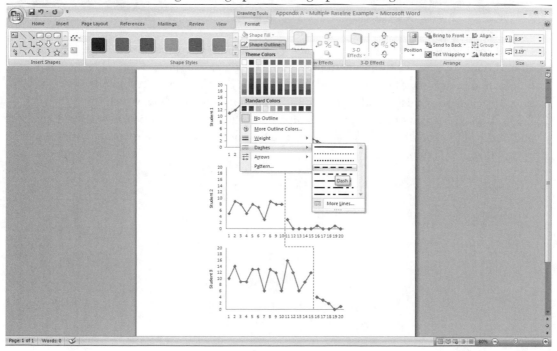

9. The final step in developing MB graphs using Microsoft Excel and Microsoft Word is the process of placing labels on both the *X*- and *Y*-axes. At this point, there is no *X*-axis label and the current *Y*-axis labels refer to each target in the MB design (in this case, an MB across-participant design, Student 1, 2, and 3). We begin with the *X*-axis. To add a label, select the "Insert" tab, then the "Text Box" button, and finally, the first option, which is a "Simple Text Box" (see Screenshot A.41).

SCREENSHOT A.41. Creating an MB graph: Creating axis labels—inserting a text box.

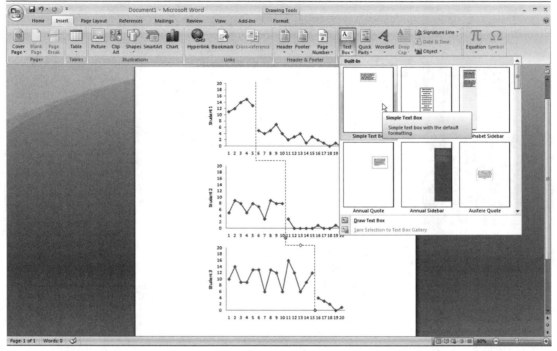

10. Step 9 creates a text box that can immediately be edited to the correct label. The text box can be altered at any time in the future by simply aiming the pointer at the text, pressing the left mouse button, and then typing in the new text. This text box can then be moved into the correct location. To accomplish this, aim the pointer at the border of the text box, which turns the pointer into a cross with arrows pointing in each direction. After this cross appears, press and hold the left mouse button, and then move the text box to the correct location. Screenshot A.42 shows the completion of this step.

SCREENSHOT A.42. Creating an MB graph: Creating axis labels—editing a text box.

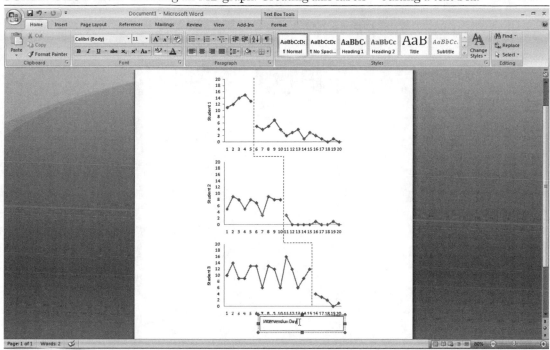

11. The final step for the *X*-axis label is to remove the border. To remove the border, aim the pointer at the text box border and press the right mouse button. This action opens up the "Text Box Tools" toolbar and the "Format" tab. The next step is shown in Screenshot A.43. Select the "Shape Outline" button and then the "No Outline" option. This removes the border.

SCREENSHOT A.43. Creating an MB graph: Creating axis labels—removing the text box border.

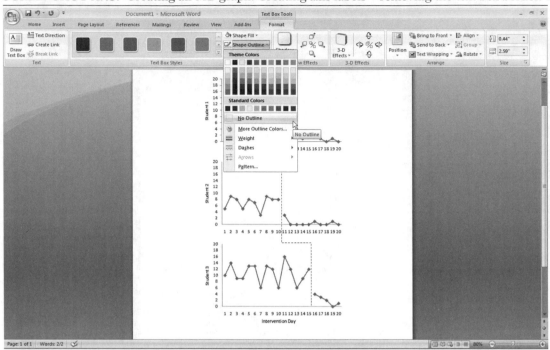

12. The process of placing a label on the Y-axis begins by repeating Steps 9–11, which creates a second label. The next step is to alter the text direction. Select the "Text Box Tools" toolbar and then the "Format" tab. As shown in Screenshot A.44, select the "Text Direction" button twice. The result is shown in Screenshot A.45. Once the text box has been rotated appropriately, simply move it to the right location. This completes the process of building an MB graph (see Figure A.3).

SCREENSHOT A.44. Creating an MB graph: Creating the Y-axis label.

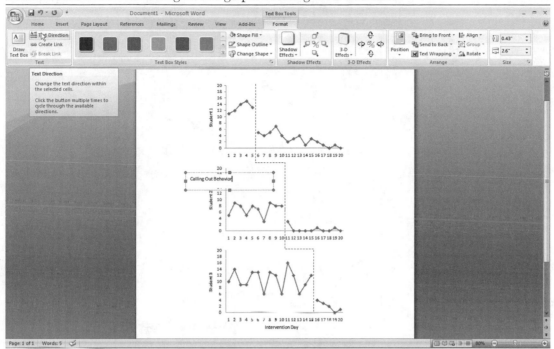

SCREENSHOT A.45. Creating an MB graph: Rotating and placing the Y-axis label.

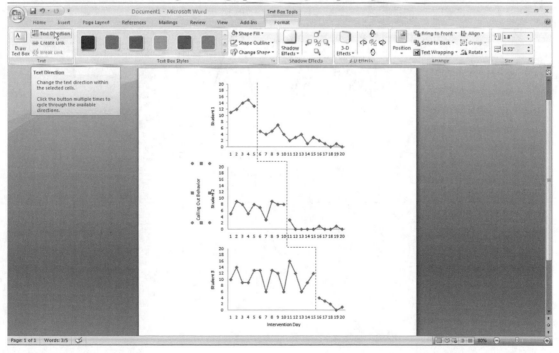

Appendix A

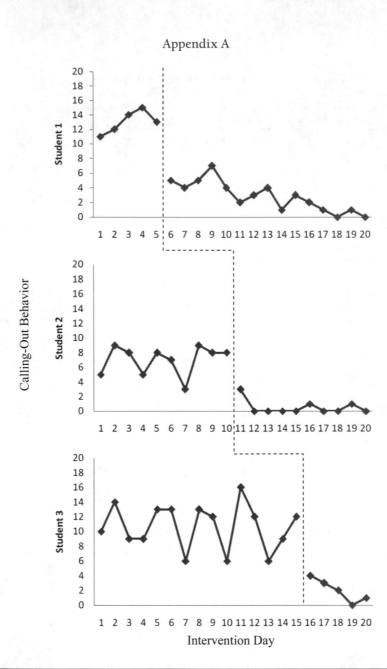

FIGURE A.3. Final MB graph.

APPENDIX B

Sample Analysis Techniques with Microsoft Excel

Another benefit of using software such as Microsoft Excel is that some analysis techniques can be accomplished rather easily within the program. In this appendix, we build on the SCD graphs presented in Appendix A to examine three simple ways to estimate level, variability, and trend. This appendix is not intended to present an exhaustive list of methods to compute level, variability, and trend. This is simply a sampling of analysis strategies that can be accomplished using Microsoft Excel. In addition, these methods are not intended to replace visual analysis. Rather, these methods are presented to assist as part of a comprehensive analysis strategy.

ESTIMATING LEVEL

1. To estimate the phase level in terms of a mean, begin by entering the outcome data into the worksheet as shown in Screenshot B.1. The data should be entered vertically in column A, with the name of the student in cell A1.

SCREENSHOT B.1. Estimating level: Data entry.

2. The mean (or any other result of a formula) is placed into any empty cell in the worksheet. In Screenshot B.2, cell B6 has been selected as it is to the right of the last data point in phase A. Next, we use the "Function Wizard (f_x)" command as shown in Screenshot B.2. Aim the pointer at the "Function Wizard" button and click the left mouse button.

SCREENSHOT B.2. Estimating level: Using the Function Wizard I.

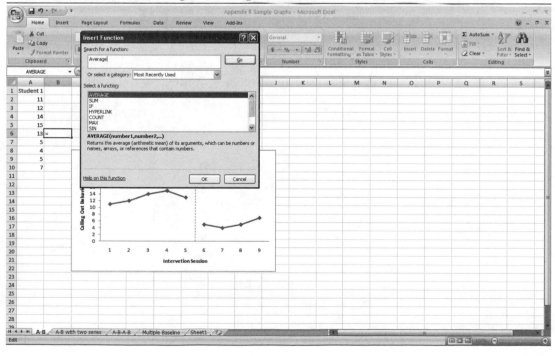

3. The "Function Wizard" menu box opens after Step 2 (see Screenshot B.3). In the "Search for a function" box, type in "Average." This searches for the "AVERAGE" function. Select the "AVERAGE" function and click the "OK" button in the bottom right of the menu box.

SCREENSHOT B.3. Estimating level: Using the Function Wizard II.

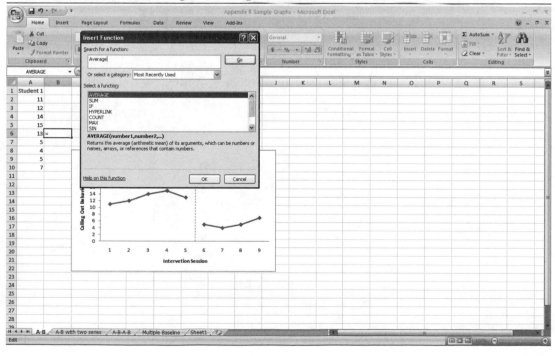

4. The actions in Step 3 result in opening the "Function Arguments" menu box. There are two
   places where information can be entered. To the right of the text box associated with Number 1
   there is a button that looks like a small worksheet. As shown in Screenshot B.4, aim the pointer
   at that "worksheet" button and click the left mouse button.

SCREENSHOT B.4. Estimating level: Function Arguments I.

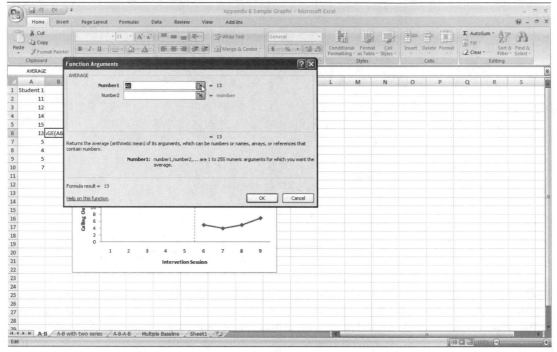

5. Completion of Step 4 results in opening a smaller "Function Arguments" menu box. Now, select
   the phase data that will be utilized in the computation of a mean. To accomplish this, place the
   pointer on the first data point (cell A2 in Screenshot B.5) and then press the left mouse button,
   hold it down, move the pointer to the bottom of the data (cell A6 in Screenshot B.5) and release
   the left mouse button. Next, close this "Function Arguments" menu box by clicking the "X" button in the upper right corner.

SCREENSHOT B.5. Estimating level: Function arguments II.

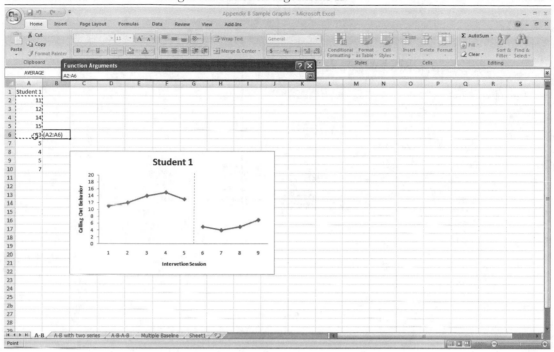

6. Finally, close the main "Function Arguments" menu box by pressing the "OK" button in the bottom right corner (see Screenshot B.6). This results in the mean of the phase being placed in the cell originally selected in Step 2 (see Screenshot B.7). Steps 1–6 can then be repeated for each additional phase for which the computation of a mean would be useful. In this example, the process for computing a mean is repeated once for phase B (see Screenshot B.8).

SCREENSHOT B.6. Estimating level: Function Arguments III.

SCREENSHOT B.7. Estimating level: Results I.

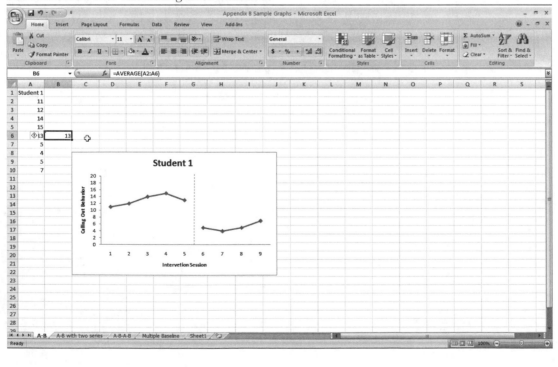

SCREENSHOT B.8. Estimating level: Results II.

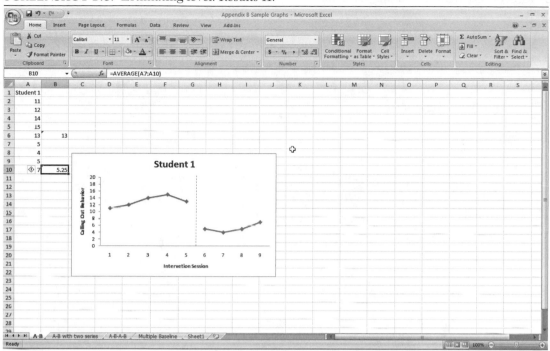

ESTIMATING VARIABILITY

1. To estimate the percentage of nonoverlapping data points (PND), a simple formula is used in Microsoft Excel. To begin, examine the data in the first comparison phase (see phase A in Screenshot B.9) and depending on the predicted effect of the intervention, select the most extreme (lowest or highest) value. In our example, the intervention was intended to reduce the rate of behavior, and thus the lowest number in phase A (11) is selected. Place this number in any cell (cell C6 is utilized in Screenshot B.9).

SCREENSHOT B.9. Estimating variability: Results.

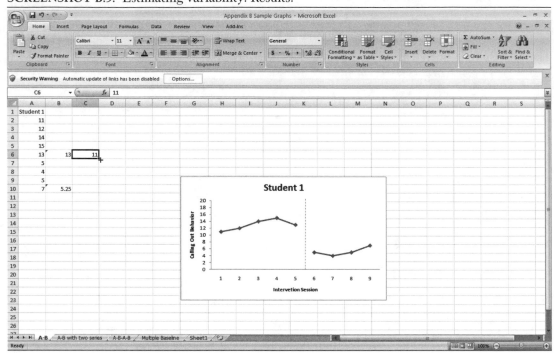

2. We again use the "Function Wizard (f_x)" command. Aim the pointer at the "Function Wizard" button and click the left mouse button. The "Function Wizard" menu box opens. In the "Search for a function" box, type in "Countif." This searches for the "COUNTIF" function that is utilized for the computation of PND. Select the "COUNTIF" function and click the "OK" button in the bottom right of the menu box (see Screenshot B.10).

SCREENSHOT B.10. Estimating variability: Function Wizard I.

3. Step 2 opens the "Function Arguments" menu box for the "COUNTIF" command (see Screenshot B.11). Notice that two text boxes require information: "Range" and "Criteria." First, select the range for the "COUNTIF" function (use the same process as Steps 5 and 6 in the Estimating Level section of this appendix). The range is the data in the second phase (phase B in this example).

SCREENSHOT B.11. Estimating variability: Function Wizard II.

4. After the range is selected, it is time to set the countif criteria. In this example, we are interested in the number of data points in phase B below the most extreme data point (lowest, or 11) in phase A. Thus, we set the criteria to <11 (see Screenshot B.12). Remember that in the case of an intervention with the goal to increase the outcome data the criteria would be > the most extreme data.

SCREENSHOT B.12. Estimating variability: Function Wizard III.

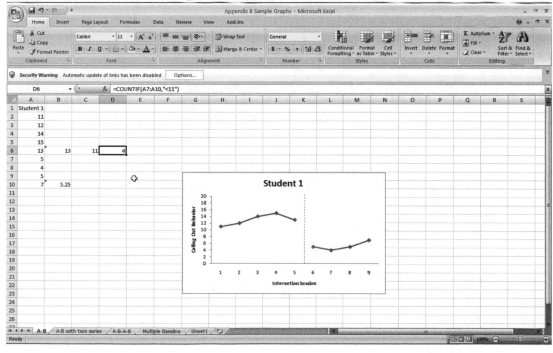

5. The result of Step 4 is shown in Screenshot B.13. In this case, all data points (4) in phase B are below the most extreme point in phase A (11). As such, the number 4 is displayed in the selected cell.

SCREENSHOT B.13. Estimating variability: Countif results.

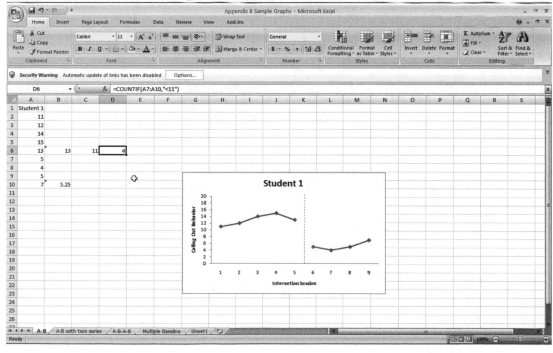

6. The final step in the process to compute PND is to turn the "COUNTIF" function results into a percentage. This is done by dividing the countif results by the total number of data points in the phase for which those results are related (phase B in this example). This is accomplished by altering the formula. To do this, aim the pointer at the "Formula Bar" and click the left mouse button. This process enables you to type the required changes to the formula. The final formula for PND is =(Countif (phase A data range, "stipulation")/number of phase B data points). In this example, the formula is =(COUNTIF(A7:A10,"<11")/4). See Screenshot B.14 for both the final PND formula and the results of this process (in cell D6). For an example where there is some overlap between phases, see Screenshot B.15. In this example, the first data point in phase B was changed to 11, which overlaps the lowest data point in phase A (11). As a result, one of the four data points in phase B now overlaps with phase A, and the PND is reduced to .75, or 75%.

SCREENSHOT B.14. Estimating variability: Computing PND I.

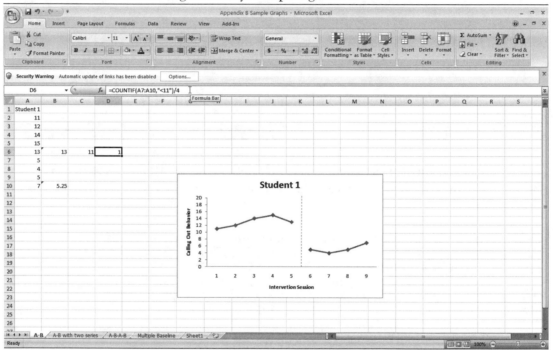

SCREENSHOT B.15. Estimating variability: Computing PND II.

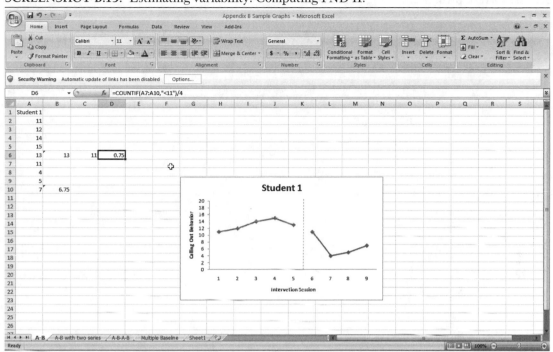

ESTIMATING TREND

1. As discussed in Chapter 6, it is a rather simple process to estimate the slope of a series of SCD data using Microsoft Excel if the interval is a consistent time unit (e.g., if sessions were used with two session intervals for each week, then the resulting slope computed with this process would be incorrect). Using the same example as in Chapter 6, we begin with the process of computing a slope. In this example, a student's reading progress was monitored on a weekly basis with curriculum-based measures of his oral reading fluency. The first five data points were collected in the baseline phase and the remaining eight data points were collected during the intervention phase, for a total of 13 weeks of data. Set up the data as in Screenshot B.16.

SCREENSHOT B.16. Estimating trend: Data entry.

	A	B	C	D	E	F	G	H	I	J	K	L	M	N
1		Baseline	Baseline	Baseline	Baseline	Baseline	Intervention	Intervention	Intervention	Intervention	Intervention	Intervention	Intervention	Intervention
2	WC/M	10	14	8	11	12	17	19	15	25	30	36	34	35
3	Weeks	1	2	3	4	5	6	7	8	9	10	11	12	13

2. We begin by computing the slope for the baseline phase. Select a cell to display the slope. In the current example, cell F4 is selected. Aim the pointer at the "Function Wizard" button and click the left mouse button. Using the Function Wizard, search for the "SLOPE" function. Next, select "SLOPE" and press the "OK" button. Screenshot B.17 shows this process.

SCREENSHOT B.17. Estimating trend: Function Wizard I.

3. Step 3 opens the "Function Arguments" menu box for the "SLOPE" command. Notice that two boxes need information: "Known_y's" and "Known_x's". Known_y's refers to the outcome data, or in our example, cells B2 to F2 (the baseline phase). Known_x's refers to the data in column A, or in our example, cells B3 to F3. Select each relevant range as in Steps 5 and 6 in the "Estimating Level" section of this appendix. The results of this process are shown in Screenshot B.18. Press the "OK" button in the bottom right of the window, and the slope is displayed in the cell selected in Step 3 (see Screenshot B.19). These steps can be repeated for each additional phase if relevant. In our example, the slope was as computed for the intervention phase (cells G2 to N2) as shown in Screenshot B.20.

SCREENSHOT B.18. Estimating trend: Function Wizard II.

SCREENSHOT B.19. Estimating trend: Final for baseline slope.

SCREENSHOT B.20. Estimating trend: Final for baseline and intervention slope.

	A	B	C	D	E	F	G	H	I	J	K	L	M	N	O	P	Q
1		Baseline	Baseline	Baseline	Baseline	Baseline	Intervention	Intervention	Intervention	Intervention	Intervention	Intervention	Intervention	Intervention			
2	WC/M	10	14	8	11	12	17	19	15	25	30	36	34	35			
3	Weeks	1	2	3	4	5	6	7	8	9	10	11	12	13			
4						0.10								3.20			

N4 ▾ fx =SLOPE(G2:N2,G3:N3)

Sheet tabs: A-B-A-B / Multiple Baseline / **Chapter 6 Slope Example** / Chapter 6 Classwide Slope

ESTIMATING TREND FOR A WHOLE CLASS

1. The advantage of computing slope in this manner is that the rate of student growth can then be interpreted by comparing it to the average for the student's respective grade and/or class. To determine a classwide mean slope value, simply set up the data as shown in Screenshot B.21. The numbers in the first three columns (A, B, and C) are the data for each student's benchmark reading assessment. For example, the first student (row 2) read 7 WCPM during the fall benchmark assessment, 10 during the winter assessment, and 31 WCPM at the spring benchmark assessment. Entered into columns E, F, and G are the numbers that represent the weeks. The first assessment occurred during the second week of the school year, the second was 16 weeks later, or the 18th week of the year, and the final one was an additional 16 weeks after that (34th week of the year). The weeks of the year can be dragged into the subsequent cells by highlighting all three boxes and dragging them into the cells below.

SCREENSHOT B.21. Estimating trend for a whole class: Data entry.

	A	B	C	D	E	F	G	H	I
1		A	B	C	D	E	F	G	H
2	1	Fall	Winter	Spring		Week	Week	Week	Slope
3	2	7	10	31		2	18	34	
4	3	4	7	8		2	18	34	
5	4	9	17	13		2	18	34	
6	5	13	16	18		2	18	34	
7	6	5	6	19		2	18	34	
8	7	13	29	71		2	18	34	
9	8	24	71	82		2	18	34	
10	9	6	35	65		2	18	34	
11	10	10	67	84		2	18	34	
12	11	10	14	38		2	18	34	
13	12	11	12	27		2	18	34	
14	13	23	60	74		2	18	34	
15	14	31	45	61		2	18	34	
16	15	5	8	16		2	18	34	
17	16	14	25	55		2	18	34	
18	17	30	88	105		2	18	34	
19	18	19	32	65		2	18	34	
20	19	24	52	82		2	18	34	
21	20	25	59	78		2	18	34	
22	21	26	60	67		2	18	34	
23	22	15.45	35.65	52.95					

2. Next, insert the "SLOPE" function in the empty column in H, use the data in cells A, B, and C as the dependent data (*Y*) and the data in columns E, F, and G as the independent (*X*) variables (see Screenshot B.22). The results of this process are shown in Screenshot B.23.

SCREENSHOT B.22. Estimating trend for a whole class: Computing slope I.

Formula bar: =SLOPE(B3:D3,F3:H3)

Function Arguments — SLOPE
Known_y's B3:D3 = {7,10,31}
Known_x's F3:H3 = {2,18,34}
= 0.75
Returns the slope of the linear regression line through the given data points.
Known_x's is the set of independent data points and can be numbers or names, arrays, or references that contain numbers.
Formula result = 0.75
Help on this function   OK   Cancel

SCREENSHOT B.23. Estimating trend for a whole class: Computing slope II.

3. Finally, drag the "SLOPE" formula into the desired cells (cells I4–I21 in our example). For analysis purposes, the class slope average is computed and displayed in cell I23. Screenshot B.24 shows the results of Steps 1–3.

SCREENSHOT B.24. Estimating trend for a whole class: Final.

References

Aaron, P. G. (1997). The impending demise of the discrepancy formula. *Review of Educational Research*, *67*, 461–502.

Alberto, P. A., & Troutman, A. C. (2003). *Applied behavior analysis for teachers*. Saddle River, NJ: Merrill Prentice Hall.

American Psychological Association. (2001). *Publication manual of the American Psychological Association* (5th ed.). Washington, DC: Author.

Audi, R. (Ed.). (1999). *The Cambridge dictionary of philosophy* (2nd ed.). New York: Cambridge University Press.

Baer, D. M., Wolf, M. M., & Risley, T. R. (1968). Some current dimensions of applied behavior analysis. *Journal of Applied Behavior Analysis*, *1*, 91–97.

Barnett, D. W., Daly, E. J., III, Jones, K. M., & Lentz, F. E., Jr. (2004). Empirically-based special service decisions from increasing and decreasing intensity single-case designs. *Journal of Special Education*, *38*, 66–79.

Baron, A., & Derenne, A. (2000). Quantitative summaries of single-subject studies: What do group comparisons tell us about individual performances? *Behavior Analyst*, *23*, 101–106.

Begeny, J. C., & Martens, B. K. (2006). Assessing pre-service teachers' training in empirically-validated behavioral instruction practices. *School Psychology Quarterly*, *21*(3), 262–285.

Berninger, V. W. (2006). Research-supported ideas for implementing reauthorized IDEA with intelligent professional psychological services. *Psychology in the Schools*, *43*(7), 781–796.

Boren, J. J. (1963). The repeated acquisition of new behavioral chains. *American Psychologist*, *18*, 421.

Bowen, J., Jenson, W. R., & Clark, E. (2003). *School-based interventions for students with behavior problems*. New York: Springer.

Bramlett, R. K., Murphy, J. J., Johnson, J., Wallingford, L., & Hall, J. D. (2002). Contemporary practices in school psychology: A national survey of roles and referral problems. *Psychology in the Schools*, *39*, 327–335.

Brossart, D. F., Parker, R. I., Olson, E. A., & Mahadevan, L. (2006). The relationship between visual analysis and five statistical analyses in a simple AB single-case research design. *Behavior Modification*, *30*(5), 531–563.

Brown-Chidsey, R., & Steege, M. W. (2005). *Response to intervention: Principles and strategies for effective practice*. New York: Guilford Press.

Burns, M. K. (2007). RTI WILL fail, unless. . . . *NASP Communiqué*, *35*(5), 38–40.

Burns, M. K., & Coolong-Chaffin, M. (2006). Response to intervention: The role of and effect on school psychology. *School Psychology Forum*, *1*, 1–10.

Burns, M. K., Deno, S. L., & Jimerson, S. R. (2007). Toward a unified response-to-intervention model. In

S. R. Jimerson, M. K. Burns, & A. M. VanDerHeyden (Eds.), *Handbook of response to intervention: The science and practice of assessment and intervention* (pp. 428–440). New York: Springer.

Burns, M. K., Ganuza, Z. M., & London, R. M. (in press). Brief experimental analysis of written letter formation: Single-case demonstration. *Journal of Behavioral Education.*

Burns, M. K., & Gibbons, K. (2008). *Implementing response-to-intervention in elementary and secondary schools: Procedures to assure scientific-based practices.* New York: Routledge Press.

Burns, M. K., Hall-Lande, J., Lyman, W., Rogers, C., & Tan, C. S. (2006). Tier II interventions within response-to-intervention: Components of an effective approach. *NASP Communiqué, 35*(4), 38–40.

Burns, M. K., & Scholin, S. E. (2008, February). *Reliability of response to intervention decision-making frameworks.* Poster presented at the National Association of School Psychologists Annual Convention, New Orleans, LA.

Burns, M. K., Scholin, S. E., Koscielek, S., & Livingston, J. (2008, February). *Reliability of decision-making frameworks within response to intervention.* Poster presented at the National Association of School Psychologists Annual Convention, New Orleans, LA.

Burns, M. K., & Senesac, B. V. (2005). Comparison of dual discrepancy criteria to assess response to intervention. *Journal of School Psychology, 43*(5), 393–406.

Burns, M. K., & VanDerHeyden, A. M. (2006). Using response to intervention to assess learning disabilities: Introduction to the special series. *Assessment for Effective Intervention, 32,* 3–5.

Burns, M. K., VanDerHeyden, A. M., & Jiban, C. L. (2006). Assessing the instructional level for mathematics: A comparison of methods. *School Psychology Review, 35,* 401–418.

Burns, M. K., Vanderwood, M., & Ruby, S. (2005). Evaluating the readiness of prereferral intervention teams for use in a problem-solving model: Review of three levels of research. *School Psychology Quarterly, 20,* 89–105.

Burns, M. K., & Wagner, D. (2008). Determining an effective intervention within a brief experimental analysis for reading: A meta-analytic review. *School Psychology Review, 37*(1), 126–136.

Burns, M. K., & Ysseldyke, J. E. (in press). Prevalence of evidence-based instructional practices in special education. *Journal of Special Education.*

Busk, P. L., & Marascuilo, L. A. (1988). Autocorrelation in single-subject research: A counterargument to the myth of no autocorrelation. *Behavioral Assessment, 10*(3), 229–242.

Busk, P. L., & Serlin, R. C. (1992). Meta-analysis for single-case research. In T. R. Kratochwill & J. R. Levin (Eds.), *Single-case research design and analysis: New directions for psychology and education* (pp. 187–212). Hillsdale, NJ: Erlbaum.

Campbell, D. T., & Stanley, J. C. (1966). *Experimental and quasi-experimental designs for research.* Chicago: Rand McNally.

Carson, P. M., & Eckert, T. L. (2003). An experimental analysis of mathematics instructional components: Examining the effects of student-selected versus empirically-selected interventions. *Journal of Behavioral Education, 12,* 35–54.

Carter, S. L., Devlin, S., Doggett, R. A., Harber, M. M., & Barr, C. (2004). Determining the influence of tangible items on screaming and hand mouthing following an inconclusive functional analysis. *Behavioral Interventions, 19,* 51–58.

Cates, G. L., Skinner, C. H., Watson, T. S., Smith, T. L., Weaver, A., & Jackson, B. (2003). Instructional effectiveness and instructional efficiency as considerations for data-based decision making: An evaluation of interspersing procedures. *School Psychology Review, 32,* 601–616.

Chafouleas, S. M., Riley-Tillman, T. C., & Eckert, T. (2003). A comparison of school psychologists' acceptability of norm-referenced, curriculum-based, and brief experimental analysis methods to assess reading. *School Psychology Review, 32*(2), 272–281.

Chafouleas, S. M., Riley-Tillman, T. C., & Sugai, G. (2007). *School-based behavioral assessment: Informing instruction and intervention.* New York: Guilford Press.

Christ, T. H. (2007). Experimental control and threats to internal validity of concurrent and nonconcurrent multiple-baseline designs. *Psychology in the Schools, 44,* 451–459.

Christ, T. J. (2006). Short-term estimates of growth using curriculum-based measurement of oral reading fluency: Estimating standard error of the slope to construct confidence intervals. *School Psychology Review, 35,* 128–133.

Cohen, J. (1988). *Statistical power analysis for the behavioral sciences* (2nd ed.). Hillsdale, NJ: Erlbaum.

Cohen, J., & Cohen, P. (1983). *Applied multiple regression/correlation analysis for the behavioral sciences* (2nd ed.). Hillsdale, NJ: Erlbaum.

Cohen, M. R., & Nagel, E. (1934). *An introduction to logic and scientific method.* New York: Harcourt, Brace.

Cooper, H. M., Valentine, J. C., & Charlton, K. (2000). The methodology of meta-analysis. In R. Gersten, E. P. Schiller, & S. Vaughn (Eds.), *Contemporary special education research: Syntheses of the knowledge base on critical instructional issues* (pp. 263–280). Mahwah, NJ: Erlbaum.

Cooper, J. O., Heron, T. E., & Heward, W. L. (2007). *Applied behavior analysis.* Upper Saddle River, NJ: Pearson Education.

Daly, E. J., III, Chafouleas, S. M., & Skinner, C. H. (2005). *Interventions for reading problems: Designing and evaluating effective strategies.* New York: Guilford Press.

Daly, E. J., III, Martens, B. K., Dool, E. J., & Hintze, J. M. (1998). Using brief functional analysis to select interventions for oral reading. *Journal of Behavioral Education, 8,* 203–218.

Daly, E. J., III, Martens, B. K., Hamler, K. R., Dool, E. J., & Eckert, T. L. (1999). A brief experimental analysis for identifying instructional components needed to improve oral reading fluency. *Journal of Applied Behavior Analysis, 32,* 83–94.

Daly, E. J., III, Murdoch, A., Lillenstein, L., Webber, L., & Lentz, F. E. (2002). An examination of methods for testing treatments: Conducting brief experimental analyses of the effects of instructional components on oral reading fluency. *Education and Treatment of Children, 25,* 288–316.

Daly, E. J., III, Witt, J. C., Martens, B. K., & Dool, E. J. (1997). A model for conducting a functional analysis of academic performance problems. *School Psychology Review, 26,* 554–574.

Deno, S. L. (1985). Curriculum-based measurement: The emerging alternative. *Exceptional Children, 52,* 219–232.

Deno, S. L., & Mirkin, P. K. (1977). *Data-based program modification: A manual.* Minneapolis, MN: Leadership Training Institute for Special Education.

Donovan, M. S., & Cross, C. T. (2001). *Minority students in special and gifted education.* Washington, DC: National Academy Press.

Duhon, G. J., Noell, G. H., Witt, J. C., Freeland, J. T., Dufrene, B. A., & Gilbertson, D. N. (2004). Identifying academic skill and performance deficits: The experimental analysis of brief assessments of academic skills. *School Psychology Review, 33,* 429–443.

Eckert, T. L., Ardoin, S. P., Daisey, D. M., & Scarola, M. D. (2000). Empirically evaluating the effectiveness of reading interventions: The use of brief experimental analysis and single-case designs. *Psychology in the Schools, 37,* 463–474.

Eckert, T. L., Ardoin, S. P., Daly, E. J., III, & Martens, B. K. (2002). Improving oral reading fluency: A brief experimental analysis of combining an antecedent intervention with consequences. *Journal of Applied Behavior Analysis, 35,* 271–281.

Education for All Handicapped Children Act. (1975). Pub. L. No. 94-142.

Erchul, W. P., & Martens, B. K. (2002). *School consultation: Conceptual and empirical bases of practice* (2nd ed.). New York: Kluwer Academic/Plenum Publishers.

Fletcher, J. M., Francis, D. J., Shaywitz, S. E., Lyon, G. R., Foorman, B. R., Stuebing, K. K., et al. (1998). Intelligence testing and the discrepancy model for children with learning disabilities. *Learning Disabilities Research and Practice, 13,* 186–203.

Fuchs, D., Fuchs, L. S., & Burish, P. (2000). Peer-assisted learning strategies: An evidence-based practice to promote reading achievement. *Learning Disabilities Research and Practice, 15,* 85–91.

Fuchs, D., Mock, D., Morgan, P. L., & Young, C. L. (2003). Responsiveness-to-intervention: Definitions, evidence, and implications for the learning disabilities construct. *Learning Disabilities Research and Practice, 18,* 157–171.

Fuchs, L. S. (2003). Assessing intervention responsiveness: Conceptual and technical issues. *Learning Disabilities Research and Practice, 18*, 172–186.

Gerber, M. M., & Semmel, M. I. (1984). Teacher as imperfect test: Reconceptualizing the referral process. *Educational Psychologist, 19*(3), 137–149.

Glass, G. V. (1976). Primary, secondary, and meta-analysis of research. *Educational Researcher, 5*, 3–8.

Graham, S., Harris, K. R., & MacArthur, C. (2004). Writing instruction. In B. Y. Wong (Ed.), *Learning about learning disabilities* (3rd ed., pp. 281–313). San Diego, CA: Elsevier Academic Press.

Gresham, F. M. (2002a). Caveat emptor: Considerations before buying in to the new medical model. *Behavioral Disorders, 27*(2), 158–167.

Gresham, F. M. (2002b). Responsiveness to intervention: An alternative approach to the identification of learning disabilities. In R. Bradley, L. Danielson, & D. Hallahan (Eds.), *Identification of learning disabilities: Research to practice* (pp. 467–519). Mahwah, NJ: Erlbaum.

Gresham, F. M. (2005). Response to intervention: An alternative means of identifying students as emotionally disturbed. *Education and Treatment of Children, 28*, 328–344.

Gresham, F. M., Reschly, D. J., Tilly, W. D., Fletcher, J., Burns, M. K., Christ, T., et al. (2004). Comprehensive evaluation of learning disabilities: A response-to-intervention perspective. *NASP Communiqué, 33* (4), 34–35. (Also published in *The School Psychologist, 59*(1), 26–29.)

Haring, N. G., & Eaton, M. D. (1978). Systematic instructional procedures: An instructional hierarchy. In N. G. Haring, T. C. Lovitt, M. D. Eaton, & C. L. Hansen (Eds.), *The fourth R: Research in the classroom* (pp. 23–40). Columbus, OH: Merrill.

Haring, N. G., Lovitt, T. C., Eaton, M. D., & Hansen, C. L. (1978). *The fourth R: Research in the classroom.* Columbus, OH: Charles E. Merrill.

Hasbrouck, J., & Tindal, G. A. (2006). Oral reading fluency norms: A valuable assessment tool for reading teachers. *Reading Teacher, 59*(7), 636–644.

Hawkins, P. R., & Dobes, R. W. (1977). Behavioral definitions in applied behavior analysis: Explicit or implicit. In B. C. Etzel, J. M. LeBlanc, & D. M. Baer (Eds.), *New developments in behavioral research: Theory, methods, and applications. In honor of Sidney W. Bijou* (pp. 167–188). Hillsdale, NJ: Erlbaum.

Horner, R. H. (2008). IES Single-Case Design Training Institute, Washington, DC.

Horner, R. H., Carr, E. G., Halle, J., McGee, G., Odom, S., & Wolery, M. (2005). The use of single-subject research to identify evidence-based practice in special education. *Exceptional Children, 71*(2), 165–179.

Hosp, M. K., Hosp, J. L., & Howell, K. W. (2007). *The ABCs of CBM: A practical guide to curriculum-based measurement.* New York: Guilford Press.

Individuals with Disabilities Education Improvement Act. (2004). Pub. L. No. 108–446.

Jimerson, S. R., Burns, M. K., & VanDerHeyden, A. (2007). *Handbook of response to intervention: The science and practice of assessment and intervention.* New York: Springer.

Johnston, J. M., & Pennypacker, H. S. (1993). *Readings for strategies and tactics of behavioral research* (2nd ed.). Hillsdale, NJ: Erlbaum.

Jones, K. M., & Wickstrom, K. F. (2002). Done in sixty seconds: Further analysis of the brief assessment model for academic problems. *School Psychology Review, 31*, 554–568.

Joseph, L. M. (2006). *Understanding, assessing, and intervening on reading problems.* Bethesda, MD: National Association of School Psychologists.

Kavale, K. A. (2001). *Discrepancy models in the identification of learning disability.* Executive summary, Learning Disabilities Summit: Building a Foundation for the Future, Washington, DC.

Kavale, K. A., & Forness, S. R. (1999). Effectiveness of special education. In C. R. Reynolds & T. B. Gutkin (Eds.), *The handbook of school psychology* (3rd ed., pp. 984–1024). New York: Wiley.

Kavale, K. A., & Forness, S. R. (2000). Policy decisions in special education: The role of meta-analysis. In R. Gersten, E. P. Schiller, & S. Vaughn (Eds.), *Contemporary special education research: Synthesis of the knowledge base on critical instructional issues* (pp. 281–326). Mahwah, NJ: Erlbaum.

Kavale, K. A., & Glass, G. V. (1981). Meta-analysis and the integration of research in special education. *Journal of Learning Disabilities, 14*, 531–538.

Kavale, K. A., Mathur, S. R., Forness, S. R., Quinn, M. M., & Rutherford, R. B., Jr. (2000). Right reason in the integration of group and single-subject research in behavioral disorders. *Behavioral Disorders, 25*, 142–157.

Kazdin, A. E. (1982). *Single-case research designs: Methods for clinical and applied settings.* New York: Oxford University Press.

Kazdin, A. E., & Kopel, S. A. (1975). On resolving ambiguities of the multiple-baseline design: Problems and recommendations. *Behavior Therapy, 6*, 601–608.

Keith, T. Z. (2002). Best practices in applied research. In A. Thomas & J. Grimes (Eds.), *Best practices in school psychology IV* (pp. 91–102). Bethesda, MD: National Association of School Psychologists.

Kennedy, C. H. (2005). *Single-case designs for educational research.* Boston: Allyn & Bacon.

Kirk, R. E. (1996). Practical significance: A concept whose time has come. *Educational and Psychological Measurement, 56*, 746–759.

Kovaleski, J. F., & Pedersen, J. (2008). Best practices in data analysis teaming. In A. Thomas & J. Grimes (Eds.), *Best practices in school psychology* (5th ed., pp. 115–130). Bethesda, MD: National Association of School Psychologists.

Kratochwill, T. R. (1978). Foundations of time-series research. In T. R. Kratochwill (Ed.), *Single subject research: Strategies for evaluating change* (pp. 1–100). New York: Academic Press.

Kratochwill, T. R. (1985). Case study research in school psychology. *School Psychology Review, 14*, 204–215.

Kratochwill, T. R., Mott, S. E., & Dodson, C. L. (1984). Case study and single-case research in clinical and applied psychology. In A. S. Bellack & M. Hersen (Eds.), *Research methods in clinical psychology* (pp. 55–99). New York: Pergamon.

Kratochwill, T. R., & Williams, B. L. (1988). Perspectives on pitfalls and hassles in single-subject research. *Journal of the Association for Persons with Severe Handicaps, 13*(3), 147–154.

Leitenberg, H. (1973). The use of single-case methodology in psychotherapy research. *Journal of Abnormal Psychology, 82*, 87–101.

Lentz, F. E., Jr. (1988). Effective reading interventions in the regular classroom. In J. L. Graden, J. E. Zins, & M. L. Curtis (Eds.), *Alternative educational delivery systems: Enhancing instructional options for all students* (pp. 351–370). Washington, DC: National Association of School Psychologists.

Lewis, T., & Sugai, G. (1996). Descriptive and experimental analysis of teacher and peer attention and the use of assessment-based intervention to improve pro-social behavior. *Journal of Behavioral Education, 6*(1), 7–24.

Martens, B. K., Eckert, T. L., Bradley, T. A., & Ardoin, S. P. (1999). Identifying effective treatments from a brief experimental analysis: Using single-case design elements to aid decision making. *School Psychology Quarterly, 14*, 163–181.

Maughan, D. R., Christiansen, E., Jenson, W. R., Olympia, D., & Clark, E. (2005). Behavioral parent training as a treatment for externalizing behaviors and disruptive behavior disorders: A meta-analysis. *School Psychology Review, 34*(3), 267–286.

McComas, J. J., Wacker, D. P., Cooper, L. J., Asmus, J. M., Richman, D., & Stoner, B. (1996). Brief experimental analysis of stimulus prompts for accurate responding on academic tasks in an outpatient clinic. *Journal of Applied Behavior Analysis, 29*, 397–401.

McDougal, J., Chafouleas, S. M., & Waterman, B. (2006). *A practitioner's guide to functional assessment and behavior intervention in schools.* Champaign, IL: Research Press.

Merrell, K. W. (2003). *Behavioral, social, and emotional assessment of children and adolescents* (2nd ed.). Mahwah, NJ: Erlbaum.

Moxley, R. A. (2007). Graphing in the classroom for improving instruction: From lesson plans to research. *Education and Treatment of Children, 30*, 111–126.

Murphy, J. J., & Duncan, B. L. (2007). *Brief intervention for school problems: Outcome informed strategies* (2nd ed.). New York: Guilford Press.

Nist, L., & Joseph, L. (2008). Effectiveness and efficiency of flashcard drill instructional methods on urban first graders' word recognition, acquisition, maintenance, and generalization. *School Psychology Review, 37,* 294–308.

No Child Left Behind Act. (2001). Pub. L. No. 89–10.

Noell, G. H., Freeland, J. T., Witt, J. C., & Gansle, K. A. (2001). Using brief assessments to identify effective interventions for individual students. *Journal of School Psychology, 39,* 335–355.

Noell, G. H., & Gansle, K. A. (2006). Assuring the form has substance: Treatment plan implementation as the foundation of assessing response to intervention. *Assessment for Effective Intervention, 32*(1), 32–39.

Odom, S. L., Brantlinger, E., Gersten, R., Horner, R. H., Thompson, B., & Harris, K. R. (2005). Research in special education: Scientific methods and evidence-based practices. *Exceptional Children, 71,* 137–148.

Parker, R. I., & Hagan-Burke, S. (2007a). Useful effect size interpretations for single case research. *Behavior Therapy, 38,* 95–105.

Parker, R. I., & Hagan-Burke, S. (2007b). Single case research results as clinical outcomes. *Journal of School Psychology, 45,* 637–653.

Parker, R. I., Hagan-Burke, S., & Vannest, K. (2007). Percentage of all non-overlapping data (PAND): An alternative to PND. *Journal of Special Education, 40*(4), 194–204.

Poling, A., & Gossett, D. (1986). Basic research designs in applied behavior analysis. In A. Poling & R. W. Fuqua (Eds.), *Research methods in applied behavior analysis* (pp. 7–27). New York: Plenum.

Poncy, B. C., Skinner, C. H., & O'Mara, T. (2006). Detect, practice, and repair: The effects of a classwide intervention on elementary students' math-fact fluency. *Journal of Evidence-Based Practices for Schools, 7*(1), 47–68.

Potter, M. L., Ysseldyke, J. E., Regan, R. R., & Algozzine, B. (1983). Eligibility and classification decisions in educational settings: Issuing passports in a state of confusion. *Contemporary Educational Psychology, 8*(2), 146–157.

President's Commission on Excellence in Special Education. (2002). *A new era: Revitalizing special education for children and their families.* Washington, DC: U.S. Department of Education.

Rathvon, N. (2008). *Effective school interventions: Evidence-based strategies for improving student outcomes* (2nd ed.). New York: Guilford Press.

Ravitch, D. (1999). Student performance: The national agenda in education. In M. Kanstoroom & C. E. Finn (Eds.), *New directions: Federal education policy in the twenty-first century* (pp. 139–146). Washington, DC: Thomas B. Fordham/Manhattan Policy Institute.

Reschly, D. J., & Ysseldyke, J. E. (2002). Paradigm shift: The past is not the future. In A. Thomas & J. Grimes (Eds.), *Best practices in school psychology IV* (pp. 3–20). Bethesda, MD: National Association of School Psychologists.

Riley-Tillman, T. C., Chafouleas, S. M., & McGrath, M. C. (2004). Brief experimental analysis: An assessment strategy for selecting successful interventions. *NASP Communiqué, 32*(6), 10–12.

Riley-Tillman, T. C., Kalberer, S. M., & Chafouleas, S. M. (2005). Selecting the right tool for the job: A review of behavior monitoring tools used to assess student response to intervention. *California School Psychologist, 10,* 81–92.

Riley-Tillman, T. C., & Walcott, C. M. (2007). Using baseline logic to maximize the value of educational interventions. *School Psychology Forum, 1*(2), 87–97.

Risley, T. (2005). Montrose M. Wolf (1935–2004). *Journal of Applied Behavior Analysis, 38,* 279–287.

Rosenthal, R. (1994). Parametric measures of effect size. In H. M. Cooper & L. V. Hedges (Eds.), *The handbook of research synthesis* (pp. 231–244). New York: Sage.

Runes, D. D. (Ed.). (1942). *The dictionary of philosophy.* New York: Philosophical Library.

Salzberg, C. L., Strain, P. S., & Baer, D. M. (1987). Meta-analysis for single-subject research: When does it clarify, when does it obscure? *Remedial and Special Education, 8,* 43–48.

Scruggs, T. E., & Mastropieri, M. A. (1998). Summarizing single-subject research: Issues and applications. *Behavior Modification, 22,* 221–242.

Scruggs, T. E., & Mastropieri, M. A. (2001). How to summarize single-participant research: Ideas and applications. *Exceptionality, 9*(4), 227–244.

Scruggs, T. E., Mastropieri, M. A., & Casto, G. (1987). The quantitative synthesis of single-subject research: Methodology and validation. *Remediate and Special Education, 8,* 24–33.

Shadish, W. R. (2007, May). *Meta-analysis of single-subject research.* Invited lecture at the Association for Behavior Analysis Annual Convention, San Diego, CA.

Shapiro, E. S. (2004). *Academic skills problems: Direct assessment and intervention* (3rd ed.). New York: Guilford Press.

Shaughnessy, J. J., Zechmeister, E. B., & Zechmeister, J. S. (2003). *Research methods in psychology* (6th ed.). New York: McGraw Hill.

Shavelson, R. J., & Towne, L. (Eds.). (2002). *Scientific research in education.* Washington, DC: National Academy Press.

Sidman, M. (1960). *Tactics of scientific research: Evaluating experimental data in psychology.* New York: Basic Books.

Silberglitt, B., & Gibbons, K. A. (2005). *Establishing slope targets for use in a response-to-intervention model (technical manual).* Rush City, MN: St. Croix River Education District.

Simos, P. G., Fletcher, J. M., Bergman, E., Breier, J. I., Foorman, B. R., Castillo, E. M., et al. (2002). Dyslexia-specific brain activation profile becomes normal following successful remedial training. *Neurology, 58,* 1203–1213.

Skinner, C. H., McLaughlin, T. F., & Logan, P. (1997). Cover, copy, and compare: A self-managed academic intervention across skills, students, and settings. *Journal of Behavioral Education, 7,* 295–306.

Speece, D. L., & Case, L. P. (2001). Classification in context: An alternative approach to identifying early reading disability. *Journal of Educational Psychology, 93*(4), 735–749.

Speece, D. L., Case, L. P., & Molloy, D. E. (2003). Responsiveness to general education instruction as the first gate to learning disabilities identification. *Learning Disabilities Research and Practice, 18,* 147–156.

Stiggins, R. (2005). From formative assessment to assessment FOR learning: A path to success in standards-based schools. *Phi Delta Kappan, 87,* 324–328.

Sugai, G., & Horner, R. (2006). A promising approach for expanding and sustaining the implementation of school-wide positive behavior support. *School Psychology Review, 35,* 245–259.

Sugai, G., & Horner, R. H. (2008). What we know and need to know about preventing problem behavior in schools. *Exceptionality, 16,* 67–77.

Swanson, H. L., Hoskyn, M., & Lee, C. (1999). *Interventions for students with learning disabilities: A meta-analysis of treatment outcomes.* New York: Guilford Press.

Swanson, H. L., & Sachse-Lee, C. (2000). A meta-analysis of single-subject-design intervention research for students with LD. *Journal of Learning Disabilities, 33,* 114–136.

Tawney, J. W., & Gast, D. L. (1984). *Single subject research in special education.* New York: Merrill.

Therrien, W. J. (2004). Fluency and comprehension gains as a result of repeated reading: A meta-analysis. *Remedial and Special Education, 25,* 252–261.

Thompson, R. H., & Iwata, B. A. (2005). A review of reinforcement control procedures. *Journal of Applied Behavior Analysis, 38,* 257–278.

Thomson, S. (1993). *Principles for our changing schools: Knowledge and skill base.* Austin, TX: National Policy Board for Educational Administration.

Tilly, W. D., III, & Flugum, K. R. (1995). Best practices in ensuring quality interventions. In A. Thomas & J. Grimes (Eds.), *Best practices in school psychology III* (pp. 485–500). Washington, DC: National Association of School Psychologists.

Todd, A., Horner, R., & Sugai, G. (1999). Self-monitoring and self-recruited praise. *Journal of Positive Behavior Interventions, 1,* 66–76.

Treptow, M. A., Burns, M. K., & McComas, J. J. (2007). Reading at the frustration, instructional, and independent levels: The effects on students' reading comprehension and time on task. *School Psychology Review, 36*(1), 159–166.

U.S. Department of Education. (1983). *A nation at risk: The imperative for educational reform.* Washington, DC: The Commission of Excellence in Education.

VanAuken, T. L., Chafouleas, S. M., Bradley, T. A., & Martens, B. K. (2002). Using brief experimental analysis to select oral reading interventions: An investigation of treatment utility. *Journal of Behavioral Education, 11,* 165–181.

Van den Noortgate, W., & Onghena, P. (2003). Hierarchical linear models for the quantitative integration of effect sizes in single-case research. *Behavior Research Methods, Instruments, and Computers, 35,* 1–10.

VanDerHeyden, A. M., & Burns, M. K. (2005). Using curriculum-based assessment and curriculum-based measurement to guide elementary mathematics instruction: Effect on individual and group accountability scores. *Assessment for Effective Intervention, 30,* 15–31.

VanDerHeyden, A. M., Witt, J. C., & Naquin, G. (2003). Development and validation of a process for screening referrals to special education. *School Psychology Review, 32,* 204–227.

Vaughn, S., & Fuchs, L. S. (2003). Redefining learning disabilities as inadequate response to instruction: The promise and potential problems. *Learning Disabilities Research and Practice, 18,* 137–146.

Wacker, D., Berg, W., Harding, J., & Cooper-Brown, L. (2004). Use of brief experimental analyses in outpatient clinic and home settings. *Journal of Behavioral Education, 13,* 213–226.

Wagner, D., McComas, J. J., Bollman, K., & Holton, E. (2006). The use of functional reading analysis to identify effective reading interventions. *Assessment for Effective Intervention, 32*(1), 40–49.

Walcott, C. M., & Riley-Tillman, T. C. (2007). Evidence-based interventions from research to practice. *NASP Communiqué, 35*(6), 16–20.

Watson, P. J., & Workman, E. A. (1981). The non-concurrent multiple baseline across-individuals design: An extension of the traditional multiple baseline design. *Journal of Behavior Therapy and Experimental Psychiatry, 12,* 257–259.

White, O. R. (1987). The quantitative synthesis of single-subject research: Method and validation: Comment. *Remedial and Special Education, 8,* 34–39.

Wilber, A., & Cushman, T. P. (2006). Selecting effective academic interventions: An example using brief experimental analysis for oral reading. *Psychology in the Schools, 43,* 79–84.

Winn, B. D., Skinner, C. H., Allin, J. D., & Hawkins, J. A. (2004). Practicing school consultants can empirically validate intervention: A description and demonstration of the non-concurrent multiple-baseline design. *Journal of Applied School Psychology, 20,* 109–128.

Witt, J. C., Daly, E. M., & Noell, G. (2000). *Functional assessments: A step-by-step guide to solving academic and behavior problems.* Longmont, CO: Sopris West.

Wolery, M., Bailey, D. B., & Sugai, G. M. (1988). *Effective teaching: Principles and procedures of applied behavior analysis with exceptional students.* Boston: Allyn & Bacon.

Wright, J. (2007). *RTI toolkit: A practical guide for schools.* Port Chester, NY: Dude Publishing.

Ysseldyke, J. E., Algozzine, B., & Thurlow, M. L. (2000). *Critical issues in special education* (3rd ed.). Boston: Houghton Mifflin.

Ysseldyke, J. E., Morrison, D., Burns, M. K., Ortiz, S., Dawson, P., Rosenfield, S., et al. (2006). *School psychology: A blueprint for the future of training and practice II.* Bethesda, MD: National Association of School Psychologists.

Ysseldyke, J. E., & Thurlow, M. L. (1984). Assessment practices in special education: Adequacy and appropriateness. *Educational Psychologist, 19*(3), 123.

Index